**ONE
DAY
I'LL
FORGET
MY
TROUSERS**

One Day I'll Forget My Trousers

Pete Murray

EVEREST BOOKS LIMITED
4 Valentine Place, London SE1

Published in Great Britain by Everest Books Ltd, 1975

ISBN 0903925 311

Copyright © Pete Murray & Jeremy Hornsby 1975

Printed and bound in Great Britain by
Redwood Burn Limited, Trowbridge & Esher

To my lovely Mum
and to my adorable wife Tricia
for their love and understanding

FOREWORD

When graphologist Fraser White was a regular on 'Open House' Everest Books published Fraser's 'Handwriting Secrets', an assortment of in-depth analyses of some of the stars who had appeared on the show. It included Fraser's analysis of my handwriting, which was read out — much to my amazement — by Leslie Phillips. To my distress my lower loops indicated that I had now "reached the stage where my sex life is simmering down". In spite of this horrific revelation I remained friendly with Fraser and, indeed, wrote the foreword to his book. It was then that Robin McGibbon of Everest suggested that I wrote my life story.

"No way," said I.

"Don't be a coward," said he.

"Haven't got the time," I replied.

"Well, we can get someone to ghost it for you. A couple of hours a week, for a couple of months, talking into a tape machine, and you'll be home and dry."

Well, I guess I'm still wet behind the ears. I agreed.

But who could I get to write for me? Who could I trust? Who could understand my humour?

I remembered a young journalist named Jeremy Hornsby who had written an article on me in the Daily Express.

I was impressed by his humour and, above all, his integrity. Jeremy, poor soul, agreed and after $4\frac{1}{2}$ months and no less than 50 hours of taping, this is the finished product.

The title of the book will perhaps bemuse all except those who know me. Those that do will probably say: "You mean he hasn't already?"

Jeremy has done a superb job of interpreting my life and my anecdotes.

In a masochistic sort of way we've enjoyed doing it. I hope you'll enjoy reading it.

Pete Murray
April 1975

Chapter One

I am not a reformed alcoholic.

I would like to make that clear right from the start. The reason is a simple one. I have never been an alcoholic. The reason for that is simpler still, in that I do not drink, nor have I ever done so.

These protestations may seem a bit previous for the start of an autobiography, but the curious fact is that of all the activities in my life, the one that appears to intrigue people the most is my lack of desire to get drunk every night. Whether this has any bearing on the size of the National Debt or our failure to win the World Cup I leave for others to judge.

I am now, however, prepared to reveal to an astonished world that the reason why I do not drink is that I do not like drink. And the reason for *that* lies in my earliest childhood. My parents, and my grandparents come to that, were publicans. Some people have Shakespeare ruined for them by having him rammed down their throats at school. With me, it's pubs. Even to this day, my idea of hell is to go into a pub even for a sandwich. I suppose it's a phobia. To me, pubs represent standing up. I mean, for some reason best known for themselves, men in pubs always seem to want to drink standing up. I just don't like standing up. I like sitting down. I don't even like cocktail parties because you have to stand up...

We came from the East End. I was born in Victoria Park, Hackney (not *in* the park, you understand, but in a house nearby) in 1925. At that time, my father, whose name was Harry, and my mother's parents, were keeping the Nottingham Arms in Plaistow.

I don't remember much about the Nottingham Arms, but I do know

1

that it has been demolished. Readers who stick with me in this tale will quickly realise that there is nothing strange about that. The fact is that looking back over this last half-century I discover that virtually every building or institution with which I have been associated has either been demolished or has changed its use. It's the exact reverse of all those houses preserved because famous people lived in them. In my case, it seems that teams of demolition contractors were simply panting for me to move out so that they could get started.

One thing about the Nottingham Arms was that it was near the West Ham Speedway and greyhound track. At that time, a football team called Thames played there. They had a few old Spurs players in the team, and that was the first football I saw and my first interest in the game. My mother's brother, my uncle Bill Reece, was a director of Thames, and used to take me to see them play. They were at the bottom of the Third Division South. And I know they had bad financial problems. But undoubtedly my support was the final straw, because after a couple of seasons they folded, and the ground has now been built on.

By then, we had moved to Chiswick, to 17, Harvard Road. I mention the address only as a warning of inevitable demolition to whoever lives there now. Incredibly, it is still standing. We shared the house with Auntie Dorothy and Uncle Laurie, and my father had to commute to work. He had left the Nottingham Arms and had taken over the Elephant, on the Kingsland Road at Dalston. That, of course, has now been demolished, and all that remains of it are some brown and white tiles at the back of the Argos discount shop.

My mother, Violet, and I would often go over to visit him at the pub, and this would sometimes entail a ride on Uncle Bill's bus. Uncle Bill had been a corporal in the First World War. Surviving both the destruction of Europe and the demise of the Thames football club, he had managed to save enough from his work at the pub to start a bus company. So Uncle Bill's bus actually *was* Uncle Bill's Bus. Just the one, to start with, the sole representative of the Renown Bus Company, which plied what is now the No. 15 route.

Soon the bus was joined by other buses. They were jolly good buses, double-deckers, with the steps going up outside at the back, and painted maroon. They were much better than the red buses of the

General Omnibus Company, which later became London Transport. I loved them. I was going to be a conductor, not a driver, because I liked the idea of working the clipboard for the tickets and of ringing the bell. That appealed to me enormously. It was a big clanger of a bell which you pulled with string. I used to get on the bus with my mother at Piccadilly and say loudly "We don't have to pay, do we Mummy, because this is Uncle's bus." God knows what the other passengers thought. In the end, of course, Uncle Bill's bus company was not so much demolished as nationalised, which perhaps comes to the same thing.

My grandparents had a dog named Blackie who showed no allegiance to my uncle's transport system. Blackie was a mongrel of indefinable pedigree. Blackie had a predilection for trams. He would get on a tram, ride to the nearest park, take his constitutional, trot back to the tramstop, get off at the appropriate place and quietly take up his position in front of the lounge bar fire. Blackie had not only settled for the good life, but was equally determined never to get hardpad. A very exceptional dog, was Blackie.

Although we often went over to the pub, I didn't see much of my father. I think that's another reason why I dislike the places. To me, a pub meant separation. They'd hardly come upstairs after lunch than they'd be back down again to prepare for the evening. But I do remember that my father always had Thursdays off, and Thursdays meant going to the Regent Palace Hotel. Well, not just that. We'd go to the pictures, or to a theatre as well. In fact, the first theatre I ever went to was the old Playhouse at Charing Cross, which is now a BBC Studio, and from where I have done many broadcasts. It was a lovely old theatre, and I think *that's* going to be demolished soon, too.

But the Great Event of Thursdays was the Regent Palace Hotel, all beautifully panelled and posh, and specifically its Grill Room. Because that Grill Room served what I reckon the best fish and chips I've ever had in my life. I didn't like meat, but I did like their fried plaice.

I suppose you could say that my parents were aspiring middle-class, in the same way that all working-class people want to get a better deal from life. They'd really had to struggle. They came from Bow, and my mother, who is a very proud woman, has told me often of the hardships of her early life.

3

She was the great influence on my life. My father could hardly ever get away from the pub, because managers would always go on the fiddle, the hand in the till, the half-crowns in the shoe. But my mother always taught me "Nobody is better than anybody else. Some are more fortunate, but none are better. You have to show as much respect to a dustman as to a vicar."

As a result, she was pefectly happy for me to play with the local kids in Dalston. I think that playing with those cockney kids was what gave me my first start in doing different accents . . . also, since a lot of them were Jewish, I picked up a great deal of Yiddish. The pub was just near Ridley Road, which was then a very Jewish area. In the Thirties it became a stamping ground for the Blackshirts. Very sinister. Very frightening. They used to come into the pub with their black shirts on, and then outside I would see them smashing the windows of Jewish-owned shops.

The Elephant had a mixed clientele. There was a saloon bar for the businessmen, but it could get pretty rough on the other side. There were plenty of fights, but at least they were straight fights, no razors, or people being beaten over the head. There was a lot of thieving, a lot of crookedness, a lot of skulduggery, but somehow it never got dirty as it does today.

My grandfather was a great character. Known and loved by all, as they say. I remember once Uncle Laurie and Aunty Dorothy came over from Chiswick to visit him. They parked their car outside the pub. When they went out again a number of things had been stolen from it. My grandfather was furious.

He never went to the police, but within half an hour he had the lot back. He figured out who must have done it, and went up to this man he suspected. "Gor Blimey Bill," said the man. "We 'ad no idea it was any relative of yours. 'Ere's all the stuff back, and 'ere's a tenner for all the trouble we caused." So we showed a profit.

At this stage, perhaps, I am less than fair to all concerned if I give the impression that my schooling was confined to the seamier side of Dalston Junction. Attempts were in hand to give me an education, although it must be admitted that schools and I have never been what one would describe as willing partners.

When I was 4, my mother had attempted to send me to a

4

Kindergarten. It was in Gunnersbury, and I was a very shy little boy, and I hated it. I hated it because there were little girls there, one of whom, as an act of welcome perhaps, picked up a bottle of ink and poured it down my back. I've had trouble with women ever since.

Reacting with what I must proclaim as commendable decisiveness, I immediately returned home and refused to return to the school under any circumstances whatsoever.

My mother wisely allowed me two years to get over the trauma of my day at school. Then, when I was six, a second attempt was made. I was sent to Gunnersbury Preparatory School, whose building still miraculously survives, though no longer as a school. I loved the uniform. There were scarlet caps with a grey patch in the middle, and red and grey socks and tie. About fifty boys attended this chic place of learning.

The word 'learning' is simply a phrase I use for convenience. My scholastic achievements were not very high. To put it another way, I was always bottom of the class. There was one brief exception to this. One term I started to show a little form at Latin, because the master, a Mr Bright, actually showed some interest in me. When exam time came at the end of term, I came top...and was promptly accused of cheating. I suppose it must have seemed to them a bit like a selling-plater winning the Derby. All my school reports carried that hopeless refrain "Must try harder."

But already I knew, and said, that I was not prepared to try harder, because what I wanted to do was to go into the theatre. As often as I could, I would go to the Chiswick Empire (which has now, as readers will guess, been demolished) and see the Variety shows. I was crazy about them. Nervo and Knox. George Robey, towards the end of his career. It seemed like a temple to me, and all I wanted to do was to go on stage, though what on earth I thought I might do when I got there, heaven knows.

Another idiosyncrasy began to manifest itself on Saturday nights, when I would listen to Music Hall on the wireless. I would stand in front of the table which carried the big old fretwork-fronted apparatus, and 'conduct' the orchestra. Now I wanted to be a conductor. (Band – not buses.) A development of this arose with visits to the Corner House in Coventry Street, where an orchestra played for

5

the tea-drinkers. I would take the straw from my orangeade and 'play' the violin across my arm. It had occurred to me that the violinist was always the leader of the orchestra, and that's what I wanted to be. One drawback to this ambition was that I knew nothing about music. I did not take music lessons, since any 'lessons' were indelibly linked in my mind with small girls and ink bottles.

To assuage these longings, my uncle Laurie, who was very handy at things, made me a miniature stage. I played with it for hours. We must have gone to every toy shop in London in search of a toy orchestra to put on the stage, and when we had it, Uncle Laurie made me a miniature cinema organ to play along. So started a lifelong ambition, which was realised a few years ago when I actually 'rode up' on the Leicester Square Odeon's organ alongside Robin Richmond.

My one test of childhood musicianship came at the age of seven. Gunnersbury boasted, if that's not too strong a word, a school percussion orchestra, with which the ears of doting parents were, at intervals, assaulted.

For some reason, I was given the freedom of the rostrum for one of these episodes, at that well-known venue, the Village Hall of St Michael's Church in Gunnersbury. I wore my red cricket blazer (obviously conscious that this was a sporting occasion), with the white flannels, the white shirt, and the red and grey tie.

It was the pronounced opinion of one and all that I 'looked awfully sweet' while conducting the assembled drums, cymbals, and tambourines. This opinion, however, was modified at the subsequent tea, at which I made it my business to serve the jam tarts by the simple method of throwing them.

In spite of this blot on the escutcheon of this budding Klemperer, I was given a special prize for my efforts...a book of Grimm's Fairy Tales. Sadly, on the day that the Brothers Grimm were to be delivered publicly to the young maestro, the young maestro caught a severe case of chicken pox. Thus was I robbed of the one occasion when I could be honoured without accusations of cheating.

At this time my closest friend out of school was my cousin, Tony King, Auntie Daisy's son. He was five years older than me, and used to take me to the pictures. We were both mad cowboy fans, and saw all the Westerns we could. But the film that made most impression on me was a horror film he took me to see at what was the Blue Hall, Hammersmith, now the Regal. God knows what it was called, but I'll never forget it. I have this vision of a man's face disappearing into a cellar. If I wake in the middle of the night, even now, I can see that face. The star of the film was Warner Oland, who later played the part of Charlie Chan, so I keep saying to myself "He was really quite a nice fellow."

I saw Tony at the weekends as well, because I was a weekly boarder at Gunnersbury. There were about six of us boarding, and it was very comfortable. Once a week, the headmaster and Mr Bright would put on a film show for the boarders. We would put on our pyjamas and dressing gowns and go downstairs and watch African natives making cocoa.

We were each allowed two baths a week. Cleanliness being next to godliness, this was presumably thought the minimum requirement for the salvation of our souls. On one particular evening, my bath night coincided with film night. I was half way through my bath when Mr Bright walked in with a man whom he introduced as Captain Something – I'll call him Captain Bloggs.

Mr Bright said "It's alright, we've just come for the champagne glasses,"…which was reasonable, since we knew that for some reason, apparent only to the logical recesses of the headmaster's mind, the champagne glasses were kept in a cupboard in the bathroom. Perhaps champagne was used as an early type of bubble bath. At any rate, Mr Bright went out with the glasses, leaving me with Captain Bloggs.

It was as I was getting out of the bath, that Bloggs started to kiss me. My instant impression was that he was some unusual kind of lunatic. I couldn't wait to tell the others about it.

"This man," I informed myself, "is quite clearly insane. However, since he has been ushered in by Mr Bright, the insanity is clearly of an official nature."

My only recourse was to get downstairs as soon as possible, which I did. But hardly had the lights gone down, and the first flickering cocoa bean appeared on the screen, than Captain Bloggs executed a fresh manoeuvre. The palpable absurdity of this behaviour, which had no physical effect on me whatsoever, but which disturbed my concentration on the basket-carrying natives, made me decide that

7

during the reel-changing I would move to another seat. Captain Bloggs obviously took this as the final rejection, because, as I learned later, he made use of Reel Two for an attempt to board one of the other boarders.

Sometime later, the news of Captain Blogg's raid upon our persons was relayed to the headmaster and Mr Bright, and we never saw the gallant militiaman again.

In 1936, my mother and father took over a pub in Cheapside called the Gog and Magog...whose fate was to be bombed out of existence during the war. That was the one pub I liked, because it had a beautiful flat above, with a roof garden, and they didn't work at weekends. In those days the City, with only about three thousand inhabitants, was just like a village. I used to commute to school on the Tube from the Mansion House to Chiswick and did my homework on the train.

That year, aged eleven, I had been moved from Gunnersbury to a neighbouring preparatory school called Colet Court. The reason was that my mother wanted me to go to St Paul's public school, for which Colet Court specialised in preparing their pupils.

My mother's reasons for this were simply that she wanted me to get the best possible start in life and speak, as she put it, "the King's English", about which she was very keen. Although this was something of a departure for natives of the East End, the rest of the family were all for it. They recognised that in those days the wearing of the old school tie was a positive asset, and they may of course have felt that the number of positive assets I had to offer were not so many that some extra help would come amiss.

So for two years I went to Colet Court. They seemed an eternity. At Gunnersbury there had been 50 boys. Here there were 400. (Colet Court, which is about to be demolished, stands on the Hammersmith Road near where St Paul's used to be before *it* was demolished.)

At Gunnersbury at least I had some sort of status. I had been on the brink of the first team at football (nowadays I suppose I might even have got on a few times as substitute), though my cricketing skills were felt to be lacking (I was hopeless). Nor had I shone at rugby. This may have been due to the fact that I only played one game at rugby. And *this* may have been due to the fact that I was sent on to play while labouring under a distinct disadvantage. No-one had told me the rules.

Thus it was that, a few minutes after the commencement, I felt distinctly aggrieved when one of the opposing team ran towards me and stuck his fist in my face. I felt this to be unreasonable. No-one had informed me that I might expect fists in my teeth. Foolishly, I had believed it to be a game, and not an incitement to murder.

The fist in my face – I confess it now – really did upset me, arriving unheralded as it did. Following my own example with the ink at kindergarten, I thereupon made it immediately clear to one and all that I had no intention of ever playing rugby again. Nor have I. But I *was* on the brink of the first team at football.

My other interest at Gunnersbury had been fighting. Although I was small enough to be known as Tich, I loved boxing and would take on anyone of any size. At Colet Court, however, it soon became clear that I would not have things my own way. I got my first inkling of this on the first day, when one of the school bullies took me out on to the playing field and stuffed caterpillars down my shirt. Fired by this example, all the school bullies then took turns to perform at my expense. I was not happy at Colet Court.

In 1937 my father died. Before the First World War he had done a lot of cycle-racing – London to Brighton and back, and that kind of thing. He was the sort of man who, after taking exercise, would never bother to put a sweater on. Then, in the War, he got badly gassed. So what with the cycling and the gassing and the fact that he was also a heavy smoker, he got TB and died, and my mother went to live at the Elephant in Dalston. My uncle, Bill Reece, became a sort of second father to me. He used to take me to Wanstead Flats and Clissold Park to kick a football about, and he also took me to the matches, no doubt to torture himself with memories of what might have been at the Thames Club.

Apart from the games at Thames, the first match I saw was a Second Division game between Tottenham and Blackburn. It was at Tottenham, and I remember thinking that the ground was very tatty...like the programmes, which were printed on a sort of pink sheet. I expect they were economising.

At any rate, the next game Uncle Bill took me to was at the Arsenal, and I immediately decided to support them because I liked the colour of their shirts. Arsenal reeked of glamour. All the big names seemed to be there, and it was there that I found my first hero, Denis Compton. He was 16 or 17 at the time, and in the reserves, and we used to go to the reserve games as well. He played football the way he played cricket, like a cavalier. He was a professional with an amateur's outlook. I think he had the right attitude.

A couple of years ago I played a charity cricket match with him, and we found ourselves batting together. It was unbelievable to me, actually at the crease with my hero. I just did all I could to stay in so that I could watch him. All the old magic, the timing, was still there. That was a genuine thrill.

Compton, in fact, was responsible for one of my minor successes at Colet Court. As well as football, I used to watch him play cricket in the holidays. And I was already turning into something of a mimic. My favourite impression was of an old radio comedian called Claude Dampier. Anyway, by watching Compton closely I managed to pick up some of his strokes.

I started to imitate him at school. The cricket master, I remember, was called Renton, and very fine-looking and smart with a brown chalk-striped suit. He made quite an impression, because all the other masters seemed to be so tatty. Mr Renton became very impressed by my style. He ordained that I should play in the house cricket matches. I failed to score any appreciable number of runs, but the failure was achieved in magnificent style.

This compensated in some small way for another schoolmaster, named Buster Reed, who was sadistic in the extreme. He taught us French, and boxing, at which he had been an army champion, or something of the sort. The kids lived in terror of this man, and it was plain that he had it in for me. One day I did a bad homework. It *was* a bad homework; of that I have never been in doubt.

But Buster Reed's reaction was to hang the homework around my neck with a string and order me to walk through the school thus garlanded. He was mentally sadistic, and loved to see kids in tears. I am happy to report that I took off the offending paper and threw it in his face. Somewhat taken aback at this revolutionary act, all he could conjure in riposte was: "Well of course there's only one answer for you. You'll be lucky to get a job as a lavatory attendant in Victoria

Station." Why he should have chosen that job, and that station, I never knew.

Since those days I've taught myself to speak French pretty well, and I've always wanted to meet that man again and speak to him in French. It was always my guess that although he knew the grammar, he couldn't speak a word of it. French master indeed! Years later I had a French mistress and she taught me far more...but that's another story.

In 1938 my mother, together with Uncle Bill, whose buses had by now been nationalised, took a pub in Bayswater called the Duke of Edinburgh. They had grandiose plans for it, but it has, as the reader will have guessed, now been demolished. I went to live with Auntie Dorothy and Uncle Laurie in Osterley, where they had moved when my father died. And in 1939, contriving somehow to concoct a few answers from my unhappy years of association with primary education, I managed to scrape through the exams and into St Paul's.

This achievement was not, of course, the one for which most people remember that year. The outbreak of war meant that my first term at St Paul's was spent in the excitement of gas-mask fittings and evacuation to the country.

We went to Easthampstead Park, at Wokingham in Surrey, the family seat of the Marquis of Downshire. But there, any resemblance between our existence and the life aristocratic ended abruptly. My previous feelings about the nature of education had admittedly been less than ecstatic. But now I was to meet Misery in person and look her square between the eyes.

It *was* miserable. It was straight out of Dickens. It was an experience for which no old school tie was ever going to be compensation. We were billeted out in various houses round the area. Some of the boys found themselves living with the warders from Broadmoor. Denied this early introduction to insanity, I was posted to a house on the edge of Wellington College. St Paul's, of course, was normally a day school, so that the masters were untrained in the niceties of keeping adolescents happy in slum conditions. It didn't help matters that the man appointed over us, a Mr Richards, was unsympathetic to boot.

We slept six to a small room. The house was unheated. We would be roused from sleep at some unearthly hour, and then have to bicycle eight miles, in what inevitably seemed to be awful weather, to

Easthampstead Park. Of course we realised that it was the war, and that things could not be perfect. But I think that even during the war there must have been comparatively few children being fed, as we were, on steamed stinging nettles.

For some, there was worse, and my salvation was the fact that I boxed, though even in that field, such success as I had may have owed more to a latent acting ability than to pugilistic skills. Soon after my arrival I had to go to the sanatorium, where I met a boy I had boxed at Colet Court. "Golly, I remember boxing you," he said. "I was terrified out of my life. Not by what you did with the boxing. But the way you looked." The fact was that I used to do all the 'moody'... snarling, jiggling the shoulders and all that. Well, soon after that, some of the younger boys from St Pauls had a boxing match with the older boys from my old school, Colet Court. I was down to fight a boy I remembered fighting before. He was a year younger than me, and I pictured him as a bit weedy, and thought there wouldn't be too much trouble.

The match took place at Wellington, since we didn't have any of our own facilities, and as soon as I saw this bloke I realised he'd put on a lot of weight. That fight was murder. It was sheer toe to toe thuggery. No impediments like the Queensberry rules were allowed to interrupt the mayhem. Right at the end of it, his hands dropped, from sheer exhaustion, and I caught him a beauty, right on the end of the chin, and knocked him cold.

Unfortunately, the bell, as they say, intervened. He was in tears when they brought him round, but I can't say I was too happy either, when I was judged to have lost on points. Years later, I knew how Henry Cooper felt, the time he put Ali down.

About twenty years later I had another reminder of that fight. I was sitting at a football match when a fellow came up to me and said: "I was at school with you." Being rather more interested in the prospects of the match than in reliving my frightful schooldays, I replied non-committally: "Oh yes?"

"Yes," he said, obviously not going to be put off. "I saw you in a boxing match. You knocked a bloke out. Do you remember?"

I nodded, pride gaining some ascendancy over the fact that Arsenal were coming onto the pitch.

"That was fantastic," he said. "The best fight I ever saw. What I wondered was, do you ever see the fellow you fought?"

I said I didn't.

"His name was Mulligan," he said.

I said: "Yes, that's right."

"Well," he said. "It's Mick Mulligan, the band leader."

I was so astonished, I don't think I even noticed the kick-off. I had worked with Mick a lot in the days when George Melly was singing with him, and neither I, nor I believe he, had ever realised that we had 'met' before. And the funny thing is, I've never seen him since, to tell him.

The boxing, as I said, turned out to be a help in hours of crisis. Some repairs were being done to our house, and eight of us were moved into Wellington College itself. Friction was instantaneous, and when one of our boys decided that his role in life was to smear one of their boys' cake with mustard, open warfare was declared. The Wellingtonians got hold of four of our blokes and tied them to beds, and having performed in a way of which Captain Bloggs would have been proud, they proceeded to administer a thorough beating up. Doubtless, I thought, this was the sort of preparation for which we have to thank the victories at Waterloo and elsewhere. Doubtless it is in these joyful memories that pride in the old school tie resides. But I couldn't see it. But I had fought one of their boys in a boxing match, and I'd beaten him, and they left me alone, though God knows we were outnumbered.

The incident took me back a couple of years to when we had the Gog and Magog. I joined the City of London Boy Scouts, and we used to go to camp (in the best possible meaning of the word) at a place near Chislehurst. It was near a priests' training establishment called St Nicholas'. The inmates used to spend nearly the whole day praying, doing their devotions, learning their scriptures, throwing incense around, and so forth.

They had just one half-hour break per day. And I have the clearest memory of how those students of the Gospel, those followers of wisdom, those devotees of Christ, spent the entire half-hour, every day, in throwing the largest bricks they could find onto the heads of the poor City of London Boy Scouts. (I am not sure about St Nicholas' state of demolition or otherwise, but I can only hope.)

Apart from boxing, my main occupation outside school hours was cross-country running. I didn't actually enjoy it at all, but it was the one certain means of escape, of getting away from awful masters and frightful conditions. All the time I was there I didn't play cricket, or rugby (for reasons which readers will appreciate…I *still* didn't know the rules), or rowing. Football they didn't play anyway. Anything you wanted to take part in seemed to involve a cycle ride of at least ten miles, and I was having enough cycling at weekends.

That was how I used to get home at weekends, by bike. Thirty-odd miles from Crowthorne to Bayswater. I would try to get a lift in a lorry and put my bike on the back, but sometimes it didn't happen, and I just had to pedal. I suppose those journeys must have taken me about four hours. Anything to get away!

I remember I had a Raleigh bike, with three speeds and celluloid mudguards. That was really IN at that time, to have celluloid mudguards. It had a saddlebag, and racing handlebars, and one of those thin and painful racing saddles. I've never been able to talk in a low voice since riding that machine.

At one point, my misery at the general existence was such that one of the older boys apparently decided that I was about to waste away. He took me over to the house where he was billeted, a really beautiful place at Bracknell. The lady said that she would be delighted to have me. I applied to the billeting master for a 'free transfer', but after some deliberations I was later informed that I could not go. It was made pretty clear that they assumed I was having some sort of an affair with the older boy, which was totally untrue. So back to Mr Richards' house I went, where things seemed to get even worse. I started organising complaints about the conditions, notably the stinging nettle diet, and was called before Mr Richards, who announced that he considered me to be the leader of a revolution. Straight out of *If*. Well, considering that I was only 14 and the rest of the boys were 18 or 19, I reckon that was pretty good going in those pre-Vanessa Redgrave days.

Soon after this, Mr Richards attempted to flog the rebellion out of me. I had thrown a piece of orange peel out of the window, intending it for the bushes. It had missed and landed in the open. Richards waited until I had covered the 8 miles to Easthampstead Park, then called me to see him and declared, like the Police Chief of some banana republic: "You have thrown some orange peel out of the window at the house."

"Yes, I have," I admitted.

"Well, after school you will return and pick up the orange peel. That will delay your return home for the weekend."

The way he said it, you'd have expected him to rub his hands together and add: "Heh! Heh! Heh!"

Well, I asked a friend to do it for me, as he was going back there anyway, but he either forgot or didn't bother, and I got flogged by Mr Richards.

No, I didn't enjoy St Paul's. The masters offered no encouragement. The spirit of the place was exemplified by the Cadet Force, the OTC, which in a school famous for producing soldiers, and considering there was a war on, should have been massively supported. Frankly, I can't remember a person joining. Non-warriors all, we'd spend our spare time going to the crummy cinema at Crowthorne, which was always breaking down, and which I am sure must have been demolished by now. Or we would go in search of fish and chips to supplement the nettles. I mean, even Clement Freud, who was there at the time, didn't have a dog in sight. It was wretched. At the age of 15 I asked my mother if I could leave.

So I said farewell to heavenly Crowthorne, and arrived at the portals of the Pitman College in Holborn. Here, as they say in those Victorian novels, I was to continue my studies. The only studying I did was of the girls there. They outnumbered the men by about ten to one, which I have always considered a satisfactory sort of ratio. Unfortunately, we were forbidden even to speak to them, let alone date them. But, a hardened revolutionary by now, I did actually take three of them out . . . not all at once, I hasten to add.

I stayed at Pitmans for about a year, and hated it, an emotion which readers will have gathered that I associate with every form of education. (Pitmans was not demolished, but a wartime bomb right outside made a fair attempt at it.)

Happily, it was during this year that I became friendly with Mrs Gisborn, a chum of my mother's. And Mrs Gisborn had *connections* . . . in the theatre.

Chapter Two

My name is not Pete Murray.

My name is Peter Murray James. True, the 'r' in Peter has come and gone at various stages in my career, for reasons theatrical or trivial or both. But the James was abandoned from the moment that I set my sights at the stage. The combination of two Christian names, I decided, would be confusing for the waiting world of admirers. They might be tempted to ask: "Peter James who?", or even worse "Peter James what?"

It wasn't really so surprising that the stage should appeal to me. My mother had been very keen on the stage herself. She had worked with Jack Buchanan, and her great friend was Elsie Randolph. In fact, many years later a clairvoyant I knew met her and told me: "She would have been a far greater star than you will ever be." Well, I never was, so perhaps that doesn't say much, but I believe that if she hadn't got married she'd have had a great career. She had what they call 'the magic'.

Her friend Mrs Gisborn had a daughter (whose name was Patricia Fox owing to Mrs G's rather complicated marital arrangements) at the Royal Academy of Dramatic Art; and one day while I was still struggling with the sex barriers of Pitmans College she said to my mother: "Your boy wants to act. He should go and see someone at RADA."

Thus it was that, still very shy, but fired with who knows what inner ambition, I made my way down Gower Street and presented myself at the temple of all dramatic wisdom. The doorman, in the practised way of all his kind who wish to make it clear immediately that they have "seen 'em all come and go, some successes, most failures," raised a barely curious eyebrow in my general direction.

"Could I see the principal, please?" I quavered, in answer to the unspoken question.

He gestured to me to wait, then returned some minutes later to usher me into the office of Sir Kenneth Barnes.

"You wanted to see me?"

"Yes, Sir."

"Well?"

"Well, I'd like to become an actor." It could hardly have been the first time he'd heard that particular line performed.

"I see. Have you done any amateur dramatic work at school?"

"No, Sir."

"Outside school?"

"No, Sir. I've never done anything at all."

Obviously shaken by this poverty of experience, he eyed me with some disbelief, then said "Well, you must have done *something*."

"Well, Sir," I stammered. "I *have* worked as an extra."

As indeed I had, courtesy of Mrs Gisborn. Mrs Gisborn knew somebody who knew somebody else, and by dint of these confusing arrangements I had contrived to join the Film Artists' Association and found myself as a film extra on the set of *The Young Mr Pitt*. I was supposed to be one of fifty students being lectured at an academy. For this I was paid £3 a day and remained totally invisible, since I was standing at the back and most of the others were taller than me.

But the extra work was in fact good experience. I would have been scared to death to go straight into a film part, and as it was I could be on the set and watch really good actors at work, like Anna Neagle, whom I saw playing Amy Johnson. The other thing I learned was that once you are working, no-one takes any notice of you, because they're all too busy doing their own thing.

My first sight of David Niven and Leslie Howard at work came in the shooting of *The First of the Few*, all about Mitchell, the man who invented the Spitfire. My heroic contribution to this epic came during the scene of the Schneider Trophy Race. Along with many others, I spent four or five days in a stand, cheering, in front of a big tank of water.

17

Admittedly, these excursions were hardly marking me as a natural successor to Olivier. A Sapling, yes. Potentially one of the Trees, perhaps not. Even a beautifully accentuated "Hooray" from the Schneider stands didn't count as 'lines'.

In fact, the only lines I ever had as an extra came in a film with Flanagan and Allen. God knows what the film was called but I was supposed to be a sound technician on a film set, and I was given the immortal piece of dialogue: "Okay for sound."

I felt that I had performed the part with some verve, and was mortified that, being so junior, I was not allowed to see the 'rushes' of the film on the following day.

I was hanging about outside the viewing room when Bud Flanagan came along and saw me.

"What's the matter, sonny?" he asked.

I explained my sorrow. "The thing is, I'd love to see the rushes. You see, it's the first line I've ever had in a film."

Bud pushed open the door. "Let the kid in," he said. " 'Ere, sonny, wanna cuppa tea?" And I saw my rushes.

He was lovely. Years later I opened a betting shop for him and for some reason I completely forgot to remind him of the incident. I regret that, now.

My other memory of that film was of a scene where Chesney Allen, who was privately a very shy man, was supposed to be playing a lover. It was right in the middle of this terrible love scene, and about the fifth 'take' because Chesney was doing it so badly, when suddenly Bud shouted out: " 'Ere, Ivor," – meaning Ivor Novello, because he looked like him, with the white tie, full tails and all – " 'Ere, Ivor, yer flies are undone." Need I say that the whole place promptly dissolved. That was Bud Flanagan.

This then was the 'experience' that I was laying at the thespian feet of Sir Kenneth.

For reasons which I have never remotely understood, I was taken on face value and accepted for RADA. I had no audition, which was just as well, because that *would* have sunk me. Perhaps it was simply that, because all the young men had been called up, they were desperately short of actors. I was 16.

In my first term I was so shy that they gave me a part with no lines to speak. I realised that this was making the best possible use of my experience as a film extra, but felt that that was not quite the purpose of my application to join the Academy. So then they gave me the part of Gratiano in *The Merchant of Venice*. It was intended, by the author that is, as a light-hearted role…"Let me play the fool: with mirth and laughter let old wrinkles come." Mirthful! I declaimed the lines with the solemnity due to Hamlet. They all burst into hysterics, and at the end of that first term I was called into the principal's office.

Sir Kenneth Barnes made his meaning as clear as a polished monocle.

"Murray," he said, "I really don't think you have a future as an actor. My advice to you is to give up. Immediately."

Now in normal circumstances a statement to similar effect would have crushed me beyond repair. But somewhere there was a spark of determination. I hastily reminded myself that unkind words of this nature had been offered to Vivien Leigh . . . and to Griffith Jones, who subsequently won the Bancroft Gold Medal.

So, summoning a meekness of which there was a plentiful supply on hand, I said: "Would you please give me another chance."

Well, as I said, they *were* short of young men, and my mother *was* paying my fees, which at £10 a week were heavy enough. So they made their second inexplicable decision and allowed me to stay.

I was especially pleased about this since I had just had my cards printed. I had been reading Noel Coward's *Present Indicative*, in which he describes how, when he first started, he had cards printed which read: "Noel Coward, Stage Actor."

I thought this was a frightfully good idea, and rushed out to have some printed with the defiant inscription: "Peter Murray James. Stage, Screen, and Radio." Why I reverted to the 'James' for the purposes of the cards I don't recall. Maybe I just wanted to fill the space. Maybe I remembered that the 'Murray' came from the fact that, before she married, my mother had fancied a drummer of that name at the Savoy Hotel. Maybe it struck me that Noel Coward wasn't, to the best of my knowledge, named after a drummer.

Whatever the reason, I used to arm myself with these cards and descend upon the various London cinemas, the Empire Leicester Square, the Plaza, the Queen's in Bayswater, the Dominion in Tottenham Court Road. I would approach the nearest attendant, and request an audience with the manager. As soon as this worthy emerged, I would thrust the card at him with all the dignity I could muster, and declare: "I am in the profession. Could I possibly have a complimentary ticket?"

I was never, ever, refused.

My great friend at RADA was called Patrick Westwood. We were always up to some ungodly activity, which would usually be planned at a tea and bun shop next to Goodge Street Station, now sadly but not unexpectedly demolished. From there, Patrick and I would descend upon the Lyons Corner House on the corner of Tottenham Court Road and Oxford Street.

Nothing unusual about that, you may think, until I tell you that he would wear a dog collar (a real one; nothing clerical about us) around his neck. To this was attached a lead, by which I would manoeuvre him into the Corner House. He would wear a pair of pince-nez on the end of his nose and play an extremely convincing idiot of the gibbering kind.

It always worked very well, because if we went to a table that was half full, or indeed if there were no free tables at all, people would always move away with great haste. The effect may have been heightened by the fact that I used to feed him by hand, and he'd slobber the food down all over his face, which admittedly was pretty revolting.

We did the same thing on trains. Compartments were always very full in those days, but we always managed to get an empty one. People seemed to have a preference for standing in the corridor when we came along . . . probably due to the fact that I had Patrick on the lead, and Patrick was pretending to be sick. In those days, I guess we acted better off stage than on. It was our first public success. We got our pleasures in these simple ways, since we were hardly rich, though my mother did give me £1 a week pocket money. This wasn't too bad for those days, especially if you could get the girls to meet you *inside* the cinema, which I invariably did.

I was still very nervous of that other half of the population, and it was as much as I could do to hold hands. That particular piece of ice had been broken a with a girl called Pat Walsh, from Pitmans. I had saved up ten shillings, and since this was to be a special occasion, I actually paid for her three-shilling cinema seat. That left four shillings, with which we had a meal. Now I was penniless once more, and since she lived in Hendon and I lived in Bayswater, my scope for further activity was limited. But I *had* held her hand, and I remember that delicious moment, far more than my defloration, years later, as the true moment of awakening.

At RADA I recall fancying madly a girl called Jeanette Redgrave (I never discovered if she was a relation), and another called Desiree Carnell (sadly, I mentioned her many years later on the radio, and her daughter wrote to tell me she had died of cancer) . . . and I have fond memories of an interesting incident when I was thrown out of Richmond Park in the company of a lady named Joan Sexton. But it was all innocent fun, and my techniques were all based on the one basic premise . . . my sheer ignorance.

At RADA, things started to go a little better . . . they certainly could not have got worse. I had a small part in a play about the Brontës, which wasn't too bad, and I felt I was getting somewhere, since I *was* actually being permitted to speak. But there was competition. During that second term, Bryan Forbes arrived. He came with a certain reputation, since he had been doing the Junior Brains Trust on the BBC with Lionel Gamlin. We assumed, perhaps wrongly, that this would involve his ego in some inflation, a state of affairs which we would have to alter.

At the moment of Bryan's arrival, I happened to be fencing, on the steps of RADA (oh yes, *weren't* we the extroverts) with one Norman Bird. Seeing La Forbes appear, I did a sort of leap down the stairs and put the foil to his neck. Mustering a full Shakespearean extravagance, I declaimed: "So *you* are Bryan Forbes, are you? So be it!"

What exactly this was meant to imply I have not the remotest idea, but it must have been a pretty frightening way to enter anywhere. In his book *Notes for a Life* Bryan recalls the incident and says that he was "not even disconcerted at Pete's attempted humiliation of me, for to be noticed at all was a kind of triumph." Well, that's true, but I still think he got the message, though there were no hard feelings, because Norman Bird, a fine character actor, subsequently appeared in many of Bryan's films, including *The League of Gentlemen*.

The real star of my time there was Richard Attenborough. He was very popular with everyone, and while still at RADA he was cast as a cowardly matelot in Noel Coward's *In Which We Serve*. Although he had been there before me, I was with him enough to be impressed, and looked at him with respect and not a little envy. (A funny thing, judgment. There was another student whom we all put down as destined for certain failure. His name was Alec McCowan.)

Soon after he left RADA, Dickie was cast in the play of *Brighton Rock*. Another member of the company was Harcourt Williams, a lovely old boy who had produced me in a play at RADA. Harcourt suggested me as the understudy to Dickie in the production of *Brighton Rock* at Wyndhams Theatre, but they didn't give it to me because they had a general feeling that I didn't have enough experience. So I suppose you could say that my first big disappointment in life was the failure to be Richard Attenborough's understudy.

During my second holiday break I went on tour with RADA, performing with Alec McCowan in *Julius Caesar*. The repertory, which was taken to schools round the country, included *The Merchant of Venice*. Mindful, perhaps, of my previous abject failure to grasp the part of Gratiano, they now cast me as Lorenzo. The general feeling was that during that tour I established a new low for the part of Lorenzo, completing, as it were, the Spring Double for The Merchant.

Unaffected by, or perhaps simply ignorant of, this debacle, I returned to RADA feeling confident enough to put a proposition to them. I wondered what the possibility would be of my getting a scholarship.

The monstrosity of such a suggestion presumably staggered them so much, that all they could say was that they would let me know during the next term . . . my first experience of "Don't call us, we'll call you."

There was at that time at RADA a man called Colin Chandler, who used to do all the scenery and was a kind of general odd-job man. He was given the task of producing a play by Ronald Mackenzie called *Musical Chairs*. The title belies the seriousness of the play, which was about a consumptive, and was set in the oilfields of Poland. Well, Colin Chandler, who was very 'nouveau vague', even by today's standards, set about casting us for the play. He went through all the parts, and finally came to the most important role, that of Josef Schindler, which had been played in the original production by John

22

Gielgud.

At this point, he took me aside, and said: "I saw you give what was possibly the worst performance I've ever seen in my life, as Lorenzo. But somewhere, tucked away, I think you've got something. I'm going to give you a part totally opposite to your character. I think you can do it."

And he gave me the part of Schindler.

It had the same effect on me that Mr Renton had produced with his interest in my aping of Denis Compton at cricket. I worked my heart out for Colin Chandler. And when we finally came to do the play I got a standing ovation, despite the rule at RADA that there should be no applause.

Colin Chandler is now Principal of the Royal Scottish Academy of Drama in Glasgow. I haven't seen him for 30 years. But I owe everything to that man. If it hadn't been for him I probably *would* have ended up as a lavatory attendant, as predicted by the infamous Buster Reed.

Now my fortunes changed. The authorities, by now no doubt totally bemused by the unpredictable nature of the Murray repertoire, delivered me my scholarship. Thus armed, I could have afforded to stay for the full two years. But that summer, 1943, I was cast in *St Joan,* which was that year's big production.

It was a trying time for me. My grandfather was at that moment lying in University College Hospital, just up the street, dying of cancer. I was given the part of Dunois, in *St Joan*, and to my delight, and some degree of astonishment, I won the RADA Bronze Medal for my performance. The medal was presented by the Queen, now the Queen Mother, so I was specially pleased that my Mum was there too. After the award, I took my prize up to the hospital ward where my grandfather lay, and showed it to him. His eyes lit up, he sat up in bed, and made what the surgeon called a remarkable recovery. He lived for another year, and the surgeon told me that if it hadn't been for the medal he would probably have died within the week.

St Joan was produced by Robert Atkins, who at that time was running the Open Air Theatre in Regents Park. He was very keen that I should go straight from RADA to join him there. It looked like a wonderful break.

23

But my efforts as Dunois had also been seen by an agent called Herbert de Leon, who was to become a great friend and one of the most marvellous men I ever met. He thought that my future lay in films.

Robert Atkins took this rebuff with all the theatrical pomp at his command. "You are", he said, "throwing up a fine theatrical tradition by moving into that hideous medium, with stupid women who can't project themselves."

I quavered, suitably. I also went ahead and joined Herbert de Leon.

Chapter Three

I never became another Cary Grant.

Nor even a second Lassie. Instant success and stardom were not, it is
fair to say, waiting open-armed on the steps of RADA. Equipped with
my bronze medal, my visiting cards, and my membership of the Film
Artists' Association, I emerged into a world singularly unaware of the
new talent available to it.

The first steps to rectify this omission came with an invitation to
meet Herbert de Leon at the Café Royal. I had signed a contract with
him, convinced that the document was an express ticket to fame. It
immediately became apparent, however, that the journey was on a
stopping train. This first stop took the form of an introduction to two
casting directors, Eric Lepine Smith, and Weston Drury. The fruit of
this meeting was a small part in a film called *Time Flies*, whose star was
Tommy Handley of ITMA fame. Did I say a small part? I exaggerated.
It was miniscule. I played the part of a stage hand. Evelyn Dahl, who
was then a singer with the Bert Ambrose band, was in the film, and the
moment of glory for which all the tribulations of RADA had prepared
me, came when I had to say to her: "You're on next, Miss Jones."

Now there are those who might consider that the line: "You're on
next, Miss Jones," was hardly a strong starting platform for an aspiring
actor. Some might go so far as to suggest that it is a throw-away line
which will inevitably be sunk without trace. They reckon without the
hardened veteran of: "Okay for sound?"

The film was directed by a man called Ford — *not* John Ford, to be
sure — who for some reason best known to himself went out of his

mind about the way I had performed these five words. He phoned Herbert de Leon.

"Herbert. I want to tell you, this boy's definitely got it. Great. Wonderful."

To me he said: "Listen Peter. You did that line just marvellously. You're going places, and if you ever want help, just tell me."

If it didn't sound rather peculiar, I would describe myself at that moment as having been radiant with happiness, if you'll pardon my cliché. It was just as well that I couldn't guess the sequel. A few years later, when I was with Rank and out of work, I went to see this man.

At first he didn't want to see me, and professed ignorance as to my identity. I sent back word by way of his equerry that "We had worked together." That, at least, got me in to see him.

"Yes?"

"My name's Peter Murray, and you said to get in touch if I needed help."

"Oh, did I? Why?"

"Well, I was in *Time Flies,* and I was the stage hand, and you were very pleased with the way I said: 'You're on next, Miss Jones.' You said I had a future. You phoned my agent, Herbert de Leon."

Never be desperate. You may get crushed. I got crushed.

"Oh, yes? I don't remember."

That was it, but it was a Lesson Learned.

Herbert de Leon, among his many other accomplishments, had a brother named Jack. Jack owned the Kew Theatre. The combination of Herbert and Jack provided my entrée into the professional theatre. Flushed with my success in *Time Flies*, I got a part in a play called *Marigold* at Kew. Jean Cadell was in it, I remember, and the Assistant Stage Manager, that starting (and stopping) place for so many hopefuls, was Richard Pascoe. My friend in the play was acted by Peter Bayliss. We were supposed to be two officers in the Scots Guards. My chief memory of that relationship was that we got into terrible trouble with the management for sending up the Eightsome Reel, an attitude which the playwright had by no means intended.

From the Kew Theatre I went to Cambridge, where I had a part in *The Idiot* by Dostoievsky. The write-up in the Times said: "This marks the debut of a young 17 yr-old actor who has a tremendous future."

Obviously the critic hadn't been to see my reels at Kew, but it was nice all the same. And London beckoned.

I was put up for a part in *The Man Who came to Dinner*, whose star was Robert Morley. It was at the Savoy Theatre, and before I knew whether I'd got the part, I took a young actress friend of mine to see it. Her name was June Whitfield, later to be a star of *Take it from Here* and a dozen other shows. Well, we had what for me was a very pleasant and memorable, though innocent, evening. Holding hands was still THE THING as far as I was concerned, and I missed about the first half of the play trying to work out how to hold her hand without offending her, in which manoeuvre I eventually succeeded. Twenty years later she was a guest on Open House, and I reminded her of our evening out.

Heartbreak for Murray. She couldn't remember a thing.

"I can remember fancying you," she said. "But I have absolutely no memory of ever going out with you."

So much for my powers of persuasion and manual dexterity.

But I did get the part in the play, the part of the boy. It had three weeks left in London before going on tour, and I remember that there was an actress in it called Laura Smith and another named Ada Dick. That was a name that appealed to me, so on the last night, before the curtain went up, I got on to the Tannoy system which went through to all the dressing rooms.

I put on what you might call my minor-bureaucrat voice and said "Mr Robert Morley is ill today, and the part of Sheridan Whiteside will be played by Miss Ada Dick."

Morley was absolutely furious, and he nearly came to blows with Hugh McDermott, who was playing the romantic lead, because he was quite convinced that Hugh had done it.

We took the play on tour. I think if I had ever been going to give up the theatre it would have been then. I've never found going on tour the most ecstatic of experiences, even in good times. But during the war, with unheated trains, the black-out, miserable digs, it became the ultimate in the disagreeable. Sheffield, Glasgow, Edinburgh, pitch black in the middle of winter. No thank you.

The situation was in no sense mitigated by the presence of Captain Ferguson, our Stage Director. He was about six foot two inches tall, weighed about 14 stone, had greying hair, wore glasses, and sported a small, greying moustache. And he was totally overbearing. I think he had been a former regular army officer. He certainly had an intense dislike for actors, which gives one to wonder how he ever came to be doing that particular job.

The company quickly nicknamed itself The Concentration Camp, due to Captain Ferguson's insistence on running the show as if it were a part of regimental orders. "Bags will be moved at 0900 hours. The company will embus at 0945."

We travelled from town to town by train, and that was my first experience of a second-class sleeper. I hadn't realised that you could find yourself bunk-to-bunk with a complete stranger. I remember three of us once being thrown into the company of a rather unreceptive girl from somewhere like Bradford. After a while she burst out: "I can't stand all you people. Can't you call each other anything but darlings and duckies?"

At the end of the journey, the digs were seldom anything to look forward to. There was one lot in Bristol where I woke in the middle of the night to find myself crawling with bedbugs. Horrified, I woke up the landlady to inform her of the wild-life situation in my room.

"Oh, isn't that terrible," she said. "You must have brought them in with you."

"I don't run a bloody circus," I told her, but she was unmoved.

Then there was Grimsby, which in the middle of wartime was well-named. Three of us got to these digs, which were pleasant enough, but I had hardly started unpacking when the landlady infiltrated my room, with what was clearly a prepared speech.

"Me 'usband's been dead two years now. And I don't know how you feel about it, but I think it's always better with yer teeth out." With that she took out all her teeth, put them in a glass, declared: "I always think it's better for kissing, don't you?" and leapt upon me.

There was only one way out of an entanglement with this monster.

"Oh, no, no, no, no," I simpered, waving an airy hand at her. "Oh no, you mustn't. It's *abhorrent* to me."

It seemed that my life theatrical was spent trying to persuade queers that I was normal, and ladies with no teeth that I was gay. At any rate, she abandoned her assault and went off to hurl herself upon the others, taking, I'm happy to say, her teeth with her.

Nor shall I forget wartime Wigan, on a Sunday. Everything closed up tight as a bank vault, with the exception of the Methodist Church and one café. Doubting whether the preacher could find any method of relieving my gloom, I decided that my particular inner man would have, for the moment, to live by bread alone. I entered the café. There was one woman, serving a row of empty tables.

"What do yer want, luv?"

"I don't know. Can I look at the menu please?"

I inspected the fly-blown sheet. It was full of egg and chips and stuff like that, which I didn't want.

I asked: "Have you got anything else at all?"

She glowed. "You're really lucky. We've got the Speciality of the 'Ouse on 'ere today, Udder Pie."

I said : "WHAT?"

She said: "Udder Pie."

"Oh no, I don't think I'd like anything like that." I shuddered at the thought.

She said: "No, you're a Southern lad, aren't yer? We 'ave different tastes up 'ere."

I ordered egg and chips.

Now nobody believed this story, until some years later, after the war, I was on a tour which arrived in Blackpool. I was sharing digs with a couple of other actors, and we had the usual greeting ...

"Well, I'd like you in by eleven o'clock. There'll be a supper waiting for you. Is there anything you specially like?"

I said: "I'm not particularly keen on fried food. I'd rather have salad, or something like that."

She said "Alright, luv."

"Oh, by the way," I said. "My friends don't believe me. Have you ever heard of a dish called Udder Pie?"

She said "Udder Pie? No. No, I've never heard of anything like that. No. Some people do have queer tastes, don't they. No, I slice my udders and put them into the salad."

I remember my own horrified silence.

"On second thoughts," I said, "forget the salad. I'll have something fried."

29

Not all the digs were bad, but you had to get to know the good ones. There was one marvellous place in the provinces – many well-known people used to stay there – which was actually a brothel. But it was also a very good digs. Unfortunately I think the lady of the house died. But that was an exception. For the most part they were awful, and they didn't believe in items like laundry. They just ironed out the dirty sheets.

Faced with all this discomfort, I fear I rather went to pieces. On one occasion I came on stage dressed in skating attire, only to find, as soon as I got on stage, that it was the wrong scene. I suppose no-one who was in the audience ever quite realised why I was dressed for the ice.

But then, I've always been absent-minded.

On another occasion, at the Lyceum in Glasgow, I completely missed a matinee. I had had to get out of my digs by noon – it was the Saturday, and we were moving on that night – and I went to the theatre to leave my gear in the skip, the big hamper for everyone's bags. I had forgotten the matinee time, and I looked out at the front of the theatre and saw: "Matinees Wednesdays and Saturdays 2.30." When I arrived happily back at five past two, I found the play already in progress and my understudy on stage. The notice had referred to the following week.

Captain Ferguson was not pleased. Captain Ferguson was hopping mad. Captain Ferguson wrote to Firth Shepherd, the impresario, outlining Murray's misdemeanours at some length (well, there was a lot to tell). I got a note from Shepherd, which, politely translated, said: "Pull your socks up or you will be fired."

I think that it must have been about that time that I started to fantasise about killing Captain Ferguson. In uncomfortable and bug-ridden attics around the British Isles, I lay in bed at night dreaming of ways in which he could be eliminated. I remember being very pleased with one idea I had. I would wait until we were in Yorkshire, then suggest that he and I should go for a ride in the Pennines. At a suitably high spot I would push him over the abyss. Then I would rush back to the nearest police station and cry "There's been a terrible accident. Captain Ferguson has fallen off a mountain."

I considered poisoning the cups of tea he drank in the wings, but poison worried me. I'd read about Crippen, and knew they traced the rat poison he'd given his wife.

I was quite clear that I didn't want to get caught, which was the reason I ruled out shooting him. But there was a rather good plan which involved some reconstruction of the stage which would facilitate Captain Ferguson's descent, headfirst and helpless, into the orchestra pit and through the bass drum. Sadly, before any of those schemes could bear fruit, the 17 weeks of the tour were over. It had not been happy. We had an American actress who unfortunately was something of a tippler and a fellow called Edward Cooper who was in the same condition, and another actress who played the nurse in the play and who actually went on stage one night paralytically drunk. Anyone who didn't start that tour off as a drunkard had every reason for becoming one by the end.

But Robert Morley sailed through the whole thing with his own unique brand of serene pomposity. He used to be a bit unkind to me about my pimples, and he was always trying to 'corpse' the other players. You'd be in the middle of a speech and Morley would whisper: "That's a nice tie you've got on tonight." But that's just him, and I learned to retaliate with such deathless on-stage sotto voce quips as "I've got a 'Penguin' for you."

After the tour proper, we went on a kind of pseudo-tour of a number of Army and Navy barracks, under the auspices of ENSA. Somebody 'up there' clearly hadn't heard the expression "Nothing's too good for our boys," because the company was promptly cut from 35 to 20 to reduce costs. Unfortunately, this reduction did not include the elimination of Captain Ferguson. On the contrary. He was now in his militaristic element, and as soon as we arrived in a camp he would don his uniform.

This caused Robert Morley the absolute horrors, since he would in any case always refuse categorically to go into an officers' mess.

This was a matter of principle with Robert, who didn't like officers as a race, and who was, I think, a professed socialist anyway. But the rest of us would troop along like ducklings in the wake of our khaki-clad Captain, and be polite to absurd young officers who poured sherry and made 'conversational' remarks like: "Yes, I know you're an actor, but what do you actually do for a living?" I have many times regretted that I could not have gone armed with that wonderful Peter

Sellers line from *Girl in my Soup*, where he is supposed to be a TV personality and someone asks: "Yes, but do you have a proper job?" He replies "Didn't you know? I perform abortions."

The reduction in the cast meant that we all had to take on extra roles. Then one day the actor playing the romantic lead had to go and get chicken pox, which was how Murray, aged 17, with a false moustache and hair heavily greyed at the sides, found himself playing opposite Ambrosine Philpotts. This rather put me in Morley's good books, since he felt I had saved the day, and thus he came to intercede for me.

We were in Wales. Wales had not been good to us. We had performed that two-act, extremely funny play in front of an audience of (for some reason) naval Scotsmen. They achieved the rare distinction of sitting through the entire offering without so much as a titter. Anyway, one evening the phone rang. It was my mother. I had been called to serve my country. I was to report to the RAF at Llanelli. Morley would have none of it. "I shall come with you, dear boy," he announced, primping himself into a Pickwickian posture.

I presented myself to the recruiting sergeant at Llanelli feeling like a schoolboy under the wing of a benevolent uncle. 'Uncle' took immediate charge.

"You cannot possibly take this boy. He's an *integral* part of my production. I cannot spare him. He cannot go. Shall need him for the next six weeks." It was not a plea. It was a statement. I said nothing. To the best of my memory, the sergeant said nothing.

The tour continued its unappreciated progress. When it ended, Morley called me to see him. He told me how pleased he was with me, and said: "When you come out of the Air Force, do come and see me. I'd love to help you."

Another Lesson. After the war, when things were hard and I couldn't get work, I decided to see Morley. He was doing a play at the Savoy, and when I sent a message in to his dressing room he agreed to see me. He was sitting at his dressing table, and seemed to be addressing me by way of his own reflection.

"Well, dear boy, what can I do for you?"

"Er, I was wondering if you could possibly . . . I mean, you *did* say that any time you could help me you would . . ."

"Did I really, dear boy? I can't remember that. I can't remember that at all. What did you do with me, dear boy? Where was this, dear boy?"

I reminded him.

"Oh, yes. Well, I'm afraid I can't help you at all, dear boy."

A little numbed, I said: "Thank you for seeing me," and went. It was rather sad, at the time. But on reflection, I suppose there was really nothing he could do. One tends to assume that because a man is in a top position he can help anyone. And often he can't. I dare say that if the right part had come along he'd have put me on to it.

But then again, he wasn't my agent. And I guess that if he had started ringing up friends and saying: "I have this young friend aged whatever I was then and can you help him?" they'd have thought straight away: "Hello! Robert's on the turn!"

But all that was after the war. My immediate desire was to get home to Bayswater, and away from the persecution of Captain Ferguson, whose charmed life had run the gauntlet of so many daydreams. Within days, the call to duty came. I was to report to the RAF at Carshalton on December 13th, 1943.

Chapter Four

I was not a war hero.

This was due less to cowardice than to the fact that I never saw the enemy. Heroics are difficult in such circumstances. It is also fair to say that Murray had decided from the start that Murray's war should be conducted with the minumum possible inconvienience to Murray.

The whole tone of the matter had been set when I had had to go for a medical 'somewhere in Acton'. The place was covered in recruiting posters which portrayed life as extremely dangerous, and they proceeded to declare me medically fit. I burst into tears.

But I did keep my wits sufficiently together to opt for the RAF . . . I reckoned they had the easiest life, and besides, they wore collars and ties.

Thus it was that I presented myself at Carshalton, which I understood to have been an old Zeppelin base. The people there still seemed full of wind, including the depressing sergeant who interviewed me. He asked me where I came from (as though *that* was going to win the war), and about my schooling (his euphemism, not mine), and about my interests. I said "Girls," which was apparently not what he had in mind. Then he asked how much I had been earning as an actor. I told him: "Eleven pounds a week," and he immediately formed the impression that I was some kind of millionaire, since he was making about four pounds if he was lucky.

At Carshalton we were kitted out and provided with uniforms. I had some consolation in finding two friends there who had been at RADA with me, Wolfe Morris, and Charles Mander, who had been fencing with Norman Bird and myself at the moment of Bryan Forbes' arrival.

Since it was approaching Christmas, we decided to put on an impromptu show for the lads, and a few of the sergeants came in to see it. They emerged declaring that we were brilliant...though we realised that this was simply because we were able to remember our lines, which *had* to be a sign of talent.

From Carshalton we were despatched by train to Skegness, in Lincolnshire. The worst part of that journey was when it was over, because we then had to walk miles from the station to our digs. We had our kitbags on our shoulders, and by the time we had got half-way there it was just all too much for me. Happily, one of my larger companions volunteered to carry my bag for me...I've always been lucky that way; I'm one of those people who, if they get a puncture, immediately meet someone to mend it for them. Perhaps I just look helpless.

We were billeted at the Villa Marina, which must have been one of the more exotic postings in the British Isles. It was a beautiful house on the front at Skegness, overlooking the sand-dunes, and its interior included two bathrooms, both of which had been smashed to pieces, and twelve wash basins, of which one was functioning. The purpose of this period in our training, however, was not the destruction of the plumbing but square-bashing. We comprised forty men, of varying backgrounds, and I shared a room with a Canadian, a fellow from Lincoln, and a Bernard Bresslaw type called Morgan. He came from Cardiff, did poor Morgan, and he suffered agonies at the hands and voice of our sergeant, another Welshman called Jones, beside whom Captain Ferguson appeared an angel in retrospect.

Every military group has one of these slightly retarded, rather sad and slow figures. Well we had two. Morgan, and a man called Cummings. Sergeant Jones used to position himself on top of an air-raid shelter and delight in making idiots of them.

I was sorry for them, but I had already learned my basic survival lesson for the forces: "Don't do anything you're told." There's a marvellous saying, something about: "Rules and regulations are to be obeyed by idiots and for the guidance of wise men." I don't know if I was a wise man, but I did immediately decide that whereas the majority would do what they were told, I would not.

This lesson derived from an early clash with Sergeant Jones. As a punishment, he ordered me to report at seven o'clock that night to scrub out the Boston Boys Home, the inexplicably-named building where we had our 'food'. I complied with this order, only to discover that there was little or no check on whether I had done so. On about 14 subsequent occasions a similar punishment was meted out to me, and I simply didn't go.

This technique I also applied to regular training. From time to time we were required to go on a route march of some 25 miles. This seemed to me an entirely disagreeable proposition, so on every occasion that it was mentioned I would simply remain in my room and read. It seemed that the disciplinarian sergeant didn't number arithmetic among his attributes, since if he had been able to count he would have known that someone was missing.

Occasionally I had to resort to more intricate subterfuge. We had to do gun drill in the Vine Hotel, and there were aspects of this that I found uncomfortable. So, when I felt particularly loath to perform with my rifle, I would throw a fit. Summoning what little histrionic ability there was at my disposal, I would do a 'free fall' such as I had learned at RADA, foam a little at the mouth, and be carried off to the sanatorium. Of course, they could never find anything wrong with me, but they were convinced that I must be in a bad way of some kind or other. On the other hand, they were so desperate for men (I use the term loosely) that they seemed prepared to put up with it.

I know a number of other actors who used similar techniques. Some used to prance around like fairies, or pansies, as they were called then. I mean, someone who has been a Welsh miner, and then becomes a sergeant in the RAF, finds it a bit difficult to cope with a recruit who flounces around and cries "Don't you *dare* talk to me like that, or I'll hit you with my handbag."

And of course, most of them weren't 'that way' at all. Harold Lang, who later changed his name to Howard Lang, worked this trick and lasted just three weeks. In the end they simply despaired, and removed him.

This training for the RAF lasted about eight weeks, during which I saw not a single aeroplane and managed to take one bath. This was at the Skegness Public Baths. A couple of years ago, when I was up there, I enquired about the fate of those baths. "Oh, they've been demolished *quite* a number of years ago," said my informant, looking at me with some horror that I could even remember the said place of ablution.

My finances had suffered a decline, as well. From £11 a week I had descended to an unprincely 25 bob, most of which went on chocolate cakes fom the NAAFI, since the Boston Boys Home was not exactly Lincolnshire's top eaterie.

From Skegness I was moved to Cranwell, though not to become an officer. I had never gone before any officer selection boards...obviously they thought that my 'fits' did not exactly recommend me for a commission. In fact, to the best of my recollection, I never even spoke to an officer the whole time of my service, if that's what you'd call it. On the other hand, when the blue RAF battledress first came out I was issued, for some reason, with one of the first specimens, with which I affected my own blue shirt and black satin tie, which I felt was rather smart. Others obviously thought so too, since I was favoured with a number of salutes which I acknowledged in the most gracious manner I could muster.

Cranwell was like a holiday camp. There were 4,000 men and 2,000 WAAFS, and there was dancing every night. They had some great groups playing. I especially remember Keith Bird, an ex-Geraldo sax player. We would get to bed at about two in the morning, and lessons would start at 9.30 in the morning, during which, exhausted by the revelries, I would sleep.

The purpose of these lessons was to turn me into an R/T operator, an arbitrary decision on their part which had been made without any reference to yours truly. The job would entail calling pilots in and so on from the ground, and my only attitude towards it was: "God forbid that I am ever called upon to perform this task." I can say, without undue modesty, that I knew nothing whatsoever about it. I suppose in a way it was my first training in broadcasting, but I was never called upon to say a word. On the other hand, I *was* supposed to learn the morse code, but it was a blank to me, and evoked the same sort of emotions I suffer when I am forced to look under the bonnet of a car.

There was a corporal in charge of us, and every weekend I'd bung him a few bob, in return for which he would forge a weekend pass for me (I had a whole stash of them saved up) and I would go home. I went in my uniform, of course, all fairly resplendent, though I don't think the family were under any illusion that I was about to save the nation.

Back at Cranwell I continued dancing, and threw a fit if it exhausted me too much to get to 'school' in time. And finally, having put in no examination papers, and remaining incapable of tapping out even an SOS in morse, I was passed as a fully qualified R/T operator.

Thus endowed, I was now required to make my way to Fairford in Gloucestershire, in a lovely part of the Cotswolds. And it was here that any understanding of the RAF's logic in its deployment of P. Murray finally deserted me. Having forced the R/T qualification upon me, they now set me to work looking after some gliders.

It was idyllic. There were six of us and a corporal, whose job it was to check the batteries and accumulators on this fleet of gliders. We had our own hut, miles from anywhere else on the station, and our only contact with the main buildings was when we picked up our pay from the clerk every week. At first the system was that we would each have one day off a week. The second man would be on the runway, checking the fifteen or so gliders that would be standing there waiting for someone to train in them. And the other four would check the fifty or so gliders parked off the runway. It was a simple enough job, and I merely thanked God that I had not been asked to perform as an R/T operator. I mean, I wouldn't have wanted to be responsible for anyone's death or anything like that…not on *our* side, anyway.

But between us we could accomplish our chores in about two hours flat. It didn't take long for the alert mind of Aircraftman Murray to realise that this was ridiculous. While one man always had to be on the runway, the work on the remaining gliders could easily be done by two men within the day. So we could have every other day off.

It was a real Dad's Army. The Corporal's name was Barnwell, and he was studying for something or other, reading day in day out, never doing a stroke. So it was easy to get him sorted out. People since the war have asked me who I was attached to (meaning which unit) and I have always replied 'Corporal Barnwell', because that was it. I was attached to him, as far as I was concerned.

Our hut backed on to a farm, and we soon became very friendly with the family there. They and their friends all had big, old-fashioned battery radios, and when their batteries ran out we kept them supplied from the glider stocks. They in turn kept us supplied with little luxuries like eggs and so on.

The sort of routine that developed was...10.30, get out of bed. Breakfast of bacon and eggs at the farmhouse. 11.00, do a couple of hours on the gliders. 13.00, lunch at the farmhouse. (Well, it was much *nearer* than the station canteen.)

Now the Corporal had agreed, after a duly democratic discussion, that there should always be two men on duty in case of an emergency. I was paired with an Irishman named Tim Dowling whose love of work approximated to my own. Put another way, neither of us liked it. But we *had* noticed that the farmer possessed a likeable horse. So we developed a new routine by which we would finish our gliders in the morning, then say to Barnwell: "Look, Corp. If anything comes up on the phone, we're in the field over there, riding." That was on our *working* afternoons. Barnwell was too engrossed in his studies to care, and the only thought in my mind was: "Thank God it's my day off tomorrow."

At weekends I would go home for three days on the by-now familiar forged passes, and I would either hitch-hike, which was easy in uniform, or use a forged rail pass if there was one available. It was on one such rail journey that I bumped into Betsy. Actually, it was not so much a bump as a grind, since we found ourselves pressed eyeball to eyeball (and that's not all) in a crowded corridor. I found her very amenable, and discovered that she was a farmer's daughter from Witney. So I developed a new habit on days off, which involved the twelve-mile train journey to Witney and a romp in the fields with Betsy. I remember her once asking me why I didn't save money by bicycling over, and myself replying that whereas I might have the energy to get over there, my resources were usually rather depleted for the return journey.

There were only two slight ways in which that hallowed ritual of the forces, discipline, ever affected me. The first was that I liked to wear my hair at some distance below regulation length, and since it was in that condition I felt it looked better without a cap. The Special Police (our equivalent of MPs,) would *keep* reminding me that they had alternative views. There was one chap in particular whom I drove close to desperation. One day he came up to me and said, "Look, I know you don't like wearing a cap, but for Gawd's sake, if you see me coming, *please* put it on."

"Very well," I said. I had discovered that if you talked to them in a way I would call a bit sproncey, they weren't too keen to 'come it' with you . . . you might always be the son of an Air Vice-Marshal.

The second occasion came when we found ourselves confined to camp for three weeks. In ordinary circumstances – and doubtless such was the intention of the upper echelons – we would not be expected to know what was going on. But a week before our confinement Tim Dowling had persuaded me to keep him company in the local pub, where I was informed by a crusty old inhabitant "You're from the camp, are you? I hear you're all going off to Arnhem." So much for security. I have a clear memory of all these commandos being brought into the camp and being kept in caged compounds like wild animals . . . and indeed, that was exactly how they seemed to us. The rumour was that they were on some sort of drug to make them fierce, and I knew I certainly wouldn't have gone in among them.

But my main concern was that for three weeks I was denied the pleasure of my romps with Betsy, by courtesy of the Fairford-Witney railway line, a branch that has, yes you've guessed, been demolished, or rather Beechinged.

Towards the end of 1944 I went on one of my counterfeit weekends home to Bayswater and while at the Duke of Edinburgh I contracted some fearful stomach bug. I lay ill in bed at home for many weeks. The RAF seemed keen that I should return to some sort of RAF establishment, rather than the comforts of home. I thought otherwise, and remained at the Duke.

In the end, however, they won. Well, there were more of them. I was taken to the RAF hospital at Ely, where doctors probed my condition. They told me that they suspected a duodenal ulcer, but this was probably because they were too polite to mention my 'history' of 'fits'. Finally they informed me that frankly it wasn't worth all the trouble in order to get me fit enough to resume my contribution to the war effort.

The doctor's advice was: "If I were you, I wouldn't go back to acting. What you need is a good healthy open-air life."

What I said was: "Thank you, Sir."

What I thought was "Considering I've spent all my time in the RAF leading the open air-life that I do, I can't see that it's done too much for me."

I had to return to my unit for discharge, and the unit had moved from Fairford to Dunmow, in Essex. I could not believe what I found.

This was at a time when, because men had been drafted from the RAF to the Army, they were now desperate for men for the RAF. I went to find my old section looking after the gliders. There still was such a section. And they looked after exactly the same number of gliders that we had. But they now numbered one flight sergeant, four sergeants, six corporals, and 26 men.

Well, we had been scroungers, true, and we had bent all sorts of rules, the six of us and Corporal Barnwell. But we *had* always done the job thoroughly and properly. What the hell those 37 men ever found to do I never knew. But I know one thing – it meant they all had to be there all the time.

It was May, 1945, and the day of my discharge, and a few minutes before I was actually due to leave I happened into the path of a particularly obstreperous Warrant Officer, who had pulled me up before. He stopped me. " 'Ere, you. Git yer 'air cut. Yer 'air's too long. The Adjutant's seen you, and you got ter git yer 'air cut."

It was a marvellous moment. Suddenly I was on stage for all those millions of junior ranks in the forces who have wanted to express their true feelings to their superior officers. I expressed my true feelings. I said: "GO and get STUFFED!"

He was, as they say, thunderstruck, not to mention nonplussed.

"WHAT! 'Oo do yer think yer talking' to? I'll 'ave you on a charge."

I smiled my most sproncey smile.

"You'll be lucky," I said. "I'm leaving. Right now."

Chapter Five

I am not a virgin.

Some might imagine that my professed dislike of drink and so on might have infiltrated other aspects of my life. I have to disillusion them.

It is true that my chastity had remained unblemished – well, only slightly spotted – throughout my RAF career. Being 'in the Service' had remained for me exactly what it is supposed to mean, though my romps with Betsy in the hayfields had given me to understand that there was more to life than holding hands.

Soon after leaving the RAF I got a job as an extra on a film whose name has fled my memory. One of the other extras was called Norma. She was a singer, and since she had not yet been demobbed from ENSA, she changed back into khaki uniform at the end of each day's shooting. I had borrowed my mother's car, one of the old Standard Tens, and although I am not in the least kinky about uniforms – especially khaki ones – I contrived to give her a lift home, one evening, to her flat in Cumberland Place.

When we arrived, she invited me to come up for a drink. Expressing a preference for tea, I followed the khaki vision up gloomy flights of stairs to the top of the house, where she sat me down and produced a bottle of wine. It was as I repeated my desire for tea that I realised what promise the situation held, and I proceeded to ply her with her own wine.

Quite quickly she became, as they say, putty in my hands, and although I am not all that keen on putty I decided that the gentlemanly thing to do would be to put out the light and help her to unclip and unbuckle her way out of the khaki trappings.

And thus Murray, a Virgo under the Zodiac, a *virgo* no longer *intacta*. I found it all quite exciting, and remember thanking the darkness for sparing my blushes when she said: "I can't tell you how lovely it is to be with a really experienced man for a change."

Many, many years later I discovered quite by chance that I had been her first lover as well, in the light of which, her praise of my efforts rather lost its validity. That may also explain why, when I approached her on several subsequent occasions with a repeat performance in mind, she refused to have anything to do with me. Obviously I wasn't quite in the Casanova class.

However . . . fortified by this emancipation, I decided to ignore the advices of the RAF medical man and plunge again into the billboard jungle. Reunited with Herbert de Leon, I found that his friend Weston Drury was as good as his word, which my show business experience hitherto could hardly have led me to expect.

Back in 1943, he had been going to put me under contract to Gainsborough films, who numbered Stewart Granger, Phyllis Calvert and Jean Kent among their aspiring stars. But Murray's war had intervened, and while Murray was being taken over by the RAF, Gainsborough were being taken over by the Rank Organisation. And it was to them, through Weston Drury's good offices, that I was now lucky enough to be contracted, for the handsome retainer of £15 a week.

Since they had no immediate need for my screen services, I was allowed to take parts in the theatre, and I did a number of plays at the Kew Theatre, which has now been demolished, and at the Intimate, Palmer's Green, which for some reason has not. The most gratifying part of this period was that when my name appeared on the theatre programmes it was suffixed by the grand rigmarole: "By kind permission of the J. Arthur Rank Organisation." This, I hoped, would give the audience the impression that I had been brought to the theatre with no expense spared. I doubt if it did.

Then, in 1946, the Rank Organisation gave me kind permission to appear in a film. It was called *Caravan* and starred Stewart Granger, Jean Kent, and Robert Helpmann.

It is easy to remember that Robert Helpmann was in the film, since there was a scene where he had to horsewhip me, and I've never been one for masochism. But the script demanded it, so who was I to argue? I played the part of a gipsy boy, and had to wear earrings (what *would* my Grimsby landlady have said!), which was how, twenty years later, I came to give Jean Kent an earring when she was the subject of This Is Your Life.

It was a very innocuous little love story, with a few pieces of 1946-style villainy thrown in, and was supposed to take place in Spain. In fact, the whole thing was shot at Lime Grove, and this must have showed, because when it was shown on television a few years ago, Pat Campbell, the Country and Western DJ and an old friend, rang me up.

"Peter," he said, "I've just seen you in *Caravan*."

He paused, and I said nothing, hoping simply that he'd be kind.

Then he went on: "I booked a holiday to Spain this year. I've just cancelled it."

From this epic, I moved to a part in the film *Hungry Hill*. I had read the book, and thought that there must be a part of some kind for me in the film. Well, so there was . . . a massive three-liner. But seldom can an actor have had to work so hard for his three lines.

I played the part of a cavalry officer, who was Jean Simmons' fiancé. But the role was far more equestrian than amorous, so Rank in their wisdom decided that I ought to learn to ride cavalry style, feeling perhaps that the techniques I had learned with the farmer's horse at Fairford fell short of the graceful. So I was despatched to Stanmore, to the riding school of one Captain Younghusband. For three whole months I cantered and galloped under the Captain's watchful eye, and by the time that filming was due I had become so proficient that he asked me to give up acting and go into showjumping.

By now, of course, I was getting quite used to people suggesting that I should give up the stage, but it certainly wasn't going to be for showjumping. I appreciated his problem . . . at that time the war had swallowed all the potential young male riders, and only women were left. But there was one drawback. I hated jumping. My idea of riding was to get aboard the beast and go like blazes.

And so, in that summer of 1946, I arrived on the set at Denham Studios or to be accurate, just outside Denham Studios, where they had built a mock-up of the Hill of the film's title. (The fact that there were plenty of perfectly serviceable hills in the area provided by Mother Nature, didn't interest them at all. If a thing could be done the hard way, they did it.)

The shooting took place at night (daylight would have been far too easy) and we came to the scene where, in order I think to quell some miners, I had to lead a cavalry charge down the hill. About 600 riders were to follow me down, and there were some 500 others on the set, well over 1,000 in all.

Murray, resplendent in cavalry finery, had come to his big moment . . . and Lady Hamilton was led forward.

Lady Hamilton was a piebald horse. Lady Hamilton was a very astute horse. Lady Hamilton was a horse who for years had been ridden as a hack in Hyde Park, and had known more idiots than I will ever know. The director, Brian Desmond-Hurst, signalled Action. I mounted Lady Hamilton. Lady Hamilton quite clearly understood that she had yet another idiot on her back. I grasped the reins and gave her a gentle kick. Nothing happened.

The director repeated his call to Action. I gave Lady Hamilton a harder kick. Nothing happened. The floodlights glared, and the 600 cavalrymen waited, and the 500 extras waited, and Margaret Lockwood and Cecil Parker and Dennis Price and Michael Dennison and Jean Simmons waited. And nothing happened.

The director repeated his call, his voice now tinged with a note of urgency. Your big hero, three months of riding school behind him, gave Lady Hamilton the biggest kick ever administered to an unwilling mount. And you've guessed it. Nothing happened.

At this point the director went raving mad. A props man was hastily summoned. And Murray, Equestrian Extraordinary, was led round to the back of the set and up the hill like a child on a donkey ride at Bournemouth.

That was the most embarrassing moment of my life.

But otherwise the film was fun. I got on very well with Dennis Price, who had a tremendous sense of humour. Dennis was very keen on riding, and the owner of Lady Hamilton, who also must have had a sense of humour, said that I could ride Lady Hamilton any time I liked. Dennis and I would ride at an old airfield near Denham, and then, of course, Lady Hamilton would go like the clappers. But my role in the film was cut to two lines, and two appearances: mounting Lady Hamilton, and riding her down the hill. And I never did find out what 'cavalry style' was.

It did have one good outcome for me. When the film appeared, my name was actually among those on the posters which they put on the backs of buses. It was the only time in my life I've ever made the back of a bus, and it gladdened me no little.

These were the days of the so-called Rank Charm School. I say so-called, because that was a name the Press gave it — not Rank. It was at the old Highbury Studios, which were then still functioning as film studios, but which have now, inexorably, been demolished. The idea was to teach us all cinema techniques, and we used to do readings from plays and so on . . . all of which I found a complete waste of time since I'd been through it all at RADA.

My contemporaries on this rung of the ladder to stardom included John Stone, and incredibly sexy Diana Dors, who was fifteen years old and all there as they say. She had, and has, a heart of gold, and has been a close friend ever since. Many's the time I've been stuck in town and bedded down in Diana's flat . . . on the sofa, I hasten to add. I think one of the reasons why our friendship has lasted is that we never had an affair (you poor fool, Murray!).

Connie Smith, Bryan Forbes' first wife was there, looking gorgeously like Hedy Lamarr, and Anthony Steel, and the daunting Christopher Lee. Christopher is the only person I know who can give you an inferiority complex on the spot, and he was no different then. He would tell you that he is the son of some blue-blooded Royal dukedom in Italy. He is. He'll tell you that he is a great golfer. He is. He'll tell you that he was a champion fencer. He was. He's one of the most annoying men I ever met, because he boasts, but with total justification. This assorted bunch was presided over by a lady called Molly Terraine. We renamed her Molly Tyrant. She was a totally unreasonable woman, and seemed to have a great loathing for young actors. Her unpleasantness was matched only by the fact that she was extremely good at her job. I had an additional reason for regretting her presence. I had been under her at RADA and had beeen banned from her classes for misbehaviour.

But Rank was good to us, and attendance at the school was the only

46

time that they ever laid it on the line and said I *had* to do something. Admittedly, we didn't appreciate it so much at the time, and I remember turning up late one morning for the Deportment Class to find the enormous figure of J. Arthur Rank himself standing outside the Studios with a stopwatch, because he thought his money was being wasted by all these young layabouts.

Early in 1947 there was a suggestion that Roy Rich should direct a Sidney Box picture. As a sort of try-out, we did the story as a play at an army recruiting hall in Ealing. Tony Steel and I were in it, which was inevitably something of a disaster since we could never work together without having hysterics, always off-stage, and frequently on-stage. But the upper echelons of Rank must have thought well of us, because it led to Tony becoming one of the biggest stars of the fifties, and for me the suggestion that I might get a part in *The Blue Lagoon*.

Jean Simmons had already been cast in it, and they were looking for a fair-haired man to be her lover. Someone suggested that Murray might be ideal, but they felt there was one drawback. I was decidedly skinny. So, having spent a fortune on turning me into an expert horseman, they now reckoned on converting me into a replica of Johnny Weissmuller, who was the current screen Tarzan.

They said: "We'll have to send you on a building-up course."

"What do you mean?" I asked.

"Well," they said, "we'll send you to a gym every day and then we'll test you for the part."

They gave me an address in Fitzroy Square, which I eventually found after threading my way through the second-hand car maze of Warren Street. I couldn't believe it. It was in a basement, and the sleaziest dump I had ever entered, short of my wartime digs in Bristol. There were a lot of boxers punching defenceless bags, and a ring, in which men appeared to be fighting each other.

At the end of the room was a tea bar, against which, or rather supported by which, leaned an old man who appeared to be falling apart. His name was Mr Klein.

"Yiss? Vot do you vant?" His thick German accent fell short of total enthusiasm.

I said "Well, I've been sent —"

"Pardon! I'm deaf. Spikk op."

"My name's Peter Murray. I've been sent by the Rank Organisation. You're going to build me up."

"Vat's dat? Oh ja. I sink ve hev somm sort communication wiz zis...Vally!"

Wally came over, a little thickset man, crippled, and with a squint. He eyed me with disapproval.

"Vally, zis is Peter Murray from ze Renk Organisation. You gotta build him op."

Wally May, it turned out, was quite distinguished. He had been the trainer of heavyweight champion Len Harvey.

He said: "Yes, well, wot do yer want doin'?"

"I've got to be built up," I said, feeling that the litany sounded more hopeless every time I uttered it.

"Oh, that's alright," he said. " 'Ave you lookin' like Bruce Woodcock in no time."

I said nervously: "Well, that's not entirely necessary. You don't need to go quite that far. But I do need some building up. Do you think you can do anything for me?"

He eyed me with the appraisal of a farmer inspecting an unfattened steer.

"Yes, no trouble at all," he said.

"There's only one thing," I said. "Look, I am very thin, and I've got a terrible complex about it. I mean, the idea of taking off my shirt in front of all these fellows with rippling muscles. Do you think you could possibly...I mean, is there a little private room where I can go?"

He raised his eyes in supplication to the gods who could have sent him such a 'right one'.

"Private room? This is it, mate."

I said: "But, stripping off in front of all these blokes..."

"You don't want to take no notice of them. Because they won't take no notice of you." He paused, then like a true boxing genius delivered the killer blow. "We get all kinds of physical wrecks down 'ere."

So for three months, Wally May put me through my paces, with weight-lifting and all, and although I never got very wide, I did get amazingly fit, and very strong. From time to time Wally, bless his sadistic soul, would put me in to shadow box with his hopefuls, whose

48

'shadow' punches came a good deal closer to the real thing than was good for my nerves.

One in particular, a big coloured guy, was a contender for the light-heavyweight championship of Great Britain and the Empire (which we still had), and although we were great friends out of the ring, he looked bloody vicious the moment he got in it. On many occasions I had to say: "Here, hold on a minute. I'm not fighting you, you know." Mick Mulligan was one thing, but this was very much another.

Eventually, fit and raring to leap into the cinematic embraces of Jean Simmons, I went for the screen test for *Blue Lagoon* and failed. The part went to Donald Houston.

Somehow, Rank's long-term enterprises with Murray seemed doomed to disaster.

Shortly after this up-building and down-bringing I took my bulging biceps along to an audition which Michael Redgrave was holding. It was for the part of Malcolm in *Macbeth*, which Redgrave was going to take to New York . . . and like all the other young actors of those days, my main ambition was to get to America.

The audition, like a cattle market, with a couple of hundred actors there, was at the Piccadilly Theatre. That was certainly one occasion when I took their "Don't call us, we'll call you" as holding no hope whatsoever; but to my surprise they did call me. It seemed that the part of Malcolm had been narrowed down to myself and one other, whose name I forget.

We did another audition, and after it Redgrave took me aside.

"I thought you gave a beautiful reading of it," he said. "But it's evident to me that you're not a Shakespearean actor by nature. It's a specialised form of acting.

"If I weren't playing Macbeth myself, and directing, I'd take you with us. As things are, I think I have to go for the more experienced man."

Well, I'd always been told what a difficult man Redgrave was, but in my case he was utterly charming to a totally unknown actor, and in spite of the disappointment it gave me a great deal of confidence. Soon after this, we heard that *The Winslow Boy* was going to America, and I auditioned for that, only to give a very bad reading and be beaten to the part by Jack Watling. I began to despair of ever crossing the Atlantic. But it was to be third time lucky. There was a play running in London called *Power Without Glory*. It had first been put on at the Gate Theatre in Notting Hill with a group of unknown actors who included Dirk Bogarde, Kenneth More, Dandy Nichols, and Maureen Pooke (now Maureen Prior) and who were all working for about £5 a week.

The play and the players — and in retrospect it doesn't seem so surprising — received every critical plaudit that was going, and they transferred to the Fortune Theatre, where for some reason, although it remained an artistic success, it was a commercial flop. But it did seem to attract a lot of visiting Americans. So an impresario named Jack Wilson, the man who had discovered Noel Coward and who had become Coward's mentor, ·decided to take it to the States. But Dirk Bogarde had been grabbed by the Rank Organisation, and Kenneth More, who had come to the Gate Theatre from the Windmill, went straight into a Noel Coward play called *Peace in our Time*, as I believe did Dandy and Maureen.

Chloe Gibson, who had directed the original production and was now to direct it in America, started to hold auditions in her Notting Hill Gate flat, through which trooped some 300 actors.

In the end, the choice for the replacement for Dirk Bogarde came down to six of us, including Laurance Payne, Linden Brook . . . and Donald Houston. Happily for me, history didn't repeat itself. When we came to the final auditions at the Aldwych Theatre Jack Wilson was there watching, and when they were over he said: "I want that boy to play the role. Tell him to come and see me at the Globe Theatre."

In company with Lewis Stringer, a well-known radio repertory actor, who had got the Kenneth More part, I went down to the Globe, which also housed the offices of H. M. Tennant.

Jack Wilson came to the door, and said with a wry smile: "Well, which shall I speak to first, the blonde or the brunette?"

Lewis Stringer, the brunette, went in first, and then it was my turn. It was a record I had heard before: "There's not going to be a lot of money in this but there will be a lot of prestige." As it happened, the money they offered, £50 a week, seemed a fortune to me anyway, prestige or not, but I manage to confine my remarks to saying how thrilled I was just to appear on Broadway.

We rehearsed for three weeks at a little place in Dean Street, and one afternoon in late November Jack Wilson came in to watch. He told me afterwards: "It's going great," and then added what to me were those magical words: "I'll see you in New York."

Chapter Six

I am not a good sailor.
Whatever blood may meander through my veins, it is certainly not that of Drake or Raleigh. My opportunity to discover this failing came on the first night that I spent aboard the old Queen Mary en voyage to New York.

She was the first big boat I had ever been on, and that initial exposure to the open sea made me violently ill, causing great merriment to my cabin-companions Lewis Stringer, and Trevor Ward who was my father in the play. So perhaps I was less than charitable, not so say delighted, when five minutes later they both flung themselves on their beds and started to moan at the roller-coaster miseries of the life oceanic.

The rest of the voyage was pleasant enough. The old Queen had been returned to full peacetime glamour after her wartime duties, and among others the D'Oyly Carte Opera Company were with us on the way to Broadway. But for me, anything that happened on board was a mere distraction to make America arrive sooner. One morning there it was, the New York skyline, just as one had seen it in a dozen movies, except that this time it was in colour.

My first impressions were mixed. On the one hand, there was gaiety in the flashing lights and neon signs that we had missed for so long in Britain. On the other, I remember being rather saddened by the sleaziness of Times Square, and thinking that Broadway looked a little like the dirtier end of the Edgware Road.

That wasn't the only reminder of home. When we arrived at our hotel, the Barbizon Plaza, my first encounter was with the elevator

52

man who immediately announced that he was from Wigan.

"How's Wigan these days?" he asked as we shot skywards.

My stomach, left stranded by the lift's take-off, was just catching up with me as I replied "Well, the last time I was there they offered me Udder Pie."

"Oh, great!" he explained with nostalgic relish, savouring the imagined luxury by taking his tongue on a tour of his lips. "God, I don't half miss that cow-heel, and tripe, and udder pie. Marvellous." I wondered vaguely how he made out with sauerkraut and blintzes.

It was the day before Christmas Eve, and they had laid on a party for us on the stage at the Palace Theatre, where the Winslow Boy was playing, so that by a strange twist I found myself greeted in New York by Jack Watling, the man who had beaten me to the part. And the title role was played by Michael Newell, with whom I was to appear in 1950.

That party was the moment when somebody on the production – I'll call him George – started to get a bit over-friendly with me. Luckily I was forewarned by Chloe Gibson who had said: "You might have a little trouble with George, because I think he's taken a very decided fancy to you. You've got to be very careful."
be very careful."

So when we got to the party I said to Joan Newell: "Stick by me, sweetheart. I don't want any embarrassing moments."

After a while I started to feel very tired and said I thought I would go home. Immediately George said: "OK. I'll get you a cab." We got outside and he started to hold my arm, which worried me slightly, and I began to thank heaven that Joan was there.

To make what I felt to be necessary conversation in the circumstances I said: "I don't know how the hell you can tell the difference between a cab and a private car. They all look the same to me."

"It's easy to tell, once you know," said George and promptly hailed a private car.

Well, that was funny, but the situation wasn't. I thought back to 1943, and an evening on Kew Bridge when a former BBC drama producer gave me what was meant as an invitation but merely served as a warning.

"You've got a marvellous future as an actor," he had said. "But you must at least be bisexual. Because until you've had the homosexual experience you'll never really be an actor."

In those days, of course, that was much more true than today. But there was no way that I could do it, and what I resented more than anything was being made to feel embarrassed at being 'straight'. More than once I've said, when driven to it: "Look. To you it's abhorrent to go to bed with a woman. Can't you understand that it would be abhorrent to me to go to bed with a man?"

I think that's why, over the years, I've been sympathetic to women, in the sense that if they have said "No" I have taken it that they meant "No." In a strange way, I've been placed in their position. However...the day after the party, Christmas Eve, we had our first visit to Sardi's, the famous show-biz restaurant. There's a right and a wrong end at Sardi's, but we were with Jack Wilson, so we were at the right end. They'd gone to great trouble to lay on a real English Christmas Day Lunch for us, including a mass of Brussels Sprouts, since they were under the impression that all British people adored the said vegetable. The fact was that all but two of us loathed sprouts, but it was nice of them all the same, and we managed to swallow our dislike, and the sprouts.

Christmas Day itself was very depressing. We were left to our own devices, so Joan Newell, Lewis Stringer and I decided to take ourselves to see Brooklyn Bridge, which we thought was the properly romantic thing to do. The trouble was that it was so bitterly cold that even the Hudson River was icing up, and I swore at that moment that I would never again complain about a British winter.

The following day we were told to pack our bags and make for the Wilbur Theatre in Boston, where the play was to open. *Power Without Glory* was by Michael Clayton-Hutton. It was a psychological drama, quite advanced for its day, about a cockney boy who goes out with a tart, whom he kills after she jibes him about his fiancée. It was quite strong stuff, and we had to take a number of 'bloodys' and 'damns' out of the script because they thought it was too strong for Boston, where the local equivalent of our watch committee was very powerful.

The night of the dress rehearsal Jack Wilson came up to me and said: "You're giving one of the best performances I've ever seen in my life. You're going to be an international star. You need never go back to

54

England." It was very flattering, though I knew that whatever happened I had to go back to England because Rank had insisted on it – though go back to *what* I had no idea.

Well, the show opened, and although we didn't do much business we did get rave reviews. Every evening George would come round and leave his overcoat in my dressing room, though at no time did he ever make what I would call a pass at me.

After about four days, however, he got flu, and stayed away, and during his absence the rest of the cast and I got used to having a tea party in the interval in the dressing room of Hilary Liddell, who played my fiancée. Some days later, George returned, and left his coat in my room as before, and during the interval we were all in Hilary's room chatting away and sipping our tea when George walked in.

"Mr Murray," he said, and paused amid a dead silence. "You know you really don't have to run away from me. I'm not going to rape you in public, you know." With that he walked out and everyone studied their feet in embarrassment.

Chloe Gibson broke the silence. "I think you'd better go and talk to him," she said.

I went in search of him, an found him in my room. "George," I said "I think we ought to get a few things cleared up here."

He said nothing, as I groped for the right words. "Look, I don't know why I've been cast in this play. But I have never given you a come-hither in any sense of the word. And I'm sorry, but if that's how you feel about the situation, it's just no-go as far as I'm concerned."

There was a pause, as he picked up his coat, then spoke two very short and very clear sentences. "You have led me on. And I will see that you are destroyed."

Needless to say, all this left a very nasty atmosphere in the company. Chloe Gibson was sympathetic, as I think the others were, but there was nothing they could do.

After two weeks in Boston we returned to New York to open at the Booth Theatre on Broadway. I remember that George Sanders and Herbert Marshall were among the first night audience, and when the curtain fell we got a standing ovation, which continued when we went on to Sardi's afterwards, where everyone seemed to want to know us and shake our hands.

Then, the following morning, the notices came out. Put briefly, the critics murdered the play. In Boston, one critic had called me the new John Gielgud, which admittedly may have been a bit strong, but in New York, only one critic, a woman, chose to like it, and credited me with "the performance of the season." All the others panned it, and what disturbed me was that in two papers I wasn't even mentioned. Well, you can like a play, or hate it, but if you are reviewing it you simply can't not mention the leading actor. But they managed. Whether it was George's doing I will never know, but it was certainly against his interests, because after about a month of struggling the play finally came off.

On February 11th I set sail back to England.

Chapter Seven

I am not a homosexual.

People have thought my behaviour a bit queer at times, and in spite of not drinking I have managed to be comparatively gay on occasions. But in sexual matters, I am strictly one of those who cry: "Vive la difference!"

And it wasn't until I got back from New York that I realised how big the homosexual club actually is. It's like a river flowing in all directions, and it certainly flowed back to London, where the rumour was that I had led George on and then hadn't played ball. That, if true, was the one unforgivable thing, and as a result of the stories I suffered for quite a long spell, and didn't get any work with the major companies.

Like other 'resting' actors at that time, I sought consolation at the S and F Grill in Denman Street. This was really a café, where everyone seemed to spend all the time on the telephone trying to give the impression that they were getting work. Occasionally established stars would come in and the word spread quickly . . . "Robert Morley's in today" or "Rex Harrison was here yesterday".

But mostly it was the young hopefuls, like Diana Dors, Roger Moore, and my friend Digby Wolfe, who was to have a big successs in Australia and later went to America and helped to start the 'Laugh-In' show. Everyone was terribly keen on America, and Bonar Colleano was the 'King' — we all wanted to be like him. I remember when I first went there after coming back from the States I bumped into Lionel Blair, and he couldn't stop talking about the American belt and tie I was wearing. Miriam Karlin was another S and F regular. She was a rather tubby lady in those days, and I fancied her like mad. I was really sorry when she decided to slim. And I will never forget the day I went down there and found myself sitting next to Beatrice Lillie.

She turned to me and said: "You're a very pretty boy, aren't you?" I went blood red and hoped against hope that she would seduce me. She didn't.

All in all it was an extraordinary group of people, who were doing all their acting in the S and F Grill, because there weren't any parts going in the theatre. It was a sort of meeting point for all our hopes and visions, but it was hardly turning the proprietors into Rockefellers, since we would go in there in the early afternoon, order one cup of tea, and make it spin out till six-thirty. So in the end they kicked us all out, which I felt was unsporting, and in any case was probably a mistake since numbers of the public used to come in to view this chimpanzees' tea party.

After some weeks of these tea-time theatricals, my employment, or rather unemployment, situation took a turn for the better. Herbert de Leon rang me up at home in Osterley, where my mother had retired after giving up the Bayswater pub. He asked me if I could still do an American accent.

By saying "still" he was harking back to 1943, when I had just left RADA and got a part with the BBC in a serial called 'The Robinson Family', which went out on the world Service. At the age of 17 I was being required to play an American Air Force Major, and I gave the Beeb the impression that I was originally American.

"What part of the States do you come from?" they asked.

"Well," I said, "of course my parents were American, and I came over here at a very early age. But I can still retain the accent."

In about the third instalment I was required to talk about the Yosemite Valley, which should be pronounced 'Yosemitty'. I said it like it's written, and they knew straight away...but by then I was into the part so it didn't matter.

Now I was being asked to repeat the charade. Herbert told me that Pathé Pictorial were going to try to sell their series to American TV. Pathé Pictorial was a very successful 'filler' for film shows. It's title sequence was always preceded by a magnificent crowing cock, long before Kentucky Fried Chicken was heard of. The narrator for these

58

'shorts' was someone very English like Bob Danvers-Walker. "Well, they don't want an English voice," said Herbert. "They want an American to narrate the films. You can do that, can't you?"

"There's only one snag...I'm not American," I said.

Herbert indicated that he *was* aware of my nationality, but added: "You just go along there and do an American accent."

So I went along, as bidden, and found all the S and F Grill's 'American' types there, applying for the job, together with some real Americans. I was interviewed by a man called Terry Ashwood, who was the big wheel at Pathé.

The question came straight away. "Are you an American?"

I took a deep mental breath and remembered the Yosemite Valley. "Yes, I am," I answered, "but I've lived in this country, and I went to RADA, and I've tried to get rid of my American accent. I think I've succeeded."

Ashwood nodded understandingly, and said:"We'll do a voice test. What part of the States are you from?"

"New York," I replied, feeling that this was a bit more anonymous than Boston, the only other place I had visited, and thanking my lucky stars that at least I could talk about the Brooklyn Bridge and the frozen Hudson.

So I did the test, and to the chagrin of the S and F gang I got the job. I did about twenty of these commentaries, at about £12 a time, but it was a vast embarrassment having to keep up the pretence, and I sweated blood trying to find real Americans (as opposed to the S and F lot) to help me with difficult pronunciations.

It was during this period of Americans that I decided to drive down to Worthing one weekend to see some chums – Bill Travers, Tony Steel, and Elspet Gray. One evening we all went over to Brighton to see a play about the trial of Jesus Christ. In this play, members of the audience took part, as members of the jury, on stage. We all volunteered, and afterwards, in a nearby café, were joined by the actors. With them was a man called Richard Pollock, who wrote for the Sunday People and was a friend of Margery Hawtrey, whose husband Anthony ran the Embassy Theatre in Swiss Cottage, now sadly demolished.

Pollock looked over at me and asked "Didn't you do a play in

America called *Power Without Glory?*"

I pleaded guilty, and he said "I've written a play called *Symphony in Violence*. I want to put it on at the Embassy in Swiss Cottage. I think there's a part in it that's just right for you."

He gave me the play, which I took back to Worthing and read. I reckoned it was a pretty terrible play, but that my part, another Cockney razor-slasher type, was not bad at all, and I decided to do it.

I got my friend Patrick Westwood (he of the dog's collar and the slobber) a part in it as my side-kick, and we set off on a pre-London tour of places like Bournemouth and Eastbourne. Now in that cast was a 29 year-old lady called Mary. She was a fabulous actress, who sadly died in a car crash about four years ago. Mary was supposed to be Anthony Hawtrey's girl friend (in real life, that is), but I fell for her completely, and we had a marvellous affair, interrrupted only by Hawtrey's visits, about which she would always warn me, since he was madly possessive and jealous. I fell completely in love with Mary, and I felt that she was in love with me. This seemed to be confirmed when, during a gap between performances, she went off to Ireland for four days. Every day she sent me a telegram with "I love you" written on it twenty times. Just that.

And then came The Lesson. Some time after she got back, I went into the old Vega vegetarian restaurant in Leicester Square (now not so much demolished, as transformed into an Angus Steak House, a sort of spiritual demolition) where I ran into an old friend who is a well-known actor.

He sat down at my table and said: "Tell me Peter, have you ever been to bed with Mary?"

Deciding to play the gentleman, I said: "No."

Then he told me: "I gave her one last night. It's the best I ever had in my life."

It destroyed me. Totally and utterly. Eventually I managed to raise the subject with her, and she didn't deny it at all. Mary, bless her heart, was a raver, and I just didn't know. Even when she told me, I couldn't believe it...my first true love that went hopelessly wrong.

At the end of 1948 I got a part in the ABC film *My Brother Jonathan*, which starred Michael Denison and Dulcie Gray. Michael was very much the blue-eyed boy of the cinema at that time, and they were both enormously kind to me. I played Dulcie's son, and years later, when she was on 'This Is Your Life,' I came on and said: "This is your son talking," and she knew immediately who it was. We always called each other Son and Mum.

Although it wasn't a big part, it was the best part I ever had in a major picture, and for the first time in my life I got fan mail. It provided another first as well, because when I went to the Empire Leicester Square to see it, the usherette said "Cor. Aren't you in it? Can I have your autograph?" I'd never been asked before. I wonder if she still has it.

The next year, 1949, I was cast as a young architect in a play called *Miss Mabel*. Mary Jerrold was in the title role, and Clive Morton, her real-life son-in-law, played a lawyer. In the play was a young actress whom I shall call Daisy.

She was the daughter of a prominent judge whom I had often seen at work since I was fascinated by law. I admired his humour and his sense of justice.

The play went on tour, and I took Daisy, whom I liked very much, to a couple of parties, though I never even got as far as a bit of necking with her. In fact, maybe I didn't treat her too well, since I always seemed to end up with some other girl, although I always made sure she got home safely.

When the tour ended, we all came back on the train not knowing whether the play would go on in London, since the Theatre was doing so well that it was very hard to get a stage to put a play on. When we got off the train I said: "Alright, Daisy, I hope to see you when we open in Town, IF we open in Town."

She said: "Yes, I hope so," and we parted.

Four weeks went by, and then the Duchess Theatre became available. We were due to start rehearsing when I got a call from my agent.

"Peter, what *have* you been up to?"

"What on earth do you mean?" I asked.

He said tersely: "I think you'd better come in to the office."

Well, Herbert had never spoken to me like that before, and it was with what they call great trepidation that I went to the office in South Audley Street. It was on the first floor, over a smart baker's shop which

61

sold beautiful home-made cakes and things.

I climbed the Regency staircase, and went through the outer office, where a girl called Diane kept the world at bay, and into Herbert's sanctum. It was a quiet, tasteful office, with a magnificent leather-topped desk, and just a few pictures, of the children of his five marriages and of Margaret Lockwood, whom he discovered and who has been with him since 1936, despite never signing a contract with him. That gives some indication of his character. He is a super, kind man, dark-skinned of Spanish or Portuguese descent, a smart dresser in an unostentatious way, and equipped by Nature with a heart of gold.

To give an idea of the sort of man he was, and is, when I got back from America, where I had been paid my £50 a week direct, I said to him that I wanted to settle up his commission with him. He wouldn't take a penny. "No. No. No," he said. "I'll get my commission later when you're earning real money. You keep it now. You need it."

I relate all this in order to emphasise my feelings at what followed. He motioned me to sit down.

"Now, Peter, have you been a naughty boy?"

I had absolutely no idea what he was talking about, and said so.

"What have you done to Daisy?"

"What do you mean 'What have I done to Daisy'?"

"Well, have you slept with her?"

"No, I have not slept with her."

"Well, what *have* you done?"

"Nothing," I said, completely baffled, racking my brains for misdemeanours with Daisy, and finding nothing.

Herbert looked at me dubiously. Then he went on, "Well…I've got to tell you. The company, that is to say Mr Clift, who's putting on the play, has asked us to withdraw you from the role. And he's bringing the matter up with Equity."

By now I was getting bewildered, and not a little angry.

"What matter?" I asked. "And under what pretext do they want me to withdraw?"

Herbert said: "Daisy is not going to be in it."

"I'm very sorry to hear that," I said. "But what's that got to do with me?"

So now the story came out. Apparently, when Daisy got the news that she wasn't going to be in the London cast, she had hysterics and told her father that she didn't care anyway, since she never wanted to see that Peter Murray again because he had been obscene, told her filthy stories, and generally behaved in a disgusting way towards her. Her father the judge had gone straight to Clift and asked him to have me removed from the play. He also went to Equity and tried to have me barred from appearing in any theatre for a period. All this without once approaching me for my version.

This was my first brush with anything vaguely connected with the law. Though I had never met him, I found it incredible that a man of so-called law and justice should condemn someone without hearing the other side of it, irrespective of whether it concerned his own daughter. Years later I was terribly sorry when she died. But him I can never forgive.

So, after some more discussion, Herbert got on to Clift. His message was simple. "I've spoken to Peter Murray. He denies that he has behaved in any way, shape, or form in a manner that could be called obscene towards Daisy. We insist that he opens in the play as stated in the contract."

So they had to take me, and the play ran about six months, which was about as unhappy a half-year as I have ever had. Any lingering sympathy that E. P. Clift, the impresario, might have had for me, vanished on the first night.

As is the wont of impresarios, he came round to congratulate the cast. Finally he arrived at the dressing room which I was sharing with Richard Warner. I was taking off my make-up as he congratulated Richard and then, reluctantly, came over to me and and shook my hand . . . which was covered in greasepaint. From that moment I was *persona* distinctly *non grata*.

There was that...and there was one other strange little twist of fate that taught me that one need never look for revenge. If one has been hard done by, my experience has been that sooner or later things get evened out.

Down among the lower echelons of the cast of *Miss Mabel* was an ageing actor who had just one line. His name was Ferguson. Yes, Captain Ferguson, my tormentor of the tour. I felt simply sorry for him. I said nothing to him about our past, nor he to me. But we each knew what the other was thinking.

And what's more...I didn't even start to fantasise about his demise. As far as I was concerned, the debt was paid by the mere fact that our positions were so completely reversed.

In September, *Miss Mabel* ended its run, which, after all that had happened, scarcely broke my heart. For the rest of the year I was out of work — sorry, resting — and then around Christmas I met an American woman called Wauna Paul, who was the impresario of a play entitled *Larger Than Life* which had been having a modest success at the Duke of York Theatre. Based on a Somerset Maugham book called *Theatre*, it starred Reginald Denny, an old English actor who had emigrated to America and appeared in the early silent movies. He had been the original screen Bulldog Drummond. The leading lady was the actress Jessie Royce Landis.

Wauna Paul wanted to take the play on tour and offered me a part. It was the only time I ever argued with Herbert de Leon, who said that at £15 a week I would be too badly paid. But I said that I'd rather do that than nothing, and took over one of the roles, along with Arthur Lowe, who played the butler in place of Laurence Naismith. Arthur, I may say, looked exactly the same then as he does today.

In the New Year of 1950 we began the tour, and I began my affair with Jessie Royce Landis. I was 24 and she was 46 and I grew up overnight. I had known that it was going to happen from the moment I first met her at the auditions, and I think she had felt the same way.

They say that every young man should have an affair with an older woman — and they're right. It's not a question of learning the tricks of the trade, or anything like that. It's simply a matter of being helped to grow up. She was a fantastic person, a wonderful actress, and enormous fun. She had a magic about her, and she turned me from an immature boy into a man overnight.

Needless to say, the tour, which ran for about four months, was endlessly happy for me. Jessie gave me more and taught me more than anyone I have ever known. She was beautiful without being beautiful, titian-haired and running to a little middle-age spread. I shall never forget her.

Our affair continued its happy course after the tour had ended, and then, in September, I went to see Herbert de Leon to ask if there was any work for me.

"How do you fancy going abroad?" asked Herbert.

I said: "It's a lovely idea, but doing what?"

"Radio," he said.

I had instant and gorgeous visions of myself as the special correspondent of Radio Newsreel in Istanbul, surrounded by beautiful spies. But reality intruded.

"Yes, but doing what?" I asked.

"Well, continuity, and announcer, and a phrase they call here I think 'Disc Jockey', whatever that means. For Radio Luxembourg. Just for for two or three months. It'll be a nice experience. Mind you, you'll have to do an audition."

So along I want to the Radio Luxembourg office in Davies Street, to see the General Manager, a man called Frank Lee, who later became the top A and R man at Decca. Lee's assistant, I recall, was a lad named Philip Jones, now Head of Light Entertainment at Thames TV.

Ushered into the presence of Lee, I was asked, almost as we were shaking hands: "What is the Number One tune in the Hit Parade?"

"Dearie" I said, not by way of making a pass at him, I hasten to add, but because that was the name of a song.

Lee was impressed. 'Dearie' was actually Number Two, but that was pretty close, especially for those days when, unless you were in the business, it was considered rather infra dig to like pop music.

So they gave me my audition. I had no idea what I was talking about. They just gave me a few records, and told me to fill in the gaps between them. But I do remember that the first one I played was 'Come Dance with Me', by Fred Waring and his Pennsylvanians. I never found out what they thought of that audition, but I do know that the job, which paid £12 a week and therefore peanuts, since the cost of living was much higher in Luxembourg, had failed to attract any other applicants.

I was on my own, and the job was mine. I bade Jessie a loving and temporary farewell, since I was 'only going for three months', and boarded the plane for Brussels.

Chapter Eight

I am not a disc jockey.

The real meaning of that phrase, which originated in America, is a man who not only introduces the records, but actually puts them all on the turntable himself, and operates the whole shebang.

I suppose you might call me an introducer of record programmes, but I never even intended to be that. When I got on that plane to Brussels, and from there the train to Luxembourg, I had no ideas of being anything but an actor. This was just to be a 'filler'.

The train was the first diesel I had ever been on, and the aroma of continental tobacco which pervaded its compartments was my first introduction to that armoury of odours with which the continental Europeans assault the Anglo-Saxon nose.

We arrived in Luxembourg after a two hour journey, and stepping on to the miserable station platform I felt no promise of immediate joys. I was met by Geoffrey Everitt, who was head of the English section of the Radio Station, and as we drove through the city it all seemed so quiet to me that I was under the impression that I had arrived in Death Valley. I had been booked into a hotel called the Brasserie du Théatre, so-named because it was near the only theatre in Luxembourg. It was a café-restaurant with a few rooms upstairs, and was run by a charming man called Herr Reissdorf. Both the Brasserie and Herr Reissdorf are now sadly gone, the one demolished, the other departed.

But the gloom of my arrival was soon lifted when I discovered that not only was Geoffrey an Arsenal supporter, but so too were Herr Reissdorf and the dozen or so regulars who managed to slip away from their wives to his café of an evening. All they ever talked about was football, which suited me fine, and they used to tune in to the Light Programme for the English football commentaries.

The following morning I went to inspect my new place of work. The Radio Station is set in a most beautiful park. It was orginally an old castle, called the Villa Longwy, but any illusions that I would be working in mediaeval splendour were shattered within minutes. The English service at that time was very much the poor relation of the French and German sections. We had the worst possible office, down in the basement near the record library. It was a most unhealthy place, dripping with water, and much as I enjoy a shower I prefer it not to be above my desk.

All the administration was done by Geoffrey Everitt, who also did a stint at the microphone when I had a night off, which was once a week, on Fridays. He had been in the army, and played a bit of professional football, and today is with MAM, the organisation run by Gordon Mills, Tom Jones, and Englebert Humperdinck.

To get the hang of things, I stayed that evening to watch Geoffrey doing a programme, and was rewarded by the best piece of advice I've ever been given.

After watching for a while I said: "I'll never be able to do this like you. I'll have to write a script."

He shook his head. "If you write a script, you'll never be able to ad lib," he said. "And I believe that no broadcaster is a real broadcaster unless he *can* ad lib. You'll make a hell of a lot of mistakes in your career (how right he was), but it will always sound more natural." So the idea of scripts was stillborn, and I've never used one.

Luxembourg, the city, was very quiet, and very formal. And Luxembourg the Radio Station was no different. People who had worked there for twenty or thirty years still called each other Mr This and Mr That. Or rather, Herr This and That, since the language is a German patois in spite of the fact that the people are solidly pro-French. The newspapers were in German, and the Station notice boards were in French, and life was complicated.

In those days, the daily English service only ran from 10.30 in the evening until one in the morning, and in fact after six at night the only people in the building would be the porter, the French announcer, myself, and the two technicians. The atmosphere was hardly what you would call riotous, and initially there wasn't much conversation either, since the French announcer, handing over to me, would talk to me in French, and it rapidly became clear to me that, in spite of having studied French for eight years, and being able to conjugate a few verbs, I couldn't conduct a word of conversation. I couldn't even ask where the toilet was.

So I got myself some Assimil teach-yourself-French records, and within three months or so I was able to hold a reasonable conversation or at any rate make suitable arrangements for relieving myself. I found that by throwing in a few colloquial phrases I could make people think I was more fluent than was actually the case. (I do an excellent 'Merde Alors!', and my 'Zut!' has to be heard to be appreciated.)

I adopted the same technique that I had used in watching Denis Compton in order to assemble a batting style. I watched Frenchmen talking in order to imitate them. My French-speaking became a very manual affair, and indeed many Frenchmen have asked me why I throw my arms around in conversation. I tell them that in order to speak their language I have to convince myself that I am a Frenchman . . . and I have to confess that many of them have not taken too kindly to this. But if the French came gradually, my life at the microphone really began at the deep end. Most evenings I would do one and half hours straight off. I would probably start with a half-hour of requests for new releases, then say goodbye, then play a different signature tune and say hello again with an hour of more requests.

On Sundays, bearing in mind the BBC's puritanical reputation on the Sabbath, we would open up at two in the afternoon. But, paradoxically, Luxembourg was then attacked for not having any culture. As a sop to these complaints, I was set to do a programme of ballet music, which may have been very cultural but was not very Murray.

Another of my less favourite pastimes was the early morning religious vigil. Every night, between midnight and one in the morning, they played a recorded hour of American hot gospel, paid for by some zealous sect of Madison-Avenue missionaries who felt that the The Word had to be brought to Pagan Europe. As duty announcer I would have to sit through this in order to sign off for the night.

One evening I thought: "It's ridiculous for me to have to sit here for a whole hour listening to this rubbish." So I decided to go to a local café for a cup of coffee. This was very enjoyable, and much more relaxing than the long-wave Bible-punching, and at about twenty to one I reckoned it was time to amble back. I had reckoned without the unpredictable Luxembourgers.

Although they are not overtly a very religious people, they will, at the drop of a hat, hold religious processions, about which they have an obsession. When I got outside the café, I was confronted by an apparently endless procession which appeared to include the country's entire population, with a few visitors thrown in.

I was horrified. There was I, and there was the Radio Station, and between us wound this human snake. They were all saying their prayers, and I think I must have said a few, urging the Almighty to get them out of the way. And still they came.

I thought: "How on earth am I going to get across? I can't just barge through these effigies of the Virgin Mary." A quarter to one. Ten to one. Seven, six minutes to one. There was nothing for it. I did the unforgivable. I dashed straight through the procession and made it to the studio in time for the last verse of the last hymn of the last gospellers.

It was just my luck to be recognised, and the following morning I was invited for a little chat with Herr Felten, the head of Radio Luxembourg. He made himself fairly clear. "This is not," he said, with what I later felt to be a nice degree of understatement, "this is not quite the thing to do. Leaving aside the question of the procession, you are not to leave the studio again while on duty."

Nor, after that, did I. Instead, I took to bringing in my own kettle and settling down with a nice cup of tea and book during the hour that the British Isles had Eternal Damnation beamed at them. I later learned that before my arrival, Teddy Johnson, later to achieve fame singing with Pearl Carr, but for two years a disc-jockey on Luxembourg, used to go down and fry bacon and eggs. This too had earned Herr Felten's disapproval. In spite of all they say, I believe that your average Briton is far more easygoing than your average continental.

After about six weeks of this initiation into the mysteries of broadcasting I returned to England. I hadn't become microphone-shy, or anything like that. It was simply that before I had left, I had been given a part in a film, and Radio Luxembourg had agreed to let me go back to do it.

The film was *No Highway,* and starred James Stewart, Marlene Dietrich and Glynis Johns. In fact it had quite a cast, because Jack Hawkins and Janette Scott were also in it, as was Kenneth More, who had a small part like mine. Kenneth was great fun. He played the co-pilot of the plane in the film, and always seemed to be climbing into the cockpit of the aircraft and making 'vroom-vroom' noises like a kid with his first toy racing car.

I played the navigator, and there was one scene in which we were supposed to be very nervous, and in which the navigator's ruler, which I was holding, broke. I had just one line with which to bolster this piece of illustrious acting.

But of course, with "Okay for sound" under my belt, fortified now by the wider cinematic experience of "You're on next Miss Jones," my ability to deliver these great one-liners was becoming (to me, if to nobody else) legendary.

Certainly my delivery did not escape the multi-racial sensitivities of the director, Henry Koster, a charming Hungarian-American-Jew. "I know this sounds ridiculous," he said, "but I was very impressed by the way you did that. Would you be interested in going to Hollywood?"

My mind flashed through the various possibilities. Was there some sinister implication behind the fact that everyone seemed so pleased with my one-line performances? Was it a gentle hint that this was considered the apex of my capabilities? And above all, like the gypsy's warning . . . REMEMBER GEORGE!

Well, I was pretty sure that Henry Koster wasn't interested in the latter angle, and as for the others, I cherished, in my youthful naiveté, the notion that one line might lead to two.

So I said that nothing would please me more.

"I'm going to put you up for a part," he said. "I really think you've got something. I'll send that piece of film to Hollywood."

A little later they took stills of me, and these too were despatched to Twentieth Century Fox. I was never auditioned, as such, but I later learned that I had come within a whisker of getting the part in *The Robe* that was eventually played by Richard Burton.

That part wasn't the only thing I lost during that little trip. Along with Michael Newell, and his girl friend, and her girl friend, I went to see Jessie Royce Landis in her current play. Afterwards we went to see her in her dressing room. It was a mistake. No-one explained to her that I was just making up a foursome. She assumed I was having an affair with the other girl. And I never saw her again.

I returned to Luxembourg in the New Year. To be truthful, I didn't want to go, but I'd given them my word, and that was that. And it was to cost me an 'r' in my name.

Soon after I got back to the footballing Brains Trust of the Brasserie du Théatre, and the tea-filled vigils of 'Bringing Christ to the Nations', I was joined at the Station by Peter Madren. Peter was a very different person to the extrovert Geoffrey Everitt and myself. He was a very good actor, who had got marvellous notices for a role he played at the Torch Theatre in Knightsbridge, now demolished. The play, by Dan Sutherland, had been well in advance of its time. It was about artificial insemination, and Peter played a cripple in a wheelchair.

I always remember him telling me how he had got all these awards for his part in *Breach of Promise*, and how the Tatler had published a full-page of him, and he had gone to the bookstall at Leicester Square Tube Station to sneak a look at it because he couldn't afford to buy the magazine. He was broke, and he went to work for Lyons at Cadby Hall as a night porter, hauling ice-cream around all night. In the daytime he would adorn himself with the second-hand suit he had bought from Ivor Novello and go to auditions.

I asked him: "Why haven't you had any offers since then, Peter?"

His reply was a classic statement about the theatre and how it works.

"I bumped into Alec Guinness one day," he said. "He talked about my success and said that he'd got a play, but that he couldn't possibly offer it to me because the part wouldn't be good enough. The truth was that at that moment I'd have taken anything. And the sad thing is, that if anybody had written another play about somebody in a wheelchair, I'd have been cast in it straight away."

Soon after Peter Madren's arrival it became obvious that there was a plethora of Peters at Luxembourg, for whom Peter West, Peter Dinely and various other Peters had recorded programmes. But as Madren and myself were the two staff regulars it was decided that one of us would have to give way.

71

The choice was made by the ancient ritual of tossing a coin, and although I can't remember who called, I know I lost. But I didn't want to undergo too radical a change, and, having run through all the possibilities from Alphonse to Zachary, I decided simply to drop the 'r'.

It was just as well, in a way. Peter Madren was far too much of a gentleman to be Pete. He made life hard enough for himself as it was, always insisting on writing himself a script, even for a request programme.

He was staunchly British, as indeed I think we all were in our exile, and insisted that we walk down every morning to the bookstall for the English papers, which were almost invariably late. Each morning, therefore, the conversation with the paper-seller was the same.

"Bonjour, monsieur, Est-ce que vous avez les journaux anglais?"
Answer: "Pas Encore."

So he rapidly became known as Pa Sencore, though I don't think he ever knew what we were on about.

Peter's Britishness was also an immediate advantage to us. When he discovered the slum conditions under which we were operating, he pushed me into an unheard of confrontation. Together we went to see the Managing Director, M. Pelvey. We informed this worthy that we considered the conditions unworkable because of the damp.

He said: "Well, I 'ave nowhere to go. I 'ave no place to put you."

"I think you're being rather anti-British," said Peter, in the tone of a man who knows how to produce a perfectly-rolled umbrella. M. Pelvey was 'orrified.

"Oh, Mon Dieu, non. I love ze British. I come to London. I sink it's a beautiful place, and I *love* ze British. We 'ave many sings to sank zem for, ze war and all zis, you know?"

I said: "Well, show your gratitude and put us in another office." And he did.

I was also relieved at Peter's arrival since I was able to convince Geoffrey Everitt that he would make a much more suitable presenter than myself of the Ballet Programme, and I was able to combine the Sunday 'Top Twenty' programme with a couple of essays, or perhaps I should say forays, into the vernacular. One of these was 'Irish Hour', which was at that time the most popular programme on the English

72

Station, with an audience of eight and a half million. I think that was because the Irish are basically a melodic people, and the requests I played for them would be country music, or waltzes, or happy-sounding razzmatazz.

I used to open the show by singing a couple of lines from 'If you're Irish, come into the parlour', and then I'd break off and say: "Ah yes, sure now, it's yer own darlin' boy Pete Murray here now. It's great to be with yer now." After a few weeks of this I got a letter from a man whom I supposed to be a member of the IRA. It was a very nasty letter, which indicated in language I will not duplicate that he didn't care for my phoney Irish accent, and that what's more if I didn't stop it he would set the boys on to me.

So on the next programme I apologised and told the listeners: "I'm terribly sorry. I seem to be offending you people in Ireland. I won't do it any more." I then read out the readable parts of his letter, which included his name and address.

A short while later I had a second letter from him. "I'm sorry if I caused you any offence," it said. "I've never been so embarrassed in my life. I've had people coming round to my door and threatening to kill me, or worse, because I've upset you. I now realise that you're not trying to take the mickey out of the Irish, and I'll be very pleased if you go on calling yourself 'Yer own darlin' boy', and will you please make an announcement over the air to tell people it has all been straightened out."

I did so. I hope he was alright. I'm the forgiving sort!

The other side of the Irish coin came on one occasion when I was walking down a street in Dublin and was stopped by a priest and asked for my autograph. "Listen to yer all the toim, Pete boy," he said. That I reckoned was the ultimate accolade, and should assure me of entry into some hereafter or other, in spite of my total inability to pronounce those impossible Irish place names like Dun Laoghaire.

My other venture into 'the voices' came with a programme called 'Log Cabin Lullaby'. On this, I never let on that it was really Murray doing the programme. I called myself Pedro, and assumed what I took to be a Texas accent (courtesy of Pathé Pictorial.) It must have been fairly convincing, because I used to get a stack of mail from American servicemen stationed in Europe, saying how marvellous it was to hear

73

the voice of someone from the old country playing the sort of music they loved.

Saddled (to coin a phrase) with this fan club of expatriate cowboys, I started to embroider the part. In those days, each programme was heralded by the famous Luxembourg gong, so I would start the programme with a spitting sound...'hht', then a pause, then the sound of the gong. "Got it good and true thar, friends. Time friends to meet yer ole pal Pedro, sittin' round the ole log fire, hyar."

I furnished Pedro with a wife, deceased, called Emily, on account of that was my own grandmother's name. "She were a great ole gal, ma Emily. Kicked the bucket now, ya know, but she sure used to cook up a rare ole hominy grits, thar, an' a great mess o' beans. Now I hev to do it all meself. All I got is me ole dawg Skipper. Hyar, Skipper, come and say a few words to the people." At that point I would bark. "That's it, Skipper, me ole pal, now you go lie down thar and let's hear a good ole Hank Williams number..." and so on. We were having the old needle-time problem even in those days, so I would fill out the programmes by doing the voices of the people on the records, a kind of multiple ventriloquist act that drove the Luxembourg technicians, who couldn't speak a word of English, to utter amazement.

I was still in the process of expanding this ridiculous repertoire when, about six months after joining Luxembourg, I got a call from London. It was Daphne Rye, from H. M. Tennant, under whose auspices I had auditioned for Michael Redgrave. Obviously they had remembered his approval, because the call was to say that they were going to do *A Winter's Tale*, with Diana Wynyard and John Gielgud. Would I be interested in a part?

"No," I said. "I'm here in Luxembourg, and at the moment I'm the only person here, and I'm under contract, and there's no way I can do it. Besides which, I could never get to London for an audition."

Half an hour later Daphne called me back. "Peter Brook, who is directing the play, is going to Brussels to supervise *Death of a Salesman*. Can you get to Brussels to meet him?"

Well, I thought that since they'd gone to so much trouble, with phone calls to Luxembourg and what not, the least I could do was to go and see him. So I agreed.

I extracted a copy of *The Winter's Tale* from the Public Library in Luxembourg, and settled down to read it on the two-hour train journey to Brussels; the circumstances were less than helpful for a proper enjoyment of the Bard.

After doing a short reading at Peter Brook's hotel, we went to the Belgian National Theatre, where I auditioned on stage. Now I am a bad sight-reader anyway, so it was hardly surprising when Peter said: "You obviously don't know the play very well." I was forced to agree.

He than asked whether, if he gave me a copy of *Macbeth,* I would remember that better. I thought I might, and did so, and he immediately decided that I was marvellous and wanted to know when I could get away from Luxembourg.

I suppose that was the most critical turning point in my career. Peter Brook was THE director in those days, and acceptance would have altered the whole shape of my future. Perhaps, who knows, it was to be the biggest mistake I ever made.

But faced with the direct question I replied: "You're not going to believe this, but I don't want to do it. I'd rather do what I'm doing for the moment. Besides, I don't think I'd ever be a good Shakespearean actor."

As I had suggested, he clearly couldn't believe it, and asked me to join him and some members of the Belgian National Theatre for lunch at a private apartment in Brussels. There he repeated his offer, and asked me if I was quite sure about what I was deciding. I said I was. The truth was that I would have been much happier if he hadn't wanted me, because I never really wanted to do it, and had only gone there out of politeness.

But the lunch was to provide me with another of LIFE'S GREAT LESSONS.

Most of the conversation was in French, of which I could hardly speak a word, at the time. I felt extremely shy and very inferior. They were discussing the Old Vic production of *She Stoops to Conquer*, and every now and then they would break off into English, which was for my benefit but which only succeeded in making me feel more inadequate. I kept quiet and tried to become invisible. Then it happened. Some one turned to me, and, with all the others silent around the table, asked me if I had seen *She Stoops to Conquer.*

To confess that I hadn't would have been too shame-making to bear. So I said: "Yes."

One little word, and then, horrors, the follow-up question.

"What did you think of it?"

"Oh well," I said lamely, "it was alright."

They knew. And I knew they knew. And they knew that I knew that they knew, that I hadn't seen that play.

I felt crucified, and from that day I made an absolute vow, that if I didn't understand anything, or couldn't contribute anything, I would say nothing; and that if someone said something, or used a word, that I didn't understand, I would say so. Why try to be what you're not? Not a great revelation, you may feel, but it took that experience to teach me.

Happily, back in Luxembourg I was enjoying experiences of quite another kind. Although the Luxembourgers are rather a staid lot, they do every year hold these masked balls, at which only the women are masked. It is the only time of the year when married women let their hair (or anything else for that matter) down, and pretty well anything goes. I did rather well out of these affairs, and met two or three quite pleasant girls, one of whom, a girl named Francoise, worked in the French Department at Radio Luxembourg.

Francoise was in fact extremely pleasant, so much so that one afternoon she and I repaired to one of the 'Listening' rooms, soundproof places where you could 'build' a record programme. Francoise and I were not, in fact, too interested in programme-building that afternoon. We were intent on seeing how pleasant we could be towards one another.

It was just as the mutual exchange of pleasantries was at its height, up against one of the turntables, as I recall, that the door burst open and the Head of Programmes, Herr Felten, came upon the scene. Herr Felten, you may recall, was the one who had expressed an earlier distaste for the way I had broken up the religious procession.

Herr Felten took me upstairs. He was quite nice about it. "We're all human," he said, in a tone more hopeful than convinced, "and I can't blame you for what you were doing. But if you wish to continue doing the things which you obviously enjoy doing, and which I hope you will continue to enjoy, may I suggest that you find somewhere else in which to do them. And if circumstances dictate that it has to be in our building, perhaps you could find somewhere less, as it were, open to inspection."

I felt, in a British way, that he'd really been rather decent about the whole thing.

Ernie — whose name, I haste to add, was short for Ernestine — provided further delights, though since she had a very strict father, who made her be home by eleven, and since I didn't get off work until one in the morning, the exchange of pleasantries became rather difficult. Also there was Colette, whose father had a little grocer's shop near the station. With her, the difficulty was not one of strictness but of smell ... the smell of garlic. Like so many Luxembourg girls, she seemed to live entirely off the strong local garlic sausage, specially designed by some Puritan butcher as an obstacle to romance.

These little frustrations were heightened for me by the fact that my room at the Brasserie du Théâtre stared across the road at the entrance to a brothel. I could see the gentlemen going in there to enjoy themselves, and here was I, an impatient bachelor, having to get up to all sorts of tricks to smuggle girls into my room. Herr Reissdorf didn't exactly encourage the practice, and besides, I've always been a bit of a prude about these things. I've never been able to take a girl to an hotel without blushing, and, especially in a village atmosphere like Luxembourg, I didn't want any girl with pleasant intentions to get a bad name.

The brothel was actually a café with some rooms above it, and one day a friend and I decided to investigate. I had a coke, and he had a schnapps, and there we sat while absolutely nothing happened. Perhaps it was a bit too much to expect a brothel to be operating at two-thirty in the afternoon. We just sat back and waited for everything to be offered to us, but nothing was, and so we drank up and left, feeling foolish, no richer in experience but certainly richer in pocket.

And then, in the summer of 1951, I met the girl in the typing pool. All the offices had those glass walls so that you could see what went on inside them, and we used to call this particular girl the 'English Girl', illogically, because she always wore a tartan skirt. She was blonde, about five foot six, with a very good figure, and a marvellously perky smile which lit up her whole face when she used it.

She always blushed when I looked at her, and her name was
Germaine.

Chapter Nine

I am not, nor was I ever, an Olympic swimmer.

Even Wally May's attempts to turn me into Johnny Weissmuller could not totally erase one particular memory of early childhood.

I used to go camping by the Thames, in the summer, with my aunt and uncle. On one of these occasions, well before I had even learned the dog-paddle, I had contrived to fall into the mighty river, and came within a stickleback's fin of being drowned. My father's (no doubt anxious) reaction to this event was to take his hand to my backside. This I felt to be both unfair and a little perplexing; I was for a while unclear as to whether he was really pleased at my escape from the deep!

So I suppose that any minor successes I may enjoy at the breast-stroke – the one I prefer, for reasons of my own – could be attributed to a subliminal desire to escape further punishment. But sun-bathing, accompanied by the occasional dip, I adore. And Germaine's father, Herr Graff, happened to be the owner of THE swimming pool in Luxembourg. I would be less than honest if I did not admit that this fact was a distinct addition to Germaine's charms. She, too, was a sun worshipper, and it got to the point where we would go out to the pool and I would do all my work there, in the lovely surroundings of Itziger Ste.

I remember, that Autumn, Wally Peterson came over to see us. I was walking through the park with Wally, husband of Joy Nicholls, and saying to him: "Life is marvellous. It's great. Germaine has a nice home, she's a lovely girl, she's got a super mother and father, and I get wonderfully well fed. On top of everything else, I get all my

79

swimming for nothing."

He stopped in his tracks, and looked at me, and I shall never forget his reply.

"The day will come," he said, "when you'll pay for every one of those swims . . . and you'll pay through the nose." He surely could not have known how right he was.

Germaine was shy, but very good company. Apart from the swimming, she had two great assets. One was that, like myself, she hated garlic, so that at least we were able to approach each other without instant revulsion. The other was that she too was a football fan, and would come to all the matches with me even when, as on one occasion, the temperature was five degrees below freezing and the game was played on a sort of ice rink.

Towards the end of 1951, Germaine and I decided to get married. She was Catholic, and we therefore had to go to see the priest, who turned out to be one of the most unchristian beings that I have ever met…though, to tell the truth, I found most of the Luxembourg clergy to be more like a squad of hard-faced commissars than servants of the Lord. They tended to confirm those early views of the church which had evolved during my cowering from the brickbats of St Nicholas.

We had a horrible meeting with this churchman, in his horrible vestry, and the first horrible thing he said to me was: "If there are any children they will be brought up as Catholics." To this I agreed, since in any case my wife's devotions fell short of the fervent, but I suppose I would have done better to have asked him what business it was of his. Because the second thing he declared was that, since I was not prepared to change my religion (whatever that was), he was not going to marry us in the church.

I did not like this priest. In fact, it was probably a good thing that we didn't get wed in his horrible church, because I might have been tempted to take one of his candles and stick it up his – oh yes and what a party the British Embassy gave for us.

The ambassador's name was Sir Geoffrey Allchin, and he and his wife threw a cocktail party to celebrate the impending nuptials. They threw the party, and I threw all caution out of the window and drank champagne. The caution went out of the window, and I went out of my skull. I got paralytically drunk. It was the only time in my life that

80

I have drunk, but I certainly made it count.

There were a lot of people there, and at the end of the party, when they were trying to get them to leave, it suddenly occurred to the muddled Murray mind that they couldn't leave until I did. But alcohol doesn't mix well with protocol. So, having gone up to my host to thank him, I remained rooted by his side and made it my business to bid a fond and gracious farewell to all the other guests. Finally, when the last farewell had been made by the swaying guest of honour, I turned with what I thought was a suitably diplomatic flourish to my hostess and intoned theatrically: "Good night, your Ladyship." Sir Geoffrey never told me how he felt about this sudden, and sodden, elevation to the peerage.

Two or three days before our marriage, I started to notice a slight change in Germaine's attitude towards me. It's hard to define, but somewhere a little voice was warning me. Then, the day before *the event*, I remember reading a Daily Mirror article about marriage, and something again told me I shouldn't be doing it. Years later, a friend told me a story which I wished I had heard before I took the plunge.

His son was getting married, and he asked him if he really loved the girl.

The boy said: "Yes."

Then he asked: "Are you really sure you want to marry her?"

The boy said: "No."

So he said: "Well, why go ahead? You don't have to."

The son replied: "Well yes, I've got to, Dad. I can't pull out, because they've got the beer in."

It was funny, but I know what the boy meant. You just don't want to hurt people.

So the wedding took place, a civil marriage by the mayor at the town hall, followed by a blessing from the horrible priest in his horrible vestry. I felt that with a blessing from him who needs curses?

My best man was Peter Madren, and my mother came over, and there was Wally Ridley, then the A-and-R manager of HMV, and Teddy Holmes of Chappells. I mentioned to Teddy that we were thinking of taking a summer holiday in Ischia.

"Oh, well," he said, "you *must* go to Capri and see Gracie Fields while you're there." We did, and I was half-way up the steps when

81

Boris appeared and threw us down them again, before I had any chance to say who I was or mention Teddy. So many people were just dropping in on them uninvited that it was driving them mad...but I hasten to add that we all met later and got on fine.

Radio Luxembourg, in its generosity, allowed me three days of honeymoon. We spent it in Paris, and stayed at one of those little hotels where the lift doesn't work properly and the plumbing is all up the creek, or vice versa. It was the kind of place which we tend, unfairly, to think of as typically French, and we loved it. But back in Luxembourg, the fact of my marriage was soon to bring me into further official displeasure.

The studio technicians were Luxembourgers and some of them had served in the German Army, though I am sure that for the most part, knowing them, it was with reluctance. But there was one, a man we called Jimmy, who I am certain must have relished the chance to have a go at Perfidious Albion. He was violently anti-British, and was always making petty little complaints against us in regard to such world-shaking trivia as recording levels. On many occasions I had had to bite back my tongue to preserve the international peace. But soon after the station switched to the medium waveband, and became the famous 208, in order to reach more listeners, our studio had to be done up.

We were temporarily removed to a pair of old studios up in one of the Villa Longwy's battlements, the other of which was given to the French service. The two technicians sat in the middle, between the two studios, and I had just introduced that day's tape of the enthralling 'Dan Dare' (Adventures of), and was walking through to talk to the French announcer when I noticed Jimmy complaining about something to his mate.

I said to him: "Why don't you make a note of the problem and send it to London?"

At that, he said something to his pal in Luxembourgish, and the other man, Charlie, laughed in a sneering kind of way. Now although I couldn't speak the patois, I could understand a bit, and I knew that he had said something derogatory about Germaine. So I told him: "Say that again, only this time, say it in English."

His response was to say something else unpleasant in the patois.

Again the other guy laughed.

"You've said something about my wife," I said. "Say it in English."

He refused, and again said something sneering in Luxembourgish, whereupon, fired by righteous anger and the exploits of Dan Dare, I whacked him across the face.

Now the situation was a little difficult. His reaction was one of total horror and, I am happy to say, a good deal of pain. The following morning the technicians held a meeting, into which I happened to walk. "What are you talking about — me?" I asked. I was informed that there were two alternatives. Either I gave Mr Jimmy a written apology, or they would demand my removal from Radio Luxembourg. I have to say that most of them seemed very embarrassed by the whole situation. I was so shaken that I neglected to tell them the reason for the blow in question, and instead was hauled in front of Herr Felten, who, following my disruption of the procession, and the incidents with Francoise, must have thought he had a real toughie on his hands.

"We don't want to lose you," said Herr Felten. That at least, I thought, was an auspicious start. I told him what had happened. "I understand," he said, "and you *could* take this further. And I will remonstrate with the man. But I'm afraid you'll have to write the letter."

So I did. I should have reported him in the first place, and what I did *was* wrong. LESSON ... Never strike one of the junior ranks. Come to think of it, never strike one of the senior ranks either. Put it this way, don't strike anybody.

The most embarrassing thing about the whole distasteful episode was that Jimmy took the chance to apologise quietly to me on his own, and thereafter was so bloody nice to me it was unbelievable. I preferred him as he was before.

Indirectly, it was the war which helped me to get *my* first request played on the air. Godfrey Winn had a request programme, which he recorded in London. Each week he gave away a bunch of roses to the subject of the best letter. Now I had always maintained that you can, if you really try, get a request played on any programme, and I put my theories to the test.

I wrote him a letter, under a false name, which I had posted in

83

England. I said that I was in the Navy, and that I knew he was an ex-naval type. I said how much I enjoyed the sympathetic approach he had towards his programmes. I said how much my mother enjoyed his programmes. I buttered him up so much you could have spread him on toast.

A few days later I had a phone call from my mother. "You'll never believe it," she said, "but I've had a request played for me by Godfrey Winn . . . and what's more, he's sent me a bunch of red roses."

Later I met Godfrey and got to like him very much. He was very amusing, in spite of his old woman image, which also didn't prevent him from being a marvellous tennis player. One day I decided to reveal my little ploy to him. He looked at me in a Noel Coward tone of voice and said simply: "How *very* ingenious."

In 1952, I started a programme with Peter Madren called 'Smash Hits'. People would write in with their favourite 'hates' and the reasons for them, and having played the record we would smash it, or at any rate one of a pile of old 78s we kept for the purpose. For some reason we used to find the whole thing so hysterically funny that we couldn't do it live, and it became the only programme that we recorded, so that some at least of the laughter could be cut out. Many years later Mick Jagger came up to me and told me that he used to listen to Luxembourg and that that had been his favourite programme and that: "My mum and I used to have hysterics over it."

Peter, as I have said, was the perfect gentleman, but around that time he was put in charge of the office as well as doing his programmes, and he was constantly being called by music publishers and record companies.

One day he came to me with a sorrowful look on his face, and I asked what the matter was.

"It's got to a pretty bloody state, this," he said.

Well, with Peter to say that, things must have been bad.

"What's the matter? What do you mean?" I asked him.

"It's just the way things are at the moment . . . I mean, the record pluggers are even phoning me at home now, right in the middle of my lunch."

I fear that the opportunity was too good for the twisted Murray mind to miss. When I got back to the flat, I had a quick meal, read the paper until I was sure that Peter would be at lunch, and then phoned him.

The call was to be from a man whom I cannot name, a very old friend who happens to be a raving queen. (I'll call him Clive Cusp.) He worked for a big music publishing company I'll call Disc Music. I made it as if it were coming from London, so that en route to Peter I had to be the Luxembourg, Belgium, and London operators. It went something like this:

His wife, Andre, who was a Luxembourger, answered the phone.

"Ja?"

Now I had to be the Luxembourg operator. "Ist der Herr Madren do vonishch cleeft?"…a rough way of writing the patois for: "Is Mr Madren there, please?"

"Ja."

"Hier ist London. Ein moment."

Peter came to the phone.

"Mr Madren?"

"Yes."

"We have a call from London for you."

"Oh God, who's it from?"

"We have a Mr Clive Cusp for you. One moment, please."

At this point I became the Brussels operator, who always used to infuriate Peter by interrupting his calls from London with: "Terminez?"

So I did a quick female: "Terminez?"

"No. I haven't bloody well started yet," said the normally patient Peter.

English operator. "Oh, London here. We have a Mr Clive Cusp from Disc records for you."

"Oh, Christ," says Peter.

Finally Clive Cusp comes on the line. "Hello, Peter."

"Oh, hello Clive. How are you?"

"Oh Peter, I'm going through such a terrible time."

Peter exuded sympathy. "I'm very sorry to hear that, Clive."

"Oh God, I really don't know whether I'm coming or going. You know, Peter, I've just got to get away."

"I don't blame you, Clive," says Peter.

85

"Well, what I was going to say, was I sort of…you know, I feel so at home with you all at Luxembourg and I thought … maybe … I could take a trip to Luxembourg."

"Oh yes, Clive? Always pleased to see you. When are you thinking of coming?"

"Tomorrow," says 'Clive' … knowing full well that Peter had a whole stack of people coming that day, including four music publishers and three record producers.

"Well, we've got rather a lot of people coming…" said Peter doubtfully.

"Don't worry. I'm not coming over to talk about business. I just want to keep out of the way, and perhaps see you a little bit. Oh, I'm having so much trouble with…with Ronald…at the moment. It's driving me mad."

"Well, I'm very sorry to hear that, Clive. Um…where would you like me to book you in?"

"Er, well I don't know Peter. You know, I just don't want to go into a hotel, and I feel so comfy when I'm round at your flat with you and, er, Andre."

Peter, who had a one-roomed flat with a sofa, went on to the defensive.

"Well I mean Clive, er you know, we don't sort of *have* anywhere…"

"Doesn't matter, anywhere will do," says 'Clive'.

Now finally Peter, being the totally nice guy that he was, agreed.

"OK then. How long will you be staying, Clive?"

"Oh, about three weeks."

There was a terrible pause.

"Well…um…I think we might be going away." said Peter.

"Don't worry, Peter. I can always look after the place, and do all the polishing for you and everything. Don't worry about a thing."

"Oh, Christ" said Peter.

'Clive' burbled on: "The thing is, I'm not just upset about Ronald, I'm terribly upset about His Lordship and all those boy scouts. Oh it really does upset me. It's given me quite a turn. Quite a nasty turn. And the reason, Peter, why I really want to be with you, is that I know that before you were married you were one of us."

86

Now poor Peter, utterly heterosexual Peter, had had it.

"Well, Clive, I do assure you...that under no circumstances...I mean, much as I am sympathetic, and although a great number of my friends are homosexual...er...I've never actually been that way at all."

I could keep it up no longer. "You'd better believe it, baby," I said. "I thought you were having an affair with Pete Murray."

"I beg your pardon," says a perplexed Peter.

"It's Pete Murray here," I said.

I will not commit his reply to paper. But there was a pay-off.

That night, Petula Clark and Joe Henderson were over in the Grand Duchy, and Peter and I and our wives were taking them out to dinner at the Cravat Hotel. Peter, who was doing a programme, joined us late, and as he came to the table he said: "God, I've just had the most terrible moment."

"What's happened?" I asked.

"Well, following your call at lunch, I had a strange fellow on the line who said: 'Er, Mr Madren, Ah I'm from Amsterdam and I'm just in Luxembourg for the day, and I'd very much like to see you. My name is Danny Something from Paxton Records.' "

"Well," I asked, "what's the matter with that?"

"It was a genuine call."

"So?"

"So I thought it was you again and I said: 'Why don't you piss off?' "

Another reason to remember that visit by Petula and Joe was the evening we all went out to one of the Luxembourg night clubs. They gave a marvellous impromptu concert, accompanied by Dick Norton, one of the disc jockeys, on clarinet, and Alan Freeman on drums...not 'Fluff' Freeman, but the one who is now one of the judges on 'New Faces'.

Alan was then a song 'plugger' with Polydor, and in fact plugged me with the first record with which I was ever plugged when I first went to Luxembourg. He has been a friend ever since, and is a super bloke, which I suppose is a plug for him!

Plugging, of course, was a perfectly reputable pastime...trying to get the disc jockeys to listen to a new record, and if possible play it. But bribery is another thing. I am always being asked about the truth behind the various scandals involving large gifts to disc jockeys for playing records. Well, it has happened, of course, but I have never been offered a penny.

The nearest I came to it was when a band leader once came up to me, thanked me profusely for playing a record of his, and slipped £25 into my pocket. I gave it straight back. I said: "It's very kind of you, but the day I can't play one of your records I'll feel obliged to do so because you've given me money. It's not that I don't need the money — I do — but I just can't accept it."

If that sounds very pious, it was actually in the interests of self-preservation. The risk of getting compromised just isn't worth it. In fact, I became known as the King of the B-Sides, because I always listened to both sides of a record, and nine times out of ten I would play the 'wrong' side...and was usually proved right. One instance that sticks out was a record by Herb Alpert called 'Lonely Bull'. The name on the B-side meant nothing to me, but some time after it arrived I was in a club in the French Alps.

I heard a record played there and thought: "That's great." I found out that it was the other side of 'Lonely Bull', and started to play it on my programme. It soon became a hit. Its name...Acapulco 22.

And of course, being completely independent in one's choice meant that one could happily give a boost to the people who really did seem good. In February of 1953 I wrote in '208', the magazine of Radio Luxembourg, predicting stardom for two young singers ... Tony Brent, and Dickie Valentine. Tony ended up with three records in the Hit Parade, quite something for those days, and Dickie of course went on to become one of the very big stars, though the record for which I was praising him, 'You belong to me,' was actually a hit for Jo Stafford. Well, you can't win 'em all.

But Radio Luxembourg had a much bigger pulling power than the BBC ever admitted. And we proved it with the David Whitfield record of 'Answer me'. "Answer me Lord above, just what sin have I been guilty of " . . . the BBC, still riddled with rather old-fashioned ideas, banned the record on account of its appeal to the Almighty. Radio Luxembourg had no such worries . . . and the record, David Whitfield's first, went to the top of the charts. We had proved our point that we could make a hit on our own.

David, of course, was delighted. One didn't *need* bribes in order to get enormous pleasure from the performers' gratitude. In fact, one of the biggest, and best surprises I ever had was when I got a phone call from Doris Day to say how delighted she was that I had played her record. I had a huge respect for her acting as it was, and she was absolutely charming to me . . . worth a great deal more than a few quid in the pocket.

I was lucky to have 'Top Twenty' as one of 'my' programmes, but in those days the charts, based on sales of sheet music, used to change much more slowly than they do now. For instance, 'Limelight' was at the top for 22 weeks, with 'Moulin Rouge' just below it.

Week after week it was Frank Chacksfield and Mantovani...it used to drive me insane, so I started playing other versions, which upset quite a number of people. But there was another side to that particular coin: I had a letter from Julie Dawn, whom I respect highly as a singer, saying: "Don't you ever give British artistes a chance? For the last ten weeks you've been playing Nat King Cole's version of 'Pretend'. I've made a recording of it, so why don't you give that a spin?" So I did.

Years later, on 'Juke Box Jury', I happened to remark how difficult it was for a class singer to record in Britain. I said that if Sinatra had been British he probably wouldn't be recording...simply because his records didn't become big hits immediately. I added that people like Julie Dawn should be given more of a chance. Julie must have been watching the show, because a couple of days later I had a lovely letter of thanks from her . . . I reckon she thought I'd forgotten the first letter!

That letter was pretty straightforward. But some of our mail was fairly way out, not to say utterly embarrassing. For example, one of the first sponsors of the Top Twenty programme was the firm of Bourjois with their perfume called 'Endearing'. Part of my job was to read out these very sexy adverts for the said scent.

That was what led Ian Parr, an Oxford undergraduate, to write to me: "Dear Mr Murray. I have been wondering about you for some considerable time. Having heard you read out the commercials for 'Endearing' perfume on Sunday night, there is now no doubt about it. You are a raving poof." Well, we did get an audience of more than nine and half million, so I suppose I couldn't expect them all to be avid fans.

The voice was one thing, the face was another. From time to time '208' magazine used to print photos of us, and one day this inspired a lady listener to write to me. She said she had been listening to my programme for some time, and that she had a wonderful mental picture of me as a distinguished man in his mid-forties, with greying temples. "And what do I find?" she asked. "A gangling youth, with a lop-sided grin." She signed herself "Heartbroken".

That gave my vanity not so much a pin-prick as a torpedo-hole!

Sometimes, however, the mail would get a little heavy. I know now what I didn't realise in those days, that there are people who hang on every word you say, and believe that every song is played specially for them...and even more so if it is romantic.

The wife of a miner in County Durham terrified me in this way. She wrote: "I've got your message. I'm leaving my husband and five children and getting the train to Luxembourg tomorrow."

I went cold. She had enclosed a photo of herself, hanging the washing up on a line with her hair in curlers, and I wasn't all that hot on domesticity anyway!

I managed to get a telegram off to her in time, telling her: "Please don't come. You are reading something into the playing of the request that was not there."

Then there was the highly intelligent and very rich woman, with a house worth £75,000 even in those days. I met her at some function and danced with her just once. She immediately got the impression that I fancied her, and that every time I played a romantic song it held a message for her. Since I didn't even select the records of the programme in question, I reckoned this was rather an unfair burden to carry.

Sometimes the letters turned to sheer fantasy. One I had was from a girl who asked me to play Leroy Anderson's 'The Typewriter', as she was a secretary. She wrote that she was a Teddy Girl from Liverpool, and that she had fantasies about getting me in bed, tying me up in gold chains, and whipping me. Ouch! Then, when I was quite exhausted, she would get me to make love to her. Phew! Funny, I never knew Liverpool Teddy Girls went on like that.

Mind you, who was I to deny her these little dreams? The trouble was that often the husbands or boy-friends would find out that their loved ones had sent me these erotic epistles, and I would get short sharp notes from them which summed up *their* attitude. For example..."Drop dead, you stinking rat."

But the greatest embarrassment arose from a very charming letter I had from a woman in Torquay, asking for a record to be played for herself and her husband on their wedding anniversary. This I happily did. Then she wrote again to say what joy it had brought to her, and please, would I send her a photograph of myself. Again, this is not an unusual request, so I sent her a picture of the 'gangling, lop-sided youth'. But unlike her predecessor, this lady obviously found the Murray mug to her liking. I started to get a number of letters from her, which I decided to ignore. But you can't win. She clearly took my reticence as encouragement, and the letters began to get, shall I say, a little too friendly. So I wrote her a brief note to say: "Please don't go on writing in this strain, because you're reading something into this that just doesn't exist."(Well, after all, her last letter *had* said: "I know you love me.")

To this she wrote back immediately, apologising profusely, and a gap of a month followed. I congratulated myself that this fantasy romance of the air-waves had been brought to a full stop. I had reckoned without the emotional fluency of her pen. The carnal correspondence re-started.

I wrote another of my "Please don't write" notes, and she hit back with another "I know you love me."

Faced with the prospect of a game of postal ping-pong, I got Clement Cave, Managing Director of Radio Luxembourg, to write to her. She wrote back to him and apologised.

Believe it or not, she then embarked on yet another string of letters, spread over a period of about eighteen months. Eventually, in spite of the fact that I ignored them all, they again became so hot that I got Clement Cave to write her another letter. This time he threatened to contact the police if she didn't stop. Again she apologised. Again we sighed with relief. Again, we did so too soon.

I now received a letter from her husband saying: "I've been brought back from Hong Kong on compassionate grounds. My wife has asked me for a divorce, and says she wants to marry you." The fact that I was already married hadn't deterred her in the least. He asked if there was any truth in it all, and went on: "I've asked my wife for any evidence, but she says that she's never met you. I asked if she had any letters from you in romantic vein, and she says she hasn't. But she claims that she knew by the tone of your voice on the radio that you loved her."

And all for playing one simple little request. Both Clement and I wrote to the husband and explained the situation, and he wrote apologising, and then, finally, I'm happy to say, the whole thing ended.

But it was ANOTHER GREAT LESSON. When you do a radio programme, your voice goes right into people's homes. And if they are at all unbalanced or emotionally upset, you can easily become the figure on whom they pin their hopes. It was a salutary reminder that, for many people, the world is a sad, unhappy, and lonely place.

Chapter Ten

I am not a comedian.
The thought of having to stand up every night in front of an audience that expects to be made to laugh, fills me with horror. On the other hand, I do enjoy off-the-cuff banter with audiences at shows I am compèring, and if I happen to raise an occasional laugh ... well that's a bonus.

Also, as readers may by now have gathered, I cannot resist a practical joke. Why this should be I have no idea, though doubtless a psychiatrist would be able to dig up some childhood deprivation or other.

I remember one evening at Luxembourg when I was in the middle of a programme and noticed the technician, a joker himself named Nicky Bilten, fiddling around with a piece of tape in the control room. I couldn't imagine what he was up to, until I started to experience the disconcerting sound of my own voice coming more and more slowly back to me through my headphones.

Instead of running the programme, and my own voice, straight back to me through the phones as usual, he was taping me and then playing the tape into the earphones ... at a slightly slower speed than normal. It's a very peculiar sensation.

So I told the radio audience what he had done, and warned them that we would play the same trick on Peter Madren, whose programme followed mine. Now Peter, as I have said, used to script every word of his show, and as Nicky started to play the trick on him he was completely thrown. He started to stutter and stumble and drip with perspiration. Just as he was about to fold up completely, I rushed into the studio and said, over the air: "What on earth do you think you're doing? What kind of programme is this? You're letting your listeners down. It's the most disgraceful performance I've ever heard in my life!"

Poor Peter, totally unable to ad lib, just sat there, utterly shaken, at which, I fear, I burst into hysterical laughter, and told him what had happened.

The explanation still couldn't galvanise him into anything approaching speech, so I told the listeners, who of course were in on the whole thing: "I think the old boy's gone to pieces. I'd better read the next card to let him recover."

For some reason, Herr Felten never said a word about it.

Mind you, I'd made a few bloopers myself in my time there, like the occasion I announced: "This is Radio Luckingbird" and another when I signed off with: "This programme has been introduced by yours truly Radio Luxembourg." Perhaps those made up for the listeners who used to write in with incomprehensible requests. We had, for instance, a number of requests over the years for some of the music from Polly Archy. You figure it out.

But the most extraordinary 'funny' came one day when I was doing a programme sponsored by a fireworks company. As I announced this, a tape was played in the background which had a lot of noise and explosions on it. The idea was to give the listeners a taste of the lovely bangs that would be theirs if they bought the product, but in fact it sounded more like the take-over of the station by the Luxembourg Revolutionary Party. So I said: "Don't worry folks. There's not going to be an explosion."

At that precise moment, the transmitter broke down, the electrics in the building went haywire, all the lights went out, and we went off the air.

Strangely, no-one called to see if we were alright. Perhaps they were just glad of a bit of peace.

For the first few months of our marriage, Germaine and I had lived at her parents' flat above the grocer's shop in the Rue Glesener. Then we moved into a flat of our own, which, though fairly miserably furnished, was quite pleasant since it overlooked the park, and had its own garden.

In the summer we spent some of the time in the house her parents had next to THE swimming pool. But our life together wasn't that good. We were both only children, and it didn't take long for the selfishness of both of us to come through. Marriage seemed to be one long argument about where the salt and pepper pots should be located. But I think most of the blame was mine...I've always been a bit messy, and not easy to live with.

I dare say that after a year we should have turned it in, but that Autumn our son, Michael, arrived. We christened him Michael because I thought that if he should ever become an actor, Michael Murray would be rather a good name. But someone else had the same idea, because years later, when he did go into the theatre, he found that there was another Equity member with the name Michael Murray. Equity rules don't allow two people with the same name, so in the end he had to change it anyway, to James. So much for Planning.

But at least the Luxembourg social round kept life interesting. The British Ambassador, with a magnanimity remarkable in view of my previous insobriety, actually invited us to a dinner party. This sticks in my mind because of my wife's decision to choose a banana for her fruit course.

My technique with this fruit, which no-one had seen fit to query, had always been to stick it straight in my mouth. But not Germaine, Oh no. Out came the knife and fork, and having peeled back the skin she started cutting it off in little bits. I was horrified. I was quite convinced that she was doing all the wrong things. I could see us being banished instantly from all available polite circles. But in fact, of course, she was doing the right thing. She had been to a good school in Belgium, where clearly the tackling of a banana had ranked high in the curriculum.

In 1953 the Embassy threw a magnificent party to celebrate the Coronation, a monument to all that was still, in those days, considered the best in British life. I doubt if they'll ever be able to afford to give one like that again.

But my memories of the social scene are in the end all overshadowed by the fact that I was lucky enough to be in Luxembourg when the legendary Perle Mesta was the U.S. Ambassador there. She was truly the Hostess with the Mostest, and it was on her life that the musical

Call Me Madam was based. She seemed to be giving a party two or three times a week, and they all had this tremendous sense of informality. There was no bull about it, and even the most humble Embassy secretary would be there.

At one of the first of these parties I went to, I sat down beside her on a sofa and said: "You're a marvellous hostess. But surely somewhere along the line you must feel you can't really trust people?"

She looked at me, with that air she had of a friendly barmaid, slightly over made-up, hair a trifle over-bubbled, clothes just a fraction larger than life. She said, "You're a very discerning young man. You must come to more of my parties." Which I did.

I met Eisenhower there, before he became President, and I recall telling him a rather risqué English story (about a couple on a bomb-site, actually), at which he laughed so much I thought he was going to have a hernia. Perhaps it's just as well I told it to him then, because it was certainly not the kind of story you tell a President.

Another guest I met there was Irene Dunne. Irene was a very strong Catholic, and her immediate desire, on arriving in Luxembourg, was to visit all the churches. I merely hoped, for her sake, that she gave a miss to the one inhabited by our horrible priest, and mused, in view of this devotion, that she should have been called Irene Nun.

In those early days of Luxembourg we had other parties to contend with...coach parties. These 208 visiting trips were organised by a man called Charles Graves, a relative of poet Robert. Charles ran the '208' magazine, in which I penned my first hesitant attempts at writing for public consumption. Looking back at these articles, they seem to devote more time to touring football teams than anything else, and that gave me one small success as a soccer seer.

Preston North End had come over to play a Luxembourg team. The big draw, of course, was the immortal Preston Plumber, Tom Finney, and like the true gentleman he was, he toned down his performance in order not to make a fool of the opposing full-back. But also in the team was a 20-yr old of whom I wrote: "This boy has got a fantastic future and will be one of the great footballers of our time." His name was Tommy Docherty, later to play for Scotland, and later still to be manager of Manchester United.

Anyway, these coach tours I was mentioning grew to incredible proportions, holidaymakers, soldiers from the Army in Germany, and so on. It got to the point where we had to pretend we weren't in. But on some occasions we would go for a trip on the coaches with them, which in that marvellously varied and unspoilt countryside was no hardship.

On one of these trips, the party decided they would like to go to see the transmitter from which our hallowed words were beamed to a waiting world.

On the way out there we were halted by a closed gate attended by an ancient Luxembourgish lady. Anxious to be helpful, and to impress the passengers with my fluent French, I leapt out and addressed her on the subject of the gate for an unnecessary five minutes. She listened to me calmly, even stoically, and then replied. In German. She didn't speak a word of French, nor I of German, so we just went and opened the gate ourselves.

When we finally arrived at the transmitter enclosure, we found it apparently entrusted to a fellow in wellington boots and an old pair of corduroys. He proceeded to take our 200 guests on a quick tour of the place, and when he had finished I turned to Charles and said: "You know, he's been very good. You must give him something."

"Sure. How much shall I give him?" asked Charles.

"Oh," I said, "Give him 200 francs, that'll be enough." 200 francs was worth about thirty shillings.

So Charles presented the 200 francs to the man, who examined it and said: "Thank you very much. That's very kind of you. I'll see that all the boys get a drink."

We thought that this was very magnanimous of him. It was only when we got back to Radio Luxembourg that we found out that our 'caretaker' was in fact John Madison, second only to the Managing Director of the whole of Radio Luxembourg.

A lot of our visitors, naturally, were in the business. For example, Hughie Green dropped in one day...literally. He was flying a plane to Frankfurt and decided that he might as well stop off in Luxembourg and meet the boys. He was making most of his living then in buying and selling planes, and I remember him telling us about the time he strayed over the Iron Curtain and was buzzed by Russian fighters. Rather him than me.

When he first arrived at the studios nobody on duty knew who he was, and the security men wouldn't let him in. In the end they got hold of Peter Madren, who identified him, and we took him out on the town. Talk? I don't think he stopped from midnight till six in the morning, but at least he was being funny. In those days he was doing his 'Double Your Money' show on Luxembourg, and he really just wanted to see what the studios were like.

Two Frankies popped over. The first was Frankie Lane, an enormous star at the time. I had hit on the idea of trying to get some of the artists from the Top Twenty over to interview, and then to introduce their own records...in a way, the dim and distant forerunner of 'Open House'. Frankie was the very first to do this, and introduced his big hit 'Jezebel'.

The other was Frankie Vaughan. My chief memory of him was that he brought his straw hat with him, and when we took him to a night-club he got up and did his act, to the total astonishment of the assembled Luxembourgers, who probably thought we were about to start the Boat Race.

And there was J.Y. himself. Jimmy Young. He was to provide me with another GREAT LESSON.

Jimmy was great fun, very personable, and we all liked him a great deal. Also, at the time he came over, we all felt rather sorry for him, because he was going through a rough time. He had earlier had a big hit with 'Too Young', but now he couldn't get a record off the starting-pad. I think he felt that Bunny Lewis, then the Decca promotions man, who also handled David Whitfield, was rather favouring David. So he came over, and talked to us, and we played some of his records, and back he went to England.

Now at that time, Tony Brent had just made a record called 'A Baby Cried'. We thought it was a diabolical song, and consigned the test record to the waste-paper basket, not even bothering to keep it as a victim for Smash Hits. By sheer chance, a few hours after this piece of private disc demolition who should turn up at the studios again, after an absence of a few weeks, but Jimmy Young, this time with his wife Sally Douglas, a singer with the Geraldo Band. Jimmy had a record he wanted to promote with us. He had just made it. And, you've guessed, it was his version of 'A Baby Cried'.

If there was a machine that could monitor inward groans, it would have blown its fuses at that moment. But we felt sorry for him, and we gave it a few plays. For my own part, I think it's the only time I've played a record that I didn't consider ought to be in the programme, and it proved that there were some records that even Luxembourg couldn't sell. It died the death.

A year passed, and Jimmy returned to Luxembourg yet again. This time things were better for him. He had made 'Man from Laramie', which was starting to be a hit, and he took the Madrens and us out to a slap-up meal, which he told us was a belated thank-you which he hadn't been able to afford before.

We were delighted, and grateful, and pleased at his success. And when, later, I finally came to leave Luxembourg, I felt that I would have at least one friend in London, especially as he had made a point of saying: "When you come to London we'll be able to see much more of each other. You must come to my TV show." And so on. I gave him my telephone number and address in London, but when I got back I heard nothing.

LESSON. That's a true statement about show business in general, rather than Jimmy in particular. When you're working with someone, you're with them. And when you're not, you're not. It's all a product of the gypsy-style of life we lead. I felt no anger, only a regret that we obviously weren't going to be the close friends I had thought, back in Luxembourg.

Of course, not all the people who wanted us to play their records took the trouble to come all the way to the Grand Duchy. Some would write to us, and one such request took me back to the days just before the war. It was in Whiteley's department store, in Bayswater, where a singer called Denny Dennis was dong a show. He was a big star then. On previous occasions at Whiteley's I had been successful in begging autographs from Hermione Baddeley and Derek Roy (who was just starting, and a big hero of mine.)

But when I approached Denny Dennis for *his* signature he said in an off-hand way: "Don't bother me, kid. I'm in a hurry."

I felt very hurt at the time, though subsequently I have come to realise that it *isn't* always convenient. In my own case, I happen to be a great runner-for-trains. I always seem to have exactly thirty seconds in which to board the last piece of British Rail machinery that will get me there on time. And inevitably, as I am in mid-Olympic dash, someone will ask for an autograph.

But now, the ironic thing was that Denny, who had gone to America to sing with the Tommy Dorsey orchestra, and had come back to England and made a record, wrote to me asking me to listen to it and consider playing it on the programme.

I remember the old adage: "Be nice to people when you are on the way up, because you might need them when you are on the way down." Shades of Captain Ferguson. I played Denny's record for him.

One of the advantages in working at Radio Luxembourg was that it was so convenient for visiting other parts of Europe. In an assortment of ill-favoured old motor-vehicles I would use my spare time to drive across neighbouring borders, visiting Trier, the birthplace of Karl Marx, or shopping at Thionville in France. When Philip Jones came over from the London office, I remember he wanted badly to see Verdun. We drove there, and I will never forget the eerie feeling of death all around, among the countless soldiers killed there in the two World Wars.

And there was Frankfurt. I had a few days off and took a trip there, which would have been enjoyable had I not had the feeling, when I passed people in the street, that mothers were clutching their teenage daughters away from my path, with something akin to fear in their eyes.

When I got back to Luxembourg, one of the girls in the office asked if I had seen a certain German magazine, of vast circulation and small repute. I said I hadn't, and she showed it to me. There was a picture of me, with Diana Dors (with whom I had never posed for photos), and a lengthy article exposing me as the wickedest rake in Europe. I would have been angry had I not been so flattered! I only bemoaned my luck that not a word of it was true.

But it was better than the unsolicited testimonial I received when we drove down to Spain on our way to Majorca. We picked up a hitch-hiker, and after some conversation it transpired that he listened to Radio Luxembourg, though of course he had no idea who I was. When I asked him what he thought of the station he said: "It's fine. But I just wish that guy Pete Murray would learn to keep his big mouth shut."

Collapse of stout disc-jockey!

As a matter of fact, that trip was a bit of disaster in other ways than the deflation of my ego. We stopped at Lyons on the way down, and when we finally arrived at the frontier we discovered that we had left our passports there. The French were very nice about it. "We accept that you have left your passports in Lyons, Monsieur," they said. "But the question is, will they accept it on the other side? You know what they're like."

We went over to the other side, Germaine very distressed by the whole thing, and me with a blinding toothache...a penalty, perhaps, for not keeping my big mouth shut. A couple of dumb-looking Spanish guards in scruffy uniforms took us to an office, where we were confronted by an absolutely splendid Spaniard, unlike any Iberian I have seen before or since.

He obviously sympathised with Germaine, who was by now in tears, convinced that we would miss our plane to Majorca. I think he probably fancied her into the bargain.

To my utter astonishment he said: "I will let you through. I am very sorry this has happened, and I believe you implicitly. You must arrange to have your passport sent to your hotel in Majorca, and you must notify me when it arrives. This is all I ask." To seal the bargain, he picked up about three dozen huge oranges from a pile which, for some unexplained reason, was sitting in the customs house, put them in a bag, and gave them to us.

My heart immediately warmed to all things and persons Spanish. But my tooth was in agony, and when we arrived in Barcelona I had it removed and committed to Spanish soil, making a mental note to inform our frontier friend that I was one molar less than the man who had entered his country.

The cavity promptly got infected, and so my first week in Majorca was spent in daily trips to Palma for treatment. It was very hot, and one day, without thinking, I travelled in shorts.

I had not realised that this was illegal. But the Spanish Civil Guard who saw me realised that it was illegal. He felt rather strongly about it. To be perfectly frank, what he did was to shout and scream at me, and force my naked knees aboard a bus, destination unknown...anything

101

to get me out of town, and to prevent the moral demolition of the ladies of Palma.

The bus finished up somewhere on the other side of the island. I confess I was not happy with this Civil Guard. I was quite unable to reconcile his attitude with that of the Beau Geste of the Border.

When I went on these periods of leave, my programmes would be taken over either by regulars like Dick Norton, or Jimmy Vivian or by special guests brought in. On one of the earlier occasions, the stand-in, whom I didn't meet before going on holiday, was a man named Warren Misel.

Everyone was very delighted that this man should have been procured for the job, but the hierarchy were a trifle unhappy at his name. "This is a very bad name to use on Radio," they said. "We can't possibly go on the air with a name like that." So, with much protestation from Mr Misel, his name was changed to Mitchell. Warren Mitchell.

He was there when I got back, but unfortunately didn't stay long. He had very strong views on religion and politics, and refused point-blank to introduce to the late night pray-in, 'Bringing Christ to the Nations'. They had to bring someone else in specially to do the announcement, and they felt that Warren was falling short of his undertakings, since the announcement of the early morning zealots was a built-in part of a Luxembourg announcer's job. Memories of my processional, and subsequent confessional, made me more than a little sympathetic.

I liked Warren. Even in those days he was something of a buccaneer and revolutionary. He had hair then, and an eye for the women the like of which I had never seen. The said eye communicated its orders to a rapid pair of feet, and Warren seemed to spend his entire off-duty hours in chasing a girl named Lulu around the office. Lulu seemed rather to enjoy the exercise, and I believe they ended up, as they say, very good friends.

When he finally went back to England, he decided to keep his new name, which I found surprising in light of his previous protests. He was an out-of-work actor, who had been hired in much the same way as myself. Indeed, in those days, the disc-jockeys always seemed to come from one part of show business or another. David Jacobs had been an actor, Jack Jackson a band-leader, Sam Costa a singer. Nowadays, of course, they can learn their trade in local radio, and actually set out with the intention of becoming disc-jockeys.

In December of 1953 I took some time off and came back to England, where I realised a long-held ambition. As a teenager, and in the Air Force (sic), I had been a big fan of the Ted Heath Band. My pet daydream was the idea of working with them.

At this time, they were doing a series of Sunday Night Concerts at the London Palladium, concerts which came to be legendary. On these occasions Ted always had a disc-jockey with him, not to compère the concert, but to talk a little about their work and make a break from the music. I was invited to do one of these shows, in a line-up that included Lita Roza, Dickie Valentine, and Dennis Lotis. It was the first time that I had ever appeared at the Palladium, and I was absolutely petrified.

I had about ten minutes to fill, so I worked out a little act, most of which involved reading some of the funnier letters I had been sent by listeners. Fortunately, people like laughing at themselves, and the letters brought the house down.

I say fortunately, because my other idea for getting a few laughs was still-born. I went out and bought a set of those joke false-teeth that you wind up, and which then make a clicking noise. I had those and a few other little props of that nature, and was about to go on stage when Ted Heath saw me.

"For God's sake, you can't do that!" he said.

"Why not?" I asked him.

"It's the Lord's Day Observance Society. You mustn't wear make-up, and if you take on any props like these, they'll bring the curtain down." I didn't have time to ask him what they did about instruments!

By the time that I'd got the make-up off, and dispensed with the chattering teeth, and managed to get myself on stage, I was shaking like a leaf. Thank the Lord for those letters.

My other memory of that first show, apart from Lita Roza's singing, and Dickie Valentine's marvellous impressions, is of going to see Dennis Lotis in his dressing room and finding him doing the Times crossword. In those days, such an activity was, to say the least, unusual for a pop singer. In fact it was unique. It occurred to me that here was a person of great erudition, and worthy of some respect.

Following this, I did a number of shows with Ted Heath up and down the country. One, I recall, was at the old Majestic at Staines, now unmajestically demolished. After the show the manager came round to see me and said, "I think you could be a star. That's a marvellous little act you've got there. I'm going to watch your future with great interest."

"That's very kind of you," I said, feeling that the praise was really due to the crazier of my correspondents.

"What's more, I like your delivery," he went on, pinioning me with his praise. "But there's just one thing that's missing."

I thought: "Oh God, not him too." Aloud I simply said: "Oh yes? What's that?"

He proceeded to explain the great gap in my otherwise, apparently, perfect existence. "When you shook hands with me, I noticed something was missing." I examined my hands. All the fingers seemed to be there. I didn't even chew my nails. What could it be? "You must become a Mason" he said. "If you want to succeed in life, you must be a Mason."

"Oh, that!" I said, relieved that he had not found some horrible blemish of which I was ignorant. "Well, my father and all my uncles have all been Masons, but I don't think that that was part of their philosophy for joining. To be truthful, I'm not a joining sort of person, and besides, I don't think I could do it properly. I mean, if there was a Masonic dinner that clashed with a football match, I'd always take the football match."

"Well, you may still get on," he said, in a fit of generosity. "But you'd get on a lot more quickly if you were a Mason."

I gave him a quick, run-of-the-mill handshake, and departed.

Eventually I got to know Ted Heath pretty well, and many years later, when he started to become ill, he asked me if I would be interested in taking over the band...as the bandleader! If that sounds like a fantasy, the fact is that it sounded a bit that way to me at the time. But it's true.

Of course, it would have been the ultimate fulfilment of my childhood dream of being a conductor, but I had to pass it up. The very idea of standing in front of those marvellous musicians, a twit being sent up rotten by them, was terrifying. I think Ted's reasoning was that once the arrangements were done, the prime need up front was a showman rather than a musician. But I funked it. LESSON... leave daydreams where they are, and don't tamper with them.

Another band I worked with in a similar capacity – if that's what you call a ten minute spot – was Ken Mackintosh's. Ken had had a big hit with 'The Creep', and I think his great ambition was to be respected as much as Ted Heath. My first stint with them was at the Palace in Reading, which due to my appearance there has met the inevitable fate.

After the show Ken said to his trumpet player, Johnny Harris: "We've used Bob Monkhouse on a lot of these shows, but he'll have to watch it now. Wasn't Pete great, Johnny?"

Johnny, no doubt anxious to keep in with his leader, said: "Yes, great Ken...great." I've never been sure how much they meant it. They probably wanted me to play their records!

My other memory of these trips home to Britain was of the first time I took a car over. It had an 'L' – for Luxembourg, not learner – plate, and I used to get so embarrassed by the helpfulness of British policemen to a foreigner that I used to assume a heavy continental accent. In America, you would ask a cop the way and you'd get the answer: "Drop dead, buddy," or the equivalent. But the British bobbies, viewed through a foreigner's eyes, couldn't have been nicer. I would say: "Sank you ver kindly. You are a ver nice person. I hev alvays heard ze British polissman is vundervoll. End so you are."

And they would reply: "Thank you very much sir, and have a happy stay in the country." It was all so pleasant that I would highly recommend foreign plates to anyone who has to do much travelling here.

On that particular trip I first met Vera Lynn. I had an old girl-friend, Pat Hartley, in the chorus at the Adelphi, and one evening she took me in to meet Vera in her dressing room. My first impression was that the 'Sweetheart' was desperately off-hand. She was sewing, and she offered me a cup of tea, and then went on sewing.

Over the years I have got to know her very well, and I have learned that she is not being off-hand, but perfectly natural. Many of the singers I met were over-nice to me when they heard I was a disc-jockey. But Vera never bothered. She was just herself, and that's the best thing about her.

Back in Luxembourg, the stream of visitors kept coming. In May of 1954 Johnny Johnston of the Johnston brothers, also a member of the Keynotes, came over with Bill Cotton Jnr, now Head of Light Entertainment at the BBC. They were partners in a Denmark Street music publishing business, and we took them out to the wine cellars at Remich to sample some of the famous Luxembourg wines. They came, they saw, they sampled…and they both passed out and had to be carried home.

Later that year David Hughes came over. He was to become one of my greatest friends, and he had a minor hit at the time called 'Never', which was written and recorded by Norman Newell, another old friend of mine. I didn't expect to like David, because of the Hollywood-style publicity he had had. Instead, I found him a lovely, simple man who just enjoyed normal everyday pleasures.

But the strain of virtually four years non-stop at the microphone was beginning to tell on me. I was desperately tired and drained of energy. So I told Clement Cave: "I must have three or four months off. I'm run dry."

Understandingly he agreed. "We'll let you have the time off… providing you promise to come back, and don't take another job." So back I came to England for my rest. At that time, the big thing on the BBC was Cyril Stapleton's Show Band Show. They, like Ted Heath, used compères, and Cliff Adams of the Stargazers, with whom I was very friendly, introduced me to Ricky Fulton, the regular compère. And Ricky, to my delight, asked me if I would like to compère a show. It seemed like winning the pools. The producer was Johnny Stewart (who is still at it), and the comedian for that show was Charlie Chester, who was enormously kind to me, and unlike many great comedians didn't mind at all if I got a few laughs. So it was a very happy occasion.

But the following day, in the now demolished Daily Sketch, a critic called Mark Johns wrote to the effect that: "I find it amazing that Pete Murray, a Radio Luxembourg staff announcer, should be introducing a BBC programme."

All hell broke loose. The BBC were terribly anti-commerical radio at that time, as were the papers, and I reckon that if I had committed suicide all they'd have said was: "A British subject named Peter Murray threw himself off a bridge in Luxembourg yesterday." Both Johnny Stewart, and Jim Davidson, the head of dance band music at the BBC, got terrible rockets for inviting this viper to sit at Aunty Beeb's matronly bosom.

I was not invited to do a second Show Band Show.

But I did do the occasional live show at various cinemas on Sundays. The first was at the Granada, Walthamstow, between the films. In those days discotheques hadn't been heard of, and it was the first time that a record programme had been done live on stage.

Had I known what I was in for I would never have accepted. The audience was 90% Teddy Boys. They were not in the slightest bit interested in my arrival on stage, and continued to hold their own, very loud, conversations.

Eventually, despairing of playing even one record before the films re-started, I yelled: "Shurrup!" at the top of my voice. There was a stunned silence. They couldn't believe it. They must have thought it was the reincarnation of James Cagney.

The breathing space of a few seconds which this bold stroke had afforded, enabled me to hit upon another of LIFE'S GREAT TRUTHS. This was: "If you can't beat 'em, join 'em," or rather, as I did in this case, get 'em to join you. I got the ringleaders up on to the stage, and told them that there would be prizes for the best dancing, miming, conducting and so on.

They were being noticed, so they were happy. I was able to play some records, so I was happy. And the rest of the audience were able to laugh at their mates making idiots of themselves, so *they* were happy. In the end, the whole lot joined in a record of Max Bygraves singing 'Gilligilliossenfefferkatzenellenbogen-by-the-sea,' which must be some sort of a record in itself.

After a few months of this Sabbath-filled sabbatical, I went back to Luxembourg, as I had promised. But I was getting very frustrated. My life with Germaine was getting very difficult. My son couldn't speak a word of English. And although I enjoyed the work well enough, I *still* thought of myself as an actor who was broadcasting as a temporary fill-in.

And in the summer of 1955, my mind was made up for me, by those old friends, pounds, shillings and pence.

When I had first gone to Luxembourg, I was earning £14 a week. And the commericals were actually sponsored radio, in the sense that there was merely an announcement that such and such a programme was brought to the listeners by courtesy of such and such an advertiser. But then they started introducing 'spots'. In other words, Radio Luxembourg would be responsible for the programme, and advertisers could have their commericals read out during the programme. These commercials were read of course, by us. I remember one that I did for Mentholatum, some stuff that you shove up your nose when you get a cold. I used to act the catarrh-filled voice, then give a big Mentholatum sniff, then a clear-voiced: "Ah, that's better."

The agents loved that, and the spots became very popular with the advertisers. So Radio Luxembourg came to an agreement with us that every time we did a commercial they would pay the minimum fee of £3 into our banks in London. But they hadn't reckoned on just how popular it would become, or how much we would make. A two-hour programme would be made up of eight quarter-hours, each with its own spot. That's £24. An average of six such programmes each per week made nearly £150, quite apart from our regular salaries and any specials we did, like the 'Smash Hits' programme, which I did for a pools firm which paid me an extra £10.

For those days, we were making a great deal of money.

Then, in early September of 1955, I got a letter from Clement Cave, the General Manager in London. The burden (and I use the word advisedly) of this letter was: "The matter of your expenses and earning power has come up. It is felt that you are making excessive money. So it is proposed that, irrespective of what you do, you will be allowed to make £20 a week."

£20 a week! They were asking us to take about a 90% cut in income. Since the money I was earning was just about the only reason I was still at Luxembourg, I thought that such a step would be, frankly, retrogressive.

I wrote and told them that, reduced to the poverty line, I would be unable to regard their proposition as a viable one. I asked them to find a replacement for me.

On a late September afternoon, I handed in my resignation, and left.

108

Chapter Eleven

I am not a nut-case.

It is true that the next few years were to awaken my interest in astrology and faith-healing, give a logic to my already pronounced leaning towards vegetarianism, and confirm my support for the Arsenal Football Club. But as far as I am concerned, the only 'odd' thing about these activities is the people who think them odd.

When I returned to England, that September of 1955, I came back to absolutely nothing. No work. No home. The situation held much room for improvement.

The first break in the work void came with a job on a comedy show written by Jack Bentley, for Radio Luxembourg. I took over from David Jacobs, who was moving on to higher things, the job of straight man to Miriam Karlin, John Blyth, and Jimmy Thompson. For each programme, recorded at the Star Sound Studios in Baker Street, I received the handsome remuneration of £10. What's more, the impact of this show was such that I have completely forgotten what it was called.

To supplement this meagre stipend, I took a job with ATV in Foley Street as a sort of back-up man to Bob Danvers-Walker, the continuity announcer, in case 'something should happen to him'...what, was never explained...or in case the studio broke down (not that I was very clear what I was supposed to do about that either). I spent most of my time there watching the programmes under the bright new banner of Independent Television, and there was one in particular, hosted by Derek Roy, called 'People are Funny'. I thought it was quite frightful, abysmal even, and thought to myself: "That's one programme I wouldn't have anything to do with, no matter what."

Meanwhile, I was about to 'finger' yet another unfortunate building. The flat problem had been solved for us by James Thomas, then of the (later demolished) News Chronicle. Jimmy sold us his flat in Norfolk Crescent off the Edgware Road, together with its furniture and fixtures.

The fixtures are no longer there because the block, of course, has now been demolished.

The change of home brought a change of fortune. When I left Luxembourg, their format had changed. Record companies now bought whole half-hour or hour-long segments, and played nothing but their own records. Decca were about to start doing this, and in spite of the fact that Frank Barnes thought, as he reminded me recently, that I was "finished and passé", I got the job of introducing the Decca programmes. It was an association that was to last for 14 years, until 1969 when the format changed yet again.

Emboldened by this return to favour, I decided to make a third change, that of my agent. To be precise, I acquired an extra one. The fact was that Herbert de Leon, who bless his generous heart had not taken a penny from me all the time I was at Luxembourg, admitted only too readily that he knew nothing about that side of the business. He was a theatre and film man, and so while I stayed with him on the off chance that someone might remember my theatrical talents, I now joined Edward Somerfield, who also acted as my personal manager. He was a real tough nut, but a brilliant agent who specialised in radio and TV, and had Eamonn Andrews and Peter West among his clients.

Hardly had I hitched my star to this entrepreneurial paragon, than he phoned me, at the end of December, to say: "Pete. I've got marvellous news for you."

Dazzled by his enthusiasm, my mind flashed through the various possibilities, stopping only slightly short of Director-General of the BBC. I urged him to communicate the glad tidings.

"We've put you up for 'People are Funny', and they want you to do it."

My inward groanometer registered a new record for blown fuses. But it was the first thing he had found for me, and I didn't want to seem uncharitable. Also, I needed the money. So I did it.

110

It was awful. It was a sort of Candid Camera, though in many ways more dicey. The idea was to get people to do silly things like pitching a tent on the Lord Mayor's lawn and staying there for an hour and a half. If they succeeded in these Herculean tasks they would be rewarded by prizes of television sets on which they might watch others performing in an equally stupid manner. It went out from such haunts of the rich and famous as the Hackney Empire, and the New Cross Empire, now demolished in favour of a petrol station.

On the other hand it was a very good deep end into which to be thrown. It was done live, and I had about 28 pages of script to learn every week, concerned with such gripping situations as the blowing up of balloons, or the mutual exchange of custard pies among the contestants.

The trouble was that, although the show went to the top of the ratings, it also became very popular with the criminal fraternity. People, claiming to be from the show, would enter other people's houses and remove their furniture and chattels...with the occupants' blessings! The ultimate in daylight robbery.

These and similar incidents caused such uproar that questions were asked IN THE HOUSE, and finally, after I had been on it for about three months, the show closed.

Undeterred by this clear demonstration of the destruction that my career was able to leave in its path, ATV shortly asked me to do another show for them. This new extravaganza was to be called 'Hit the Limit'. The limit is exactly what it did hit...rock bottom. 'People are Funny' had been *Titus Andronicus* by comparison.

The whole tone of this unfortunate episode was set when I first met the producer, Reg Watson, who later became the producer of 'Crossroads'.

His opening remark, which I considered to be on the defensive side, was: "I can't explain the rules to you."

Now, readers who followed my one-game rugby career will know what I feel about situations where the rules are not explained. I am agin' them. I sympathise totally with those who are expected to compete in such circumstances.

So I replied: "If you can't explain the rules to me, how am I expected to explain them to the contestants?"

111

Watson mulled this point over in his mind. No immediate answer seemed to present itself, because he replied: "Well, *somehow* we've got to get it across. THEY want to do the programme."

Such was the inauspicious start to what may well have been the worst programme ever on television. Again it was live, but this time, spurning the delights of the Hackney and New Cross Empires, they chose to relay them from a series of works canteens in the Birmingham area. This was also the only area on which, since ATV had the franchise there, the idiocies were inflicted.

I remember that there was something to do with a dart being thrown at a board, following which, various questions were asked. But I didn't understand it then, and I certainly couldn't explain it now. I made a complete muck of the whole thing, but, like the rugby matter, I accept no responsibility. If they wouldn't tell me the rules, how could I play to them?

This misery continued for six weeks. On the seventh week, I went up to Birmingham as usual on the appointed day, and as I walked in I saw Reg Watson.

"Hello. What are you doing here?" he asked.

Wondering whether perhaps this was an off-camera rule of the game that I hadn't yet learned, I said mildly: "What do you mean?"

"Well, hasn't anyone told you?"

Now it so happens that I clean my teeth every day with the right toothpaste, so I knew it couldn't be *that*. So I said that clearly no-one *had* told me.

Reg put the matter succinctly. "You've been taken off the programme."

This situation made me unhappy. Very unhappy. My unhappiness communicated itself to them, and I think they too were unhappy. They told me that that day's programme was to be done at the Ideal Home Exhibition in Birmingham, and that my place would be taken by Jerry Desmonde. I said that that was the first I had heard of it, and indicated that I was becoming unhappier by the minute.

So they said: "Tell you what we'll do. We'll put you on with Jerry and thank you for having been on the programme." This they did, and having done so presented me with what I took to be the consolation prize of a Kenwood Mixer. Since the nearest I get to cooking is

112

pouring water over a tea-bag, this was no consolation whatsoever. I said as much to my agent. My agent said that he had been told, but that he didn't want to hurt my feelings!

"That's all very well," I said, "but how the hell do you think I felt when I got there?" He had no answer. Maybe they had told him about the Kenwood Mixer...certainly he never asked for a percentage on it. This debacle left me, naturally, pretty despondent, though thank goodness Decca had now decided to run two Luxembourg programmes a week, so at least I was making reasonable money. But then, in July of 1956, dear old Herbert de Leon came to the rescue.

The de Leon phone-call seems to have been my lifeline in times of need. This time he said: "I think there's a play you might be interested in."

I asked what it was, and he said: "Have you ever read the book 'The Last Enemy', by Richard Hillary?" I hadn't, but Herbert went on: "It's a wonderful book. Peter Graham Scott of Rediffusion (later producer of 'The Troubleshooters' and 'The Onedin Line') has got a burning desire to get it on as a play."

The book was based on the true story of Richard Hillary's own experiences as a Spitfire pilot. It was about how he got his face burnt, had plastic surgery, and finally came to terms with humanity.

My rivals for the plum part of Hillary himself included Michael Bryant, Francis Matthews, and Dinsdale Landen. We were auditioned in Peter Graham Scott's office. They all got parts in the play...but I got the part of Hillary. I couldn't believe my luck, but there was one final hurdle. Hillary's mother and father had insisted that they should be allowed to meet and vet the person who was going to play their son. I went to meet them at their little flat in Crawford Street. Their son had gone on flying after his surgery, and was eventually killed in the war, and I remember their great worry about whether they would be able to keep their flat on a small fixed income. Happily, I got on very well with them, and we started filming...it was a one and a half hour play, but about 35 minutes of it had to be pre-filmed.

There was one sequence at an RAF station about getting burnt in a Spitfire, which was pretty nasty, and there was another at Maidenhead. Hillary had been a good oarsman and rowed for Oxford, and we were supposed to be in pre-war Germany in a rowing match. Maidenhead, and particularly its bridge, was bedecked in Nazi flags. I had been given some rowing tips by a gentleman who had had the courage to escort me in a trip in a double-sculls boat.

But the tips didn't include how to deal with harassment from the shore. As we approached Maidenhead Bridge, a choleric Colonel appeared, and started screaming at us. "This is most disgraceful," he yelled. For a moment I thought he was referring to the sight of such a novice in a rowing eight, but then he went on: "I've just been in the war for five years to get rid of those bastards, and you bloody Nazis are here now!" He just couldn't understand it at all.

In spite of these little local difficulties, the play was a huge success. Had I written the notices myself I couldn't have asked for anything better. One critic called it "TV's Finest Hour." It was nominated for best play of the year, and myself for best actor.

I got appreciative letters from dustmen, doctors, judges, lawyers, and a host of others actors, and I got another, much smaller part in a TV play called *Gertrude Maude*, with June Thorburn. And then, nothing.

Even now when I'm interviewed I'm often asked: "Why didn't you do more acting after *The Last Enemy*?" The answer is that that's how the business works. It was a repeat, for me, of Peter Madren's experience after his success in a wheelchair part. This time, it was the case that if they'd had another part about someone getting his face burnt, I'd have got it. It's ludicrous, but it's true. About five years after it I met Peter Bridge, the impresario. He told me: "I saw you in that play. It was the best thing I've seen on television. I feel guilty about not offering you anything since then, but my God, I'm going to make up for it now."

Well, he did try, but the play he offered was either unsuitable, or I wasn't available, or something, and instead I got one appearance in an episode of 'Maigret'.

But you can't live on other people's five-year guilt-feelings, and at the time I was just grateful that I had the Decca programmes on Luxembourg to keep me going, especially as my private life was starting to go to shreds.

Early in the year my grandmother, Emily Jane Reece, had died at the ripe age of 89. She had been a super lady...a right 'goer' up to the end. Even when she was in her eighties she had worked at the 'Duke of

Edinburgh' in Bayswater, where she was dearly loved.

Naturally we went to her funeral, and as we were getting ready I saw that Germaine had put on a red dress. Now I don't give a damn what anyone wears to my funeral, but as far as that old lady was concerned I felt it showed a lack of respect, especially from a member of the family.

I know that this must sound rather puritanical from someone whose life-style may seem to the outside world to be anything *but* that. The truth is that in many ways I *am* a bit conservative and puritan. I think a lot of it stems from the fact that I am a Virgo. I have come to be a great believer in Astrology, and Virgo is by nature a puritan, a bachelor, a loner. I remember that when I was a kid I was insanely in love with Deanna Durbin, but when I saw pictures of her in magazines my affection for her was totally romantic, and not in the least physical.

These attitudes probably owed something also to the way my mother thought. She was always a little worried about what the neighbours might think, and I've probably been brought up to like things being done 'properly'.

Whatever the reasons, I was furious with Germaine for putting on the red dress, and we had a terrible argument about it. In the end she changed into a black costume, but as far as I was concerned her whole attitude had spelled the beginning of the end for us.

So the year had started badly, but with *The Last Enemy* I had been forcibly reminded of how much I enjoyed acting, and how much I wanted to go on acting. I was determined never to do rubbish like 'Hit the Limit' again, especially having seen poor Jerry Desmonde, my successor, come to similar grief through a similar inability to impart the rules to the contestants. (They then got a third compere, and 'changed the rules', though since no-one knew what they were in the first place, it beat me how they were able to change them).

But now, at the end of 1956, came the one offer I really dreaded, the last thing in the world I wanted to do...a television musical pop show.

I was invited to a caravan at Shepherd's Bush, since the Television Centre was not then completed, where I was introduced to Jack Good and Josephine Douglas, the co-producers of the proposed show. They outlined the basic format of the idea.

115

It was to be a magazine pop show for teenagers, and it was to be called '6.5 Special'.

Chapter Twelve

I am not the oldest teenager in the business.

I leave that distinction, so often levelled at 'senior' disc jockeys, to others. I hope I never was. And I certainly never intended to be. I wanted to act, and I wanted nothing to do with television pop shows, whatever they were called.

I talked to Jack and Josephine in that little caravan, and at the end of our chat I was hired on the spot. And that really put *me* on the spot, because I didn't want to do it. But of course, in the end I was delighted that I did.

That was a marvellous show to be involved with. For a start, although it was supposed to be for teenagers, it was actually for the whole family. There was something for everyone. I think in a way, and from the degree to which people still talk about it, that it was the most successful series television has ever seen.

Josephine Douglas was already very well-known. She had appeared on a number of TV panel games, which were very popular then. She was younger than I, and very talented. She was one of the few people to be given the special contract that allowed her to appear and produce at the same time. She was a bit more 'straight' and clean-cut in her outlook than Jack, with whom she took turns to produce the show. In 'her' programmes she would always include some film — she *loved* filming — which would usually be a bit educational, about someone's hobby, or mountaineering and other masochistic exercises.

Jack was more adventurous. One week we'd do the whole show as if it were an American Army 'Stage Door Canteen' kind of show. The next week we might all be dressed up as part of Robin Hood's gang.

117

Even if an idea flopped and appeared a total disaster, it always had some magic about it, because Jack had some magic about him. He was thickset, wore glasses, and seemed at first acquaintance frightfully-frightfully upper class. He had been President of the Oxford University Dramatic Society.

In fact, he came from Palmers Green, and one day, after the show, some fellow with a thick cockney accent came up to me and said: "Oi fink yer know moi cousin."

I asked him who this cousin was, and he said: "Jack Good. 'E's done well for hisself 'cos 'e went to Oxford and learned to talk proper."

The other great asset to the show was Freddie Mills, the boxer. He was one of Britain's few former World boxing champions, and he had an outsize personality to match. He was as well-loved as Henry Cooper is now, for similar reasons, and at the same time he had a sense of showmanship like the wrestler Jackie Pallo. He started off by doing a sports spot each week, in which he interviewed some well-known personality, but although that was eventually dropped, Freddie stayed on. Just because he was Freddie.

When we started, I was certainly the least known of the three regular performers on the show, and Freddie was kind even about that. Early on in 1957, the three of us went on some big charity car rally with all the stars of the day. There were crowds to welcome us everywhere. But no-one knew me, and no-one asked for my autograph. (This is starting to sound like 'The Little Match-girl'. Don't worry. There's a happy ending.)

Freddie said jokingly: "Don't worry, son. One day somebody will know you." Half an hour later we stopped at a café for tea and someone came up to Freddie and asked for his autograph.

Then he looked at me. I thought: "Fame at last" as he said: "I know you, don't I?" I smiled what I thought would appear to be a self-deprecating little smile. Then he got it. "Yeah, I know, you're the outside-left of the Strollers, aren't you?" The Strollers was a little amateur football team I played for at the time. But at least I'd been recognised!

And at least I'd been recognised correctly. On a day's filming some months later, at a beautiful little village near Eastbourne, Jo Douglas and Freddie were kept busy signing autographs all the time they were not on camera. My own signature remained singularly unsought.

Eventually, an old Scotsman came across to me and said: "I know you."

"Really?" I said, secretly delighted by the kindness of this Celt.

"Aye. Never miss it," he said. "Every Saturday night. It's great. What's the name of it…oh aye…6.5 Special. Aye, and I know your name too. You're Jo Douglas!"

But the best thing about the show was the musical mixture. On the very first programme we had my old chum Dennis Lotis (he of the Times crossword), Lonnie Donegan, and Tommy Steele. Like the show itself, nothing was 'typical'. You just didn't know what to expect. Lonnie, who had been with the Chris Barber Band, was a marvellous guitarist. Tommy, on the other hand, was not. In fact he was pretty crummy, and would be the first to admit it. He was so bad that when he came on the show he would mime his guitar-playing while a good player performed off-stage. Another guitarist of moderate talents was Marty Wilde. His real name was Jim Smith, which I suppose could not be considered an ideal show business star name. But his bus-driver dad must have been pretty strict with him because he was one of the most polite people I ever met. He called us all Sir, or Madam as the case might be. He was starting to be a big star, and even today does very well in cabaret round the clubs. My main memory of him was the size of his guitar. It was enormous…pretty well in inverse ratio to his ability to play it.

The musical spectrum ranged from the great blues singer Big Bill Broonzy, then a very old man, to classical guitarist Julian Bream. If you didn't like Rock and Roll, you could listen to jazz musicians like Ted Heath, Humphrey Littleton, Chris Barber, Johnny Dankworth and Cleo Laine.

A great deal of the programme was ad-libbed, but there was a catch-phrase I coined to start the whole thing rolling: "It's time to jive on the old 6.5." This immortal piece of poetry was to stay with me for many years…even the dustman used to shout it at me, though what he expected me to do about it I have no idea.

And we had guest comedians, like Bill Maynard, and Mike and Bernie Winters, to liven things up. And they did. When we started each show we were never *quite* certain how it would end up.

119

So 1957 was a very happy year for me, but in one tiny respect it was not happy for Shaw Taylor. To this day he doesn't know that I was responsible.

Shaw was working as a continuity announcer at ATV. One Saturday night I was watching television along with the singer Ronnie Carroll, when Shaw made an announcement. He said "Tonight, in the cast of 'Saturday Spectacular', will be that lovely curvaceous Ronnie Carroll." He obviously thought it was Diahann Carroll, later David Frost's girl-friend.

So I phoned up ATV and assumed my solicitor voice.

"I wonder," I said, "if perchance I might speak to the continuity announcer. He has made, according to my client, a slanderous statement."

The operator, flustered, said: "Well, er, I'll put you through to the duty officer."

This worthy now came on the line, and I repeated my demand.

"What is it about?" asked the Duty Officer.

"I have had my client on the phone in a most irate manner," I said, as my 'client' rolled around the floor laughing helplessly. "It seems that this continuity announcer has inferred that my client, who is as masculine as they come, is in fact a homosexual. The words used were, I believe, 'The lovely curvaceous Ronnie Carroll.' "

"I see," said the Duty Officer. "If you would wait a minute, I'll get the announcer concerned."

Now Shaw Taylor comes to the phone, audibly shivering.

"Yes?"

"Oh, Solomon Sternberg here," I said, endowing myself with the most solicitor-sounding name I could think of. "Mr Ronnie Carroll is my client, and I would like to know exactly what you said."

"Oh, it's all a dreadful mistake," said Shaw. "All a dreadful mistake, and I want to apologise most sincerely."

"Yes, I understand that," I said. "But you do realise that this was a great slander, affecting the character of my client. My client has taken great exception to this, and, intending to take out an action against you."

"Oh, no, please no, nothing like that," said Shaw. I could almost feel the perspiration coming down the line. I mellowed.

120

"Well, Mr Taylor," I said, "as you know my client is Irish, and they do tend to get a little inflamed about things. I do understand that it was a mistake, and that you thought it was the girl singer, so if you will leave it with me for a few minutes, I will telephone him and try to mollify him."

"Oh, thank you Mr Sternberg," said Shaw, all a-tremble.

Five minutes later, with Ronnie still convulsed, I called back.

"Mr Taylor, I have now spoken again with my client, and he has decided to accept my advice and your apology. But please do not make the same mistake again. That would be most inadvisable, since I would certainly be unable to restrain him."

"Oh thank you, thank you. How can I thank you enough? Anything I can do for you…" said Shaw.

I suppose it's me who should be worrying, now that he'll find out who it really was!

'6.5 Special' became so popular that we decided it would be a good thing to take it on tour. We asked the BBC for permission to call it '6.5 Special', and they refused, which since they owned the name they were entitled to do. So my agent and Jack Good put their heads together and came up with the sparkling idea that we should call the show 'Stars of 6.5 Special'. About this, apparently, the BBC could do nothing.

It was a great success, though in fact the one thing we couldn't afford was to have the real stars, like Marty Wilde or Terry Dean. They would have been far too expensive for our humble pockets. So we just had ourselves and a few unknowns, including a rather bad trumpet player called John Barry, later to become famous as leader of the John Barry Seven, and composer of the James Bond theme…and a singer no-one had ever heard of called Adam Faith. All the scripts for the sketches were written by Trevor Peacock, now a very fine playwright and National Theatre actor.

On top of all this, they also decided to make an 'official' film of '6.5', but if you saw it today you would not get a true idea of the show. It was full of people like Petula Clark, what I call 'clean' people. It had a romantic story line, and a girl called Diane Todd who sung very sweetly, and the rest of us thrown in just to prove it was something to do with the show, though in fact it wasn't. It just didn't swing.

Certainly it didn't swing like the time we took the show to Paris.

We did it from a jazz cellar on the Left Bank, with marvellous musicians like Sidney Bechet and Stephan Grapelli. But the show itself was something of a disaster. It was the first time that I had worked with French Television, an experience I would describe as a living nervous breakdown.

The producer from the French side was a charming man called Jean Christophe.

He was a very well-known TV producer, and has since become big in films, but my chief memory of him was his lisp, which, with the prevailing chaos, resulted in him shouting "Thilenth...THILENTH" every few minutes. The situation was compounded by the fact that Dennis Main Wilson, the equally eminent British producer, insisted on giving all his directions to Jean, who spoke perfect English, in French.

Now Wilson's vocabulary extended just about to "Ou est la plume de ma tante?" delivered in a thick Surrey accent, so eventually and in desperation I implored him: "For goodness sake speak to him in English."

"No," said Dennis. "I'm in France, and I believe in speaking the language of the country." This, incredibly, he believed himself to be doing.

The Bedlam was at its height when the French Electricity Service finally collapsed under the strain and all the lights went out, so that the screams of "Thilenth!" were conducted in total darkneth. But it did add a certain sense of being in a Parisian night club.

Of course there were little local difficulties even in London. One of Shirley Bassey's first TV appearances was with us. We wanted her to do the first and last numbers of the show, but although she was in no way the star then that she is today she still wouldn't agree. She said: "No. I'm the star of the show, and I do the last two numbers. I'm not going on before that." Nor did she.

Another fabulous singer we had was Michael Holliday. After the show he came up to Freddie and myself and said: "I'm starving. Let's all go and have something to eat. I know a place round the corner called The Green Man, where they do wonderful food." So we all set off in search of this local haute cuisine, and we'd got about half a mile down the road when Michael suddenly stopped. "Oh Christ, I've made a terrible mistake," he said. "I thought we were working in

122

Wood Green." At that moment we were emerging into Shepherd's Bush.

That April I had a rather greater misfortune than a misplaced nosherie. Peter Graham Scott, who had directed *The Last Enemy*, cast me with Adrienne Corri in a film called *Breakaway*. My hope was that it would prove the break*through*. But the night before I was due to start filming I got, of all things, MUMPS! I caught it from my son, Michael, and he caught it from his friend Matthew, who was Dickie Henderson's son, and went to the same school, and who gave it to *his* father. I never found out what it cost Dickie, but it cost me my part in the film.

Shortly after this the BBC, kindly ignoring the ignominies I had suffered on 'People are Funny' and 'Hit the Limit', offered me a series called 'Place the Face'. Why they chose me I never knew. Perhaps someone at the Beeb had seen my mump-misshapen features. The series was an American idea, and was done live. A well-known personality would be confronted by someone set in a mock TV screen. This would be someone from their past, and the guest would have to question the 'face' to discover where they had met.

The embarrassment was total. The series, as a result, became another notch in my totem-pole of disasters. In all the twelve weeks I cannot remember anyone succeeding in guessing who it was.

But I do remember poor Christine Truman being presented with someone she had played tennis against, in some obscure corner of the British Isles, at the age of about ten. Of course she couldn't guess. Nor could Billy Cotton, the late bandleader. The 'face' turned out to be that of a Sergeant-Major who had been with him in the First World War. Billy was, to put it at its best, terse with this man. The reason, as he confided to me after the show, was that: "I couldn't stand the bastards at that place anyway."

I met Bill a few weeks later, and he told me that after a career of never having a rude letter in the mail he had now been deluged with them because he had been rude to this ex-soldier.

I was not happy with 'Place the Face'.

Towards the end of 1957, Jack Good decided to leave '6.5 Special'. The BBC had said that he could not go on doing the road show *and* the programme, and they gave him the choice of giving up the road show or quitting. He quit. And from that moment the show began to disintegrate. In the following February they decided they wanted Jo and Freddie to leave the show. My agent, Edward Somerfield, also acted for Freddie, and tried to get him retained. They refused. Then he told the BBC "If you are going to do this, you will have to pay Pete Murray a lot more money." The BBC refused, so I too left the show.

It made headlines in all the papers, and the whole atmosphere was very unpleasant. Jim Dale took the show over, and it ran for about another nine months, but it was never the same. No-one else could do what Jack Good and Jo Douglas had done. It had been their baby, and once they were gone the party was over.

Having bust up with the BBC, I was now about to bust up with my agent. He was a brilliant agent, but the trouble was that I had signed some sort of contract with him which virtually gave him power of attorney over me. In other words, I had to do the work that he told me to do.

What that amounted to, immediately following '6.5 Special', was a series of pilots for quite frightful programmes. The word 'pilot' has a certain irony in this context, since I don't believe that any of these programmes ever got off the ground. Nor do I remember what any of them were called, so undistinguished a bunch of rubbish were they.

The exception to this was a pilot for a show called 'Sam and Pete'. Jack Good produced it, and it was supposed to be a sort of battle of the age groups between Sam Costa and myself, with yours truly, believe it or not, representing youth. I remember it involved Sam and me in making a number of cracks about each other, and a great deal of shouting from the audience, partly to cheer the two of us and partly to indicate favour or disfavour with various records.

It was all fairly noisy and harmless, and really not a bad programme, but it seemed unlikely to put me in line for any serious stage parts. And the stage was still where I wanted to be. So I said that I wouldn't do it. Rather like a Christmas pantomime, my agent then indicated: "Oh yes you will," and I came back with an "Oh no I won't," and I left him, and he sued me, and the whole thing was finally settled some two years later.

Hardly had I left Edward than I was contacted by Tom Sloan, Assistant Head of Light Entertainment at the BBC. It was Tom with

124

whom Edward had battled during the death throes of '6.5 Special', and now I was summoned to his office, where he said: "Now that you're no longer with Somerfield, we're prepared to offer you other work." It was a kind of ironic compliment to my ex-agent; clearly the BBC didn't relish another fight with him.

The work in question was a fairly new programme called 'Come Dancing'. The suggestion was that I should compère it. I thought it over and came to two decisions. One was that a weekly tripping of the light fantastic was not exactly my cup of tea. The other was that the programme didn't have much of a future. How wrong CAN you be? I turned the offer down, and the show provided Peter West with work for the next fourteen years.

I don't really regret it, though at times when jobs have been hard to find I have occasionally mused over the money it would have meant. But that's not everything, and I still don't think I would really have been right for it, though I'm not knocking the show, and indeed, on the times that I've appeared on it in a minor capacity I've enjoyed doing it.

But I did acquire a new agent. Leslie Grade made me some spectacular promises about having my own 'Spectacular', and other fantasies. I weighed these daydreams against the lesser blandishments offered by other agents, and decided to join the Grade Organisation, very much on the grounds that in a world full of promises you might as well ally yourself with the biggest, even if nothing happens. (And very little did!)

The brothers, Lew an Leslie, were already becoming legendary, and there was a marvellous story about Lew at that time which is probably apocryphal but which certainly *ought* to be true. The story goes that Lew went to a theatre where he saw an act that he thought was absolutely marvellous. After the show he went round to the dressing rooms and said to the group concerned: "You're fantastic, boys. You're marvellous. I've got to handle you. Who handles you? I'll buy the contract."

The startled group replied. "You handle us, Mr Grade, and you have done for the last ten years."

My union with the gentle brothers Grade was shortly celebrated by my election, together with Jack Jackson, as the top disc-jockey of the year. I hasten to add that this was not the result of Grade string-pulling but of the vast vote held every year by the New Musical Express. Year after year I had come second, but now, thanks probably to '6.5 Special' I had actually made it, and went along to the Albert Hall to introduce the winning singers and musicians at the traditional NME concert. I remember that the top girl singer was Petula Clark, and that her opposite number was Cliff Richard, then still only 17 or 18. He came on in a sort of salmon pink coat and a fit of shyness so total that I was unable to get a word out of him. Flushed with success, the top disc jockey now allowed himself to be talked into making a couple of records himself. This was foolhardy in the extreme, since to all the other things that I am not I MUST add that I am not a singer.

The first was for Decca, a version of 'My Fair Lady', which Decca knew was going to be a very successful show. Along I went to the studios in Hampstead in the company of Vera Lynn, Jack Warner, the Beverley Sisters and the Stargazers.

Now, I had never heard the music at that time, and suddenly I had the words of 'The Rain in Spain' dumped in my lap, with instructions to perform them in the company of an orchestra which was already playing away like mad and clearly anxious to get home early.

"I can't possibly cope with this," I said, totally ignorant even of the identity of Professor Higgins, whose part I was playing. "It's quite impossible."

But of course, nothing is impossible for a big record company once they have decided to cover a rival's record. They sat me down in front of a gramophone and played me the Rex Harrison original a couple of times. I heaved a sigh, decided that if I could imitate Denis Compton I should be able to manage Rex Harrison, and 'took him off' as best I could.

Decca put the record out as an EP, which did very well, which is more than I did. Foolishly, I took a flat fee of £30, under the mistaken impression that no-one could be so crazy as to want to pay good money for my vocal talents. I dread to think what this misunderstanding of the human race must have cost me.

The second record sprang from the programmes that I was doing for Decca on Luxembourg. At this time I was doing three, four, and sometimes five shows a week for them, which got a bit boring since they would include the same records each time, with a couple of new ones thrown in and the order jumbled about. So I decided to do what I'd never done before and write a script.

One of the props I invented to help me in these little endeavours was a girl called Mabel, played with distinction by P. Murray.

I aimed the scripts at the nearest thing I could see as an audience, the blokes in the recording studios in London, and they seemed to like them, because it turned out after a while that they would go home and actually listen to them a second time when they went out on the air. Fired by what I felt to be this ultimate accolade, I allowed the interviews between Pete Murray proper, and Pete Murray Mabel, to get a little heavy on the 'double entendre', and there is still in existence a collection of the huge chunks that had to be hewn out of the programmes in order to get something approaching decency. But Mabel became very popular, and I was persuaded to make a record, produced by my old friend Leslie Conn, in which I played Mabel and Brian Matthew played my lover.

There was sweet music playing beneath the dulcet tones of this unlikely duo, and the record must, without doubt, be the most embarrassing ever foisted on a luckless public. What worked on radio simply did not work on record. (A MAJOR LESSON.)

About five years later, when I was doing a late night programme, Sean Kelly, after reading the News, announced that he was going to get his own back on me by playing the record. This, to my total horror, he proceeded to do.

SECOND MAJOR LESSON...if you ignored the first major lesson, don't let any of your mates know about it.

That summer, BBC Radio, in the shape of producer Derek Chinnery, asked me to do a series for them. But there was a snag. He said: "We'd like you to give up your work on Radio Luxembourg. As you're working for the Decca Record Company we can't employ you until you stop. The other companies would say you were biased."

I enquired how much they were prepared to offer me in compensation for giving up this major source of my income.

"Thirty pounds for each half-hour programme," said Derek.

I then asked for how long I would be contracted to earn this massive sum.

"Thirteen weeks," said Derek.

"You've got to be joking," said I, well aware that he wasn't. "I can't live on £30. I'd love to work for the BBC, but I'm not that stupid."

There the matter rested for a few weeks, during which time I did a programme on the BBC World Service which didn't seem to worry a soul. Clearly the sophisticated Peruvians, Papuans, and Patagonians would be less worried about my 'bias' than the primitive Britons. Then they again asked me to leave Luxembourg. Again I refused. Now they brought the redoubtable Anna Instone, then Head of the Gramophone Department, into the argument. And Anna semi-relented. She said: "OK. If we write to all the other record companies and they give us permission, then we'll use you." It must have been the only time in its history that the BBC has made such a deal...the very *idea* of letting outsiders give the yea or nay to one of its programmes!

Well, sure enough the other companies all replied that they had no objections, and we agreed that I would do a Sunday night programme from 10.40 pm till midnight. It was called 'Pete's Party', and the first one went out on August 8th, 1958. I remember vividly that Germaine and I went on the river at Maidenhead with Peter and Andree Madren, and I lay in the sun and kept saying to myself "I'm doing my first BBC radio programme tonight." I was very excited.

The programme was a breakthrough in many ways. It was the longest DJ show that the BBC had ever put out. And it opened the way for people like Jack Jackson, Sam Costa, and David Jacobs to combine working for the BBC with Luxembourg.

My first producer on 'Pete's Party' was Denys Jones, with whom I'm still working today on 'Open House'. And it was Denys who reminded me, during the writing of this book, of an early hassle.

We were in the office at the BBC Western House, as it was then, when the phone rang. Denys took the call and grimaced as he passed the phone to me. "It's Decca," he said. What everyone was frightened of was about to happen.

It was Beecher Stevens, who was responsible for my show on Luxembourg. Now at that time Decca had released a version of the song 'Volare' by the McGuire Sisters. And Beecher gave me to understand that he considered it my duty to play this record on the BBC.

"Beecher," I said, "you're a dear old chum, but I'm working for the BBC. You pay me for doing Luxembourg programmes, which I do to the best of my ability, and there my duty to you ends."

"Where's your loyalty?" asked Beecher.

I said: "It certainly doesn't lie in playing an inferior record of a song. There's only one version of 'Volare' that counts, and that's by Dean Martin. And that's the one I'll play."

If that sounds very self-righteous, the fact is that it was the only way to act, and in reminding me of the story Denys told me that he believes it was a key moment. If the conversation had gone any other way, the whole story of disc-jockeying on the BBC might have been different.

Denys has come to be a good friend over the years, in spite of being subjected to one of my little flights of telephonic fancy. He is the Chairman of the BBC Tennis Club, and when I rang him up one day, for no particular reason, and without any plan, that imp got in among my tonsils again, and I assumed a sultry girl's voice.

"Could I speak to Mr Jones, please?"

"Speaking."

"Oh, my name is Beryl Brewster."

"Oh yes?"

"Yes, and I'm with the Hurlingham tennis club."

"Yesss," says Denys, all eager.

"Now I believe you're the secretary of…"

"Yes I am," Denys, authoritatively.

"Well, I thought it would be great fun if we could get together and have a bit of a match between the BBC and Hurlingham."

"Oh, that would be wonderful," enthused Denys.

"Then we could have a spot of dinner in our beautiful club…"

"Oh, absolutely marvellous," says Denys. "My ambition is to play at Hurlingham. Wonderful."

"Yes, well to talk over the matter and get everything sort of tied up," croons 'Beryl', "do you think we could possibly get together?"

"Yes. That would be lovely. We could have a bite of luncheon together," says Denys in his tennis-hierarchy voice.

"Well, that really wasn't what I had in mind, Mr Jones," I simpered.

Denys paused. "Well, what *did* you have in mind?"

"Oh, I thought a sort of romantic, candlelit dinner somewhere,

where we could sort of *really* get to know each other. You know what they say in tennis... 'Love-All'."

"Yes, yes well, er I, well um," spluttered Denys. "You see I am a very happily-married man, an I wouldn't want to er get er um involved in any way at all."

"Oh I say," sighed 'Beryl'. "What a shame."

"Yes, well I mean a lunch would be lovely, but a candlelit dinner and so forth... I mean it wouldn't be quite..."

"Well, it's just a great pity, that's all," pouted 'Beryl'. "Because I rather think you might have fancied me. Wouldn't you like to know what I look like?"

"Well yes, alright," says Denys.

I dropped my voice about four octaves, and said: "I look exactly like Pete Murray."

There was the pause, and then the usual reply. "You bastard."

That was unscripted, of course, but the programme had to be scripted and rehearsed for its whole length, including the playing of the records. The BBC insisted on it, and they also insisted on seeing the script three days before transmission. I tried to write as colloquially as possible, and although I was known as the King of the Double-Meanings (not filthy, you understand, just a bit naughty) I still managed to get away with a lot because so much depended on the inflection a word was given.

The BBC concentrated on other aspects of my writing. On one occasion a script came back from the censors with a note to warn me that a certain page was amended. I turned to it, and couldn't believe my eyes.

I had written: "I think this bloke is going to go a long way —— The farther the better." They had crossed out the word 'bloke' and had written: '*Chap* might be more appropriate.'

The other, slightly sickening thing about having that programme, was that suddenly everyone wanted to know me again. When I had had my own programmes on Luxembourg, playing the records I wanted, everyone was always ringing up, sending invitations, wanting to give presents, and so on. Then, when I came back from Luxembourg, the telephone suddenly stopped. Now it started again, all those people who had been good old mates and whose friendship had suffered a three-year hiatus which happened to coincide exactly with the period during which I didn't have my own programme. A curious coincidence.

The one exception, a great and honourable exception, to this was my friend Leslie Conn. Leslie was a music-publisher, who later came to handle all Doris Day's music in this country. In all that time there was never a week went by without him ringing to invite me to some lunch or film show. I couldn't always go, but he never stopped inviting me, even though I could be of no possible use to him. He was, and is, a real friend.

1958 had been quite a year for change, and on top of everything else I decided to have my image altered a bit, not in the modern PR use of the word, but the actual Murray mug. I had suffered very badly from acne, which had left some scars on my face. This had all started as a kid from my desire to consume tin after tin of condensed milk.

Now the Almighty did not design the bloodstream to carry pint after pint of condensed milk, and as a result I got terrible skin trouble. That in turn, I think, was one very strong cause of my shyness. It wasn't much help with my film career either. The studio lighting was pretty crude in those days, and I was often being told:"We'd love to use you, but what about your skin?"

What with that, and Robert Morley's harassment of my pimples, I decided to get something done about it, and I went to the Queen Victoria Hospital at East Grinstead to have what they call a 'scrape job.' In my case it wasn't too successful, and I had to wait for vegetarianism to tidy up the meteor-bombarded landscape of my condensed-milk countenance.

But at least I was able to enter 1959 with some visible improvement, for which I was pleased, since I was now launched on yet another TV series for ATV in Birmingham. They just never gave up, did they? This latest brainwave was called 'This is Your Chance', though I reckoned that on previous experience it would be my chance to notch up another disaster. It was an 'Opportunity Knocks' type of programme, on a knock-out basis, with a final and so on and so on. The main interest in it lies in the fact that it was the first time that the Black and White Minstrels then known as the George Mitchell Singers had been used on a TV series, and I started my long friendship with members of the group like Tony Mercer and John Boulter, who later found fame in black and white.

This show was not destined to win any Oscars for reaching new heights of light entertainment. On the other hand, I must admit that it did not quite plumb the depths inhabited by the ghostly wrecks of 'Hit the Limit' and the like.

So when it ended I felt a sense of relief, which was probably what enabled Leslie Conn to 'con' me down to Southend. Well, it wasn't exactly a con. Southend Corporation had asked me to go down to the end of their pier on a Sunday at the end of April in order to present a record programme.

It was a sort of forerunner of a discotheque, and I had no desire to do it. Leslie persuaded me otherwise. The fact that they were going to pay me £125 probably helped as well, though when I discovered what I was in for I would willingly have sold the job back to them at a profit to them.

I drove down to Southend with Peter Pritchard, the man from the Grade Organization who was handling me, and it wasn't until we arrived that we realised that, Sunday in those days being Sunday, no dancing was allowed.

Thus it was that yours truly found himself in a sort of Palm Court at the end of Southend Pier, equipped with a gramophone and a pile of records. Some 25 people duly paid their money and entered this place of dismal entertainment, and remained for two hours, during which I talked to them, played records and felt thoroughly miserable. The misery was compounded by the fact that the contract stipulated my return on the following Sunday, when 14 people came in, supplemented by a further half dozen with their noses pressed against the salt-drenched windows. I felt I was letting them down, myself down, and Southend Corporation down, and I determined never to repeat this gloomy experience.

So it was with some hesitation that I listened to Leslie Conn's next proposal. He had been going on for some time about a record programme that he had seen in America, and which he wanted to buy and bring over here for me to take part in. But the stage was *still* calling me, from increasingly afar, and I told him that I didn't want to do any more pop shows.

132

But Leslie was determined, and persuaded the BBC to try out a pilot for the show. Its name was 'Juke Box Jury'.

Chapter Thirteen

I do not hate David Jacobs.

I do not even dislike David Jacobs. The truth of the matter, I have to confess, is that David Jacobs and I are very good friends. But listeners and viewers back in those days might have been forgiven for thinking otherwise.

When I started doing 'Pete's Party', David had a programme on the Saturday evenings. The BBC, in its collective wisdom, decided that we ought to plug each other's shows. David would have to say, "Don't forget to listen to Pete's programme tomorrow night," and I would similarly have to urge them to tune in to him the following week.

After a while, we started to find this an extremely boring way of passing the time, so we decided to insult each other instead. We thought the listeners might find this more interesting than the mutual back-slapping that had been going on. And it succeeded. Some people wrote in to say that the only reason they tuned in was to hear what frightful insults we had dreamed up for each other.

It was a trick that Crosby and Hope had done in the States, but it was the first time that it had been done over here, and we thoroughly enjoyed ourselves. And of course we were only able to do it *because* we were good friends.

And then came 'Juke Box Jury', with David in the chair, and myself a member of the panel along with Alma Cogan, Frances Day, and Digby Wolfe, my old friend of the S and F Grill days. We did the pilot, and apparently they were pleased with the result, because six weeks later, in June, they started a thirteen-week run. The panel that first night was Alma, Gary Miller, Susan Stranks and myself.

It was put out live, and the atmosphere at the TV Theatre in Shepherd's Bush was incredible, with an audience filled to overflowing. David and I had decided that we would continue our radio rivalry and ribaldry, and we worked out a little set-piece. After being rude to each other throughout the programme, at one moment towards the end I said: "David, I don't know why you're like this to me. I think you're wonderful. I really do."

"Thank you very much," said David, launching me into our set-piece.

"You've got a tremendous future in the toilet at Leicester Square," I said.

And back came the answer: "Mention my name and you'll get a good seat!"

The trouble was, we had actually arranged that I should mention the cloakroom at Victoria Station, (shades of Buster Reed), but somehow I got confused, and of course the word 'toilet' in those days was possibly more objectionable on the 'box' than a four-letter word would be today. On top of that, we had, egotistically, assumed that everyone would have heard our running battle on the radio, which of course they hadn't.

The phones immediately started ringing like there wouldn't be a tomorrow, the BBC hierarchy were tearing their hair out, all the newspapers were on the line, and in the middle of it all one lady Zionist called and spoke to David and accused me of being anti-semitic. When he assured her that we were in fact the best of friends, she declared that he was only saying that to protect me.

I think that if I hadn't had a thirteen-week contract, I would have been removed forthwith in deference to public protest, but after a few weeks people started to get the idea that it was all in fun. And the show was a huge success.

It was about this time that I first met Jimmy Savile. I had, and still have, this great friend called Pat Campbell, an Irishman, an Arsenal supporter for all that, an ex-member of the Four Ramblers group, an ex-exploitation manager ('plugger' to you) for Decca, and an ex-ex-extraordinarily funny man in his own right.

Pat said to me one day. "There's a great character I know called

Jimmy Savile. He's the manager of the Mecca dance hall in Leeds, the Locarno. You've got to meet him."

Instead of his usual doss-house, Jimmy was at that moment ensconced in the velvet-and-silk luxury of the Savoy, whither we proceeded. We were ushered to his bedroom, where I was mildly astonished to be introduced to this character sitting up in bed (for preference, not illness), smoking a cigar, and wearing tartan hair! My immediate reaction was that he was totally insane, but Jimmy has this knack of turning horror into a sort of respect. He is a very clever flatterer, as I quickly found out with his: "Privilege to know you guv'nor. I never thought I'd meet THE Pete Murray."

Soon after this faintly unorthodox meeting, Pat Campbell and I were due to go to Leeds to play in a charity football match. With us was Tommy Docherty, who was to referee the game, but it was Pat who made the fatal suggestion that we should take the opportunity of going to stay with Jimmy.

My first impression of Maison Savile was one of complete disbelief. To get to the front door one needed to be an expert in jungle warfare. I'm six feet tall, and the grass towered above my head. Having fought our way in, we found a house sparsely furnished with a number of packing cases and young ladies.

Everyone stood around for a while, uncertain as to the next move. So I tentatively suggested: "Is it possible to have a cup of tea?"

It now appeared that Jimmy had just the one cup and saucer and the one spoon. "If I have a lot of cups and saucers here," he explained, "I get all the punters coming round for a free cup of tea. So if you want a cup, you can have THE cup and saucer, and then pass it round. That way it saves money . . . guys and gals."

To supplement this liquid refreshment there was no food except for a tin of Macintosh's toffees, which was duly passed around with the cup and saucer.

Thus fortified, Jimmy announced: "I'm going off to the gaff now," by which he meant the Locarno. On the assumption that the seats there would be softer than Jimmy's packing cases, we decided to go with him. Besides, I knew that the Locarno, which had been something of a white elephant for Mecca, had been turned into a goldmine within three or four weeks of Jimmy's arrival.

Certainly his technique was amazing. He would play some Elvis Presley, Cliff Richard and so on, then suddenly there would be dead silence. Jimmy would announce: "Right, That's it. That's the lot. Standing around and listening time now," and on would go an excerpt from Tchaikowsky's 'Swan Lake'. I reckon if anyone else had tried that, they would have been booed off the stage . . . if the dancers were feeling friendly, that is. But with Jimmy they just stood there, transfixed.

After this demonstration of his powers of mob-control, he took us to a meal, and then decided it was time to go home. It was only when we had fought our way back in, past the Rolls, the E-Type and the bubble-car waiting patiently to be used, that we realised that the sleeping arrangements were decidedly dodgy.

Some quick calculations revealed that there were far fewer bedrooms than people wishing to occupy them. At this discovery, Pat made an immediate and unequivocal dash for the only available single room.

It was then that I discovered, with a certain discomfiture, that I would have to spend the night in bed, albeit a double-bed, with Tommy Docherty, then of the Arsenal, that same 'promising kid' I had praised in my column at Radio Luxembourg.

My disinclination to sleep with Tommy, lovely footballer though he might be, was compounded by the fact that his leg was in plaster. However, there was just nowhere else, so in we climbed. It seemed to me that I had hardly fallen asleep when I was rudely awakened by the plastered Docherty, who apparently had every intention of assaulting me.

It transpired that he had had some sort of a nightmare, and believed me to be in the nightmare with him. I leapt out of bed and fled downstairs, to be followed shortly by the somnambulist Scot who had himself been awakened by my shouts of fear.

We were greeted by the sight of Jimmy Savile, his long cigar at the ready, his tartan hair a thing of beauty in the night, surrounded by a bevy of the young ladies of Leeds. It was all too much for Tommy.

"Hello, girls, here we are!" he cried. One of the girls alone paid him any attention. She looked up from the protective embrace of the Prophet of the Locarno, and in a thick Leeds accent she proclaimed: "Go away! You're revoltin'. I love Jim."

Pat Campbell, of course, thought the whole affair was hilarious. But then, he revels in that sort of situation. As a practical joker I'm not in his league. I got one of my early inklings of this when we went down to Portsmouth for a football match. We happened to go into a sweet shop, and suddenly out of his mouth came this incredibly pansy voice as he said to the astonished lady assistant: "Excuse me, could I have a bar of Bounty, and please could you tell me where I can find the sailors?" I'm sure she believed him.

His great strength is that he can remain totally deadpan. I remember once a conversation with two girls who were sitting opposite us in The Beverley, a vegetarian restaurant off Oxford Street which we used a lot.

We got talking to them, and they were asking me about what I did. Then they turned to Pat and asked what he did.

"Well, I'm a female impersonator," said Pat.

"Don't believe you."

"Oh yes I am," said Pat. "I work at Danny La Rue's place."

"That's a load of rubbish."

"Oh, it is, is it? Well, you can be my guests any night, except for next week."

"Why not next week?" asked one of the girls.

"Well, as a matter of fact I'm going to Copenhagen next week for the operation. A bit off here, and a bit on there, and Bob's your auntie!"

I can always tell when Pat is about to launch into one of his little spectaculars. He gets a sort of look in his eye. I saw it once when we were in there, having a meal, with everyone around us minding their own business. Then Pat started.

"Of course, it's quite remarkable what they've done in this restaurant."

"Really?" I said, not having the first idea what was coming.

"Yes. Don't you realise that all the waitresses here are on parole?" The conversation around us drops a few decibels. One or two ears are starting to focus in our direction.

"Yes, it's quite remarkable," says Pat. "All out on parole. They've all been in Holloway. The Manageress here is a probation officer, and she has given work to all these ex-convicts."

Now I'm involved. "Yes, that really is remarkable," I said. "What sort of things were they in for?"

Pat turned a beady eye on an approaching waitress, an arthritic old girl who shuffled along in carpet slippers.

"Well, for example, what was she in for?" I asked.

"Assault and battery," said Pat.

At this point there is dead silence in the restaurant ... the place is very small, and close, and everyone sits with everyone else, so all our conversation had been monitored. And then came the clincher. Our regular waitress, Helen, came across to us, and Pat looked up at her and asked: "How long have you been out, Helen?"

I'm sure she misheard, or misunderstood, but straightaway she replied: "Oh, about six months."

All around us there is the clatter of knives and forks on plates, and from behind us there comes an extremely posh voice as a man turns to me and says: "I hope you'll forgive me saying so, but I couldn't help overhearing what you were saying. What wonderful work this woman's doing with these convicts. It's quite remarkable."

"Yes," I agreed. "It's *quite* remarkable."

"I really must interview her and talk to her about it," the man went on. "You see, I'm a prison visitor."

And like Uncle Remus' Tar-Baby, Pat Campbell he just sat there and didn't say nuttin'.

Nor did the girls ever seem to catch on. I went in there alone one day and one of the girls asked me: "What ever happened to that lovely big Irish fellow who used to come in? "She was referring to a friend of Pat's, a former Olympic athlete. I told her I didn't know.

"Isn't it a pity about him," said the girl.

"What do you mean?" I asked.

"Well, about the fact that he prefers boys to women."

"Oh God, haven't you girls learned yet? I suppose Pat Campbell told you that. What did he say?"

The girl blushed. "He told us the fellow was going out with a coalminer in Kent."

In the midst of these and similar distractions I found time to do a sketch with Tommy Steele in a Spectacular (his, not mine) for the indefatigable ATV. I mention this only because it was recorded at the

Empire, Wood Green, which since then has duly died of demolition.

And at the end of 1959 I nearly went the same way. I had been booked to appear for a week at the Bristol Hippodrome, in a variety show put on by Peak Freans, the biscuit people. The cast included the Eric Delaney Band, Cyril Fletcher, and Marguerite Patton, who was to do some cooking. My job was to provide the link between the members of this motley bunch.

Now, when I was a boy, my uncle had given me a book by Harry Benjamin called 'Everybody's guide to nature cure'. I had been impressed by this book, and determined, should I ever fall ill, to follow its precepts rather than those of orthodox medicine. And by chance, shortly before departing for the Peak Frean fiesta, I had eaten at the Vega restaurant in London and had noticed an advertisement for the Towerleaze Hydro at Bristol. I decided that this would be a good chance to try out Harry Benjamin's ideas, and that it would be more interesting than an hotel. Besides, Bristol in those days was not noted for the electrifying nature of its winter social life, and I thought that the treatment, massage, osteopathy and so on would help to pass the time between the biscuit beanfeasts.

So I made the necessary arrangements, and was due to arrive on Monday, December 7th. On the 5th, the Saturday, I went to a football match at Chelsea, and started to feel rotten, a condition I could not entirely ascribe to Chelsea's performance at the match. I went to bed early, and the next day felt like death. I never knew how I managed to stagger through 'Pete's Party' that night.

The following morning I made my way to Bristol, dropped some bags at the theatre, stayed for the band-call and made a note of my spots in the show, and shot off to the Hydro.

On my arrival, which was just for the purpose of leaving my baggage, I was examined by a naturopath who declared that I was in a very run-down condition. Anxious to prove his point, I promptly collapsed and passed out. When I came to, they informed me that they "didn't know what was the matter with me, but that I was in a very bad way." At this stage, I could have told *them* that.

That evening I insisted on getting to the theatre, and somehow staggered through the show. Immediately it was over I rushed back to the Hydro, where they informed me that I was very ill and running a temperature.

The following day they put me on a fruit diet, and gave me massage and so on, and on the Wednesday I again insisted on going in to do the matinee. And that was the last I saw of the Peak Frean Variety Show.

My stay at the Hydro was to last not one week, but five. I had severe hepatitis. I lost two stone. My urine was like man-made Coca-Cola. I never felt so ill in my life. But it was also to change my whole way of life.

Sam Wade, who ran the Hydro, was a man of 76, but he looked like 55 and still played a keen game of tennis. He was a down-to-earth character, by no means a fanatic, and he said to me: "I'm not a complete vegetarian myself, but my advice to you for the next year, if you want to get the full benefit of the treatment we've given you, is to stay on a raw diet. No cooked food. No eggs, no coffee, maybe one cup of tea a day, but no orange juice or anything acid. It's basic common sense . . . your body is in a highly acid condition, so you must stick to alkaline food."

This in fact had been the basis of the treatment they gave me, together with periods of fasting for up to about four days. And for me it certainly worked. In the preface to a book she wrote, the singer Hildegarde used a quote which says: "The doctor of today must be the dietician of tomorrow. If not, the dietician of today will be the doctor of tomorrow." I believe that is absolutely true.

I know a lot of people think that nature cures are a fad, vegetarianism is a fad, that anything even slightly outside orthodox medicine is a fad. But it's not so. Health farms are not just for people to lose weight without having to try. I am utterly convinced that if we all learned to live properly, and eat properly, and not be governed by our palates, we would be a much healthier race of people.

END OF COMMERCIAL. Sorry about that. It's just something I happen to believe in passionately. And if I can't say it in my own book, then when CAN I say it?

I must also add, sadly, that although the principles of Towerleaze have remained with me ever since, the place itself two years ago paid the inevitable price for its association with me. It was demolished.

My marriage to Germaine was about to go the same way. I came home to Norfolk Crescent from Towerleaze Hydro on January 17th,

1960. Pat Campbell met me, and drove me back to the flat, where Germaine was waiting.

"You look terrible," she said.

"Yes, I feel terrible," I said. "I've got to follow a special diet."

"What sort of diet?"

"Well, I've got to stick to raw food ... grapefruit, lemons, grapes, and things like that."

Her reply shook me rigid. "If you want that sort of food, you'll have to go out and get it yourself." I thought for a moment that Pat was going to hit her, but instead he went out to buy a basketful of the said diet.

It was the last nail in the coffin of our marriage. We were never really suited to live together, and as I have said before, it was probably more my fault than hers. But we always liked each other. A few years later, when I was involved in a very public piece of nastiness with another woman, Germaine was the first to phone to say how sorry she was. And in about 1968, when she was about to get remarried, she rang me in tears.

She had discovered that she had a growth on her breast, and she was terrified that she would have to have it taken away. I arranged for her to go to the Champneys nature cure farm, and happily, after six days of fasting, it had gone. Today I would say that we are very good friends.

But then, there was nothing to do but to split up. Michael was away at Wycliffe College, a boarding school: Germaine went off to Brussels, and I got a flat in Montagu Mansions through the help of Tony Lewis, who was Danny Williams' manager at the time. A little later Norman Newell, my song-writer friend, moved in to the block, and then Peggy Mount, and finally Beryl Reid, so it became quite a theatrical coterie.

Before I moved there, Germaine asked me for a divorce. I was quite prepared to give her one, but my solicitor said: "She has no grounds for divorce. But you could divorce her for desertion." I said that I didn't want to do that.

In the event, grounds were obtained for Germaine by a sleuth who noted the presence, during my first night in Montagu Mansions, of a showgirl named Christine. It was hardly a comfortable, or indeed an intellectual, episode.

Since I had just moved in, there was hardly any furniture. So I

142

deposited the television set in the middle of the floor, and like the chieftains at some Red Indian pow-wow, Christine and I sat cross-legged on the floor to watch 'Panorama'. At the end of the programme I remarked: "I found that very interesting."

"I 'aven't understood a bleedin' word," declared my consort.

But her stay there had been noted by some freelance 'Kojak', who confronted me some days later at my solicitor's office. I agreed with his description of events, and signed a paper to this effect.

"That's very good," said the sophisticated sleuth. "Now while you've got your pen out, would you mind signing an autograph for my wife. She's a fan of yours."

That brush with matters legal was soon followed, by chance, with a brush with matters illegal.

Now, ever since I was a kid I've always been on the side of the law. Not for me the cowboy with the black hat and the black horse. Roy Rogers and Trigger were my heroes. "Crime doesn't pay" was the message of my youth. And I think I remained a good Boy Scout despite the harassment of the budding clerics of St Nicholas.

My chance to play the goodie came one evening, when I was entering Danny La Rue's club (building now demolished . . . sorry about that, Danny.) My way was barred by two bouncers who were trying to remove a 'heavy' who'd been soaked with a bottle of champagne by another heavy from a rival gang.

"I'll kill him," screamed this worthy, with a good deal of serious intent.

The spirit of Baden-Powell loomed large before my eyes. The battle-cry "Be Prepared" rang in my ears. I stepped forward.

"I wouldn't do that, if I were you," I said to the struggling hood. "If you've got a score to settle, do it in your own time. If you start something now, the Law will get you. It's not worth it."

He looked at me hard. I prayed, extremely fast. Then he said: "Yeah, you're right." And with that he disappeared.

The niterie notables were so grateful that I was given my evening on the house, and was treated more or less as the incarnation of James Bond. Some months later I was coming out of another late-night establishment having put away at least three cups of tea, and feeling no ill effects . . . I can really hold my tannin. Suddenly a car-load of heavies pulled up, and I was summoned across the pavement. Fortified by the tea, I managed to contrive a nonchalant saunter in their direction.

"Don't remember me, do yer?" said the driver.

"No, I'm afraid not," I replied.

"Three months ago. In a club. Bottle of champagne all over me whistle."

"Ah yes, I remember," I said, grateful to have passed the first part of the interview.

The driver got out of the car and ushered me round into a little alleyway. "This is IT," I thought. "What would Roy Rogers do now?" I was just about to whistle for Trigger, when he said: "You got me out of a lot of trouble that night. I'd like you to be my guest tonight for dinner."

"I've eaten," I gulped, trying to sound grateful and suave at the same time.

He lowered his voice. "Look, you got anybody givin' you any bovver?"

"Bother?"

"Yeah, bovver. You know what I mean. Look Pete, tell yer what, if you want someone givin' a goin' over, me and the boys would be pleased to oblige. All down to the firm. Gor nicht."

I must have looked puzzled.

"Yeah, gor nicht. Fer nothin'. On the 'ouse. Got anyone in mind?"

"Well, actually no," I said, adding what was supposed to be a flippant rider . . . "no-one except perhaps David Jacobs."

My new-found ally leapt at the chance. "You want 'im doin' over?"

"No, no, no," I said, horrified at what I might have started. "It was only a joke."

"Oh," said the heavy, in a tone of grievous disappointment. "Pity. I was lookin' forward to 'avin a go at that 'ooter of 'is."

Surely it must now be believed that David and I are good friends.

Aside from these diversions, Peter Pritchard *was* also getting me work. Soon after I came back from Towerleaze I had a couple of guest appearances on 'Juke Box Jury', though not as a regular panel member. On one of these they played the Russ Conway record, 'A Royal Event'. I made a comment to the effect that I was not very keen on

144

records designed specially to cash in on real royal occasions … in this case, the wedding of Princess Margaret to Anthony Armstrong Jones.

Well, Russ, as I found out later when I got to know him much better, is incredibly sensitive, and he rang me in tears. "Oh Pete, Pete," he said. "You've got it all wrong. I wrote that piece to celebrate the anniversary of the Theatre Royal in Norwich."

"Come ON, Russ," I said, "it's a marvellous coincidence if that happens to coincide with Princess Margaret's wedding."

.He was terribly upset, and I was upset that he was upset. We were all upset. But I meant what I said. I felt the same way about the record 'Golden Coach'. Anything like that makes me sick. A specially-commissioned semi-classical piece by someone like Malcolm Arnold is one thing. But a sheer piece of pop to cash in on a coronation or whatever is another.

There was at that time, every week on television, a half-hour series' called 'Man from Interpol'. It starred a man with whom I had worked at the Kew Theatre, called Richard Stapeley. He had gone to America and returned equipped with a brand new name, Richard Wyler, and a brand new American accent. He was unhappy when I reminded him that we had worked together, and that I knew he was an Englishman from Brighton.

The occasion for this reminder came when I got a guest part in an episode of the series. It was a major role, around which the story revolved, which consisted almost entirely of the repetition of the distinguished piece of dialogue, "Let me outa here … Let me outa here." I was a convict, situated, as readers will have gathered, behind bars.

This essay in escapism cannot have been all bad, because the Danzigers, who made the series, now required me to take part in three of their films. I use the word 'films' only as a rough guide to what they produced. I once met them, and I believe they were American brothers of some kind, who owned the May Fair Hotel and made films over here in about three weeks, and then sold them to American television.

The first of these epics was called *The Lonely Woman*. It starred Jean Cadel, who had been with me in *Marigold,* the first play I ever did at the Kew Theatre. I only had a small part in the film, playing opposite, I think, a lady named Christina Greig. What the plot was I can't remember at all, and I doubt if I knew at the time. But I do remember the readthrough we did at the May Fair Hotel before we were actually committed to celluloid. One of the gangsters (there were *always* gangsters) in it was played by Dick Emery. In order to add a little depth to his paltry part, Dick suggested that he should play it as a queer, and his demonstration of what it would sound like had us in fits. I mean, it's hard for "Stick 'em up, buddy," to sound convincing when delivered in the sort of mincing tone that later became famous with 'Ooh, you are awful!' The Danzigers insisted that their gangster should be the genuine 'butch' article.

We did these films for peanuts, which from the Danzigers' point of view was the idea of the whole exercise, but even peanuts are better than no peanuts, so now I accepted a role in *Escort for Hire*. I played one of a pair of out-of-work actors (a role in which I was well-rehearsed!) who join an escort agency to provide escorts for ladies.

A little earlier that year I had seen a Dean Martin film in which he never took his hat off. With some degree of unoriginality, I decided that it would be a good gimmick if *I* never took my hat off in this film. They allowed us quite a lot of leeway in the playing of our roles, even to the extent of inserting large quantities of our own dialogue, and although they had baulked at Dick Emery's homosexual heavy they let the hat business go through, and I kept it on throughout. It was a funny little turned-up job, which I even wore in bed, which was alright, since bedroom scenes in those days were less than torrid.

Not long ago Freddie Starr told me he had seen me in *Escort for Hire*, and that he had thought it one of the funniest things he had seen. I decided to take the remark at its face-value and assume that he was praising my performance. I hope he was.

The Danzigers certainly liked it, because now they offered me the lead in a film called *Transatlantic*. They sent me the script (I use the term loosely) and after reading it I decided that it was probably the biggest load of rubbish I had read in my life.

BUT . . . it was the chance to make all my dreams come true. I was to be a FBI agent, with the white raincoat, the Alan Ladd hat, tough clichés sidling out of the corners of my mouth. The full bit. I just couldn't refuse it, and a right chapter of disasters it turned out to be.

Most of my stunts were done for me by Ray Austin, nowadays a well-known film director. But there were one or two fight scenes which were in close-up, and which I therefore had to do myself. In one of these I was supposed to hit a guy called Neil Hallam, quite a well-known actor.

Now of course these fights are faked. You take a swing and you just miss the man, and they put in the noise afterwards. But on this occasion I swung, and Mr Hallam stepped forward a fraction, and I caught him right on the jaw.

Mr Hallam went out like a light.

It later transpired that this situation had made Mr Hallam rather unhappy. He confided as much to his hairdresser, who also happened to be my hairdresser. He confided as much to me. He said: "You'd better not let him see you. I think I'd better book you in at a different time. He's after you, you know. He's after you."

This made *me* unhappy. In a proper fight I wouldn't have lasted half a minute with the man.

Soon after this unintended mayhem, there was a scene where I was due to hit another actor over the head with a bottle. They intended that I should pretend to hit him. I actually did hit him. To this day he still gets dizzy spells, or so he always tells me when we happen to meet.

He sued the film company, but I don't know whether he got anything from the insurance. I doubt it.

Certainly they were not covered for the next disaster. I contracted laryngitis. "Go ahead and make the picture," they said cheerfully. "You can dub your voice in afterwards." It was very necessary, since I sounded like a poor imitation of Louis Armstrong. Happily, my experience with commercials and so on made the dubbing easy, and the technicians were delighted. Unhappily, the Danzigers were saving money on this too, and when the film was processed, the words were all out of 'sync' … synchronisation.

But at least my friendship with the studio technicians paid off in the final disaster. One evening we arrived at the dénouement of the whole gripping tale, the bit where I had to reveal the murderer. It wasn't scheduled for that particular day, but since they'd got through all the bits that *were* scheduled, they decided to chuck that one in as well. They worked fast, those Danzigers, and they didn't believe in retakes if they could possibly help it.

147

I had about half an hour to learn my lines, a whole page of deathless prose, and I just couldn't do it. And to crown it all, it happened to be an 'early night'. In the film business they have one of these nights each week, when they lock up at 5.30, come what may, no overtime, and a definite date with the girl-friend, or even the wife. Early nights are sacrosanct.

Well, I fluffed, and messed it up left, right and centre, and it got close to 5.30, and I could see time running out, and I knew it would cost them a bomb if they had to do it the following day. To put it concisely, I was panic-stricken.

Crisis time was about to happen, when the shop steward of the ACTT, one of the most militant unions, came up to the director.

"I want a word with you," he said.

"What about?" asked the director.

"You're not going to get this shot in time, are you?" said the union man.

"It doesn't look like it," said the director.

"Well, I've had a word with the ETU boys, and because it's Pete we'll go on till 7 o'clock."

I could have cried. I honestly think that that was the most marvellous and heart-warming experience I ever had. And what's more, they were all Watford supporters, and they knew where my affections lay!

My girl-friend in the picture was June Thorburn, who had suffered the same fate in *Escort for Hire,* and that was about the only part of the film that wasn't a disaster. That, and the salad. The films were made at the Danziger Studios at Elstree, which, though not demolished, are no longer film studios. I was still on a raw food diet, as I made my recovery from the hepatitis, and I gave the canteen the recipe for the salad I needed. It included grated carrots, grated cheese, lettuce, tomatoes, beetroot, grated onion, dates, raisins, and sliced bananas.

Soon other people started asking for it, and in the end they called it the 'Pete Murray Salad' and put it on the regular menu.

I would say that was the only successful thing about that particular slice of cinematic history. I never saw any of the films. They never gave the actors a preview, because the budgets would never run to the hire of a preview theatre. And any inclination I might have to go and see one in the cinema was removed by a girl-friend of mine at the time,

Nicky Young. Nicky rang me up one day and said: "I've just seen you in *Transatlantic* at a cinema in Islington. They were throwing things at the screen."

My destiny clearly did not lie in being the British Alan Ladd.

Chapter Fourteen

I do not like blind dates.

I am one of those customers who believes strictly in viewing and approving the goods before purchase. And my ideas on the subject were confirmed by the one occasion on which I dabbled. Like my experience with rugby, once was enough.

At that time, I employed a telephone answering service. To pick up any messages, I would have to phone them between nine in the morning and six at night. There was one girl in their office who had this marvellous, sexy type of voice, and one evening she phoned me at twenty past six ... outside office hours.

"You're a naughty boy. A very, very naughty boy," purred this voice.

"What have I done?" I asked.

"I've had to stand up a date for you."

"Oh, I'm very sorry," I said, "but why is that?"

"You haven't phoned in for your messages, and there are some very important ones." And she proceeded to list them for me.

For the next twenty-four hours I allowed myself a few fantasies about this lady, and decided that with such a voice she could be nothing short of stunning. So the following evening, at a quarter to six, I called her.

"I'm a good boy today, aren't I? I'm calling in time for the messages."

"Yes, you are. You're a very good boy," came the honeyed tones.

"Well, I'd like to show my appreciation. I'll be home at 7.30. Would you care to join me for a drink?"

Yes, she'd be delighted. Thank heavens, some little warning voice also prompted me to phone Pat Campbell.

"Pat, I've got a mystery coming round. I don't know what she looks like, but she's got a fabulous voice and might be rather nice. Just in case, give me a call at a quarter to eight so that I can make a moody if necessary."

At 7.30 sharp, the voice arrived. Let's put it this way: she wasn't my type.

"It's such a thrill meeting all these people I talk to on the phone," said The Voice. "I love to meet them. I'm always being invited out, you know. I was at the Ritz only last night. And the Berkeley, or was it the Dorchester, the night before that."

She then proceeded to give me a sort of tourist guide of London night-spots, together with the celebrity list who had been inveigled into escorting her to them. I was already feeling desperate, when Pat rang.

"How goes it?"

"Oh Christ," I said, "NOW don't tell me."

"You're in trouble," said Pat.

"I can't possibly come out now," I said. "I've got a friend round here. I'm sorry if the recording went wrong, but that's your bloody look-out. I'll do it again for you tomorrow morning. NO. I bloody well won't. No, I'm not going to go out again tonight. What do you mean? They have to be flown out tonight? What time? Oh God, all right. What time do you want me?" A brief pause while I worked out how early I could make it without being too unkind to the poor 'Voice'. "Okay, then, nine o'clock."

I turned to The Voice. "I guess you heard that. I'm so sorry. Anyway, have another drink."

Perhaps as a suitable and symbolic penance for this episode, I found myself chairing a series called 'Laugh Line'. I took over from Peter Haigh, and I might as well not have bothered. The gist of this piece of sparkling television was that a panel of comedians were given a story, to which they had to add a punch-line at the end.

As far as I was concerned the programme was yet another disaster to swell the growing list of HORRIBLE HAPPENINGS in my personal television history. I lasted about eight weeks, and was then replaced by my old friend Digby Wolfe. Generously, he remained my friend. I never warned him!

Fresh from that disaster, I was now invited to take part in the pilot of a projected new situation comedy series called 'Happily Ever After', a title which might have been designed for me by way of condolence. My leading lady was the adorable Dora Bryan. The show was the property of NBC of America, but directed by a Briton, Francis Essex, now head of light entertainment at ATV.

It was a very good script, by one of the people involved in the 'I Love Lucy' show, and Dora and I enjoyed ourselves thoroughly. We did this pilot show at the now-demolished (of course) Wood Green Empire, and it was then flogged around by a gentleman named Gordon Harbord, a respected agent in the legitimate theatre. Dora and I were very keen that the BBC should buy the series, because there was no doubt that in those days their comedy output was vastly superior to that of independent television. Indeed we were both prepared to take a cut in salary to ensure that the BBC did it.

But all in vain. The series was bought by ABC, who then had the franchise for the Manchester area. This meant that we would spend five days a week rehearsing at the Duke of York's Barracks in Kings Road Chelsea (which for a fee was prepared to lend itself to situations marital rather than martial), and then leap aboard some form of transport to do the show proper at the studios in Didsbury, Manchester. (The barracks, I am surprised to record, are still standing. The studios are not.)

It was another disaster. Not because it was a bad series. I think it was good, with Dora at her ebullient best. We certainly had fun doing it. But they did it on the cheap . . . even the studio sets creaked, and had gaps in them, and the television public was becoming sophisticated enough to notice these little things, in spite of the sterling efforts of the director, Philip Jones.

On top of everything else, the programme was not networked at the same time all over the country, and in London went out at 3.30 on Sunday afternoons, a way of guaranteeing that it would *not* get into the ratings. Nor did it. After seven weeks, ABC decided that it did not fulfil the hopes that they had been unprepared to back with cash, and it folded.

I felt very sad. My role as Dora's doctor husband had been an unusual one for me, and I had enjoyed it. But it was beginning to seem as though I had the same effect on shows as I clearly did on buildings. To cap it all, I had been banned from 'Juke Box Jury', because the BBC would not countenance my appearing on both channels at once.

But at least I had Decca and Radio Luxembourg to thank for continuing my five programmes a week, the one form of employment that seemed impervious to my destructive gremlins. And even that had its moments, thanks to the indefatigable Pat Campbell.

Pat was doing a Country and Western show on Luxembourg, and shortly after Christmas he told his audience that as a freaky, not to say money-saving, essay in interior decoration, I was intending to paper the walls of my flat in old Christmas cards. I would, said this joker, be grateful if listeners would send me any they had to spare. To spare! I was inundated with regiments of reindeer and enough fir trees to reforest Alaska. The bonus post-Christmas mail must have kept the Post Office out of debt for the year.

I decided to retaliate. Pat Campbell, I announced on one of my programmes, was trying to build up the world's biggest collection of bottle tops. He would be thrilled if listeners would send him any they had. I sat back and waited. But that wily Irishman did me again. He phoned the Post Office, and asked them to send his mail for the next month, not to Radio Luxembourg, but to re-address it to his flat at 31, Montagu Mansions. And guess whose flat *that* was!

We recorded these programmes at the Radio Luxembourg offices in Hertford Street. Early in 1961, just as 'Happily Ever After' was getting under its disastrous way, I had to pop in there, and parked my car, a Renault Floride, outside. It was rear-engined, and something of a novelty on London streets. I was in there barely five minutes, but when I came out, a traffic-warden was in the process of giving me a ticket.

"What do you think you're doing?" I demanded.

"Giving you a ticket," he said, rather obviously.

"But I've only been here five minutes," I protested.

"Don't give me that," he said. "You've been here a lot longer than that." He marched to the front of the car, paused with the air of a Wellington about to win Waterloo, then placed his hand majestically on the front of the car.

"See?" he boasted, a Maigret about to pin his victim. "It's cold."

153

I walked gently towards him, took him by the hand, and ushered him round to the back of the car.

"Feel that," I said. "Quite warm, isn't it?"

He was furious, but I didn't get a ticket.

I bet I didn't get his vote in the Top DJ poll either. That year I got 16,644 votes, which was exactly 63 less than David Jacobs, and put me in second place, a position I was to occupy for about the next five years. But I can truthfully say that I was in no way saddened by this 'setback', any more than I had been overly proud when I was number one. The fact of the matter was that the people who got the votes were those who had mass-audience programmes on television. I would bet that 99% of the people who voted in those polls had never heard David or me doing a radio DJ show. It was simply a question of how many 'Juke Box Jury' or 'Top of the Pops' shows we had done. And that is very much what I think about these polls even today.

For me, as it happened, more televisual pop was on its way. As 'Happily Ever After' was on its way to becoming 'Unhappily Never Again', ABC, undaunted, invited me to be the host of a new series, 'Thank Your Lucky Stars'. It was really not a bad programme, musically, and had the great advantage of being made at Teddington, a world away from the creaking sets at Didsbury.

What's more, it did not die an instant death. It ran for a number of years. But not with me. I did the first thirteen shows, between March and June of 1961, and felt it had gone rather well. I certainly didn't expect to be taken off it. I was. When it came back in the Autumn, Keith Fordyce and Brian Matthew did it together.

Actually, I was a little bit hurt by this. I wouldn't have minded if someone had told me they wanted a change. As it was, I read it in the papers. GREAT LESSON. Never expect nothing from nobody, especially if it's a television company. Alternatively, don't read the papers!

Some consolation soon came along, though, with parts in a couple of TV series. The first was in 'Boyd, Q.C.', which starred Michael Dennison, with whom I had worked in *My Brother Jonathan,* and who had witnessed my cavalier catastrophe in *Hungry Hill.* I played the part of a footballer who had committed a foul and killed another footballer. Bearing in mind my real-life standard of football (of which readers

154

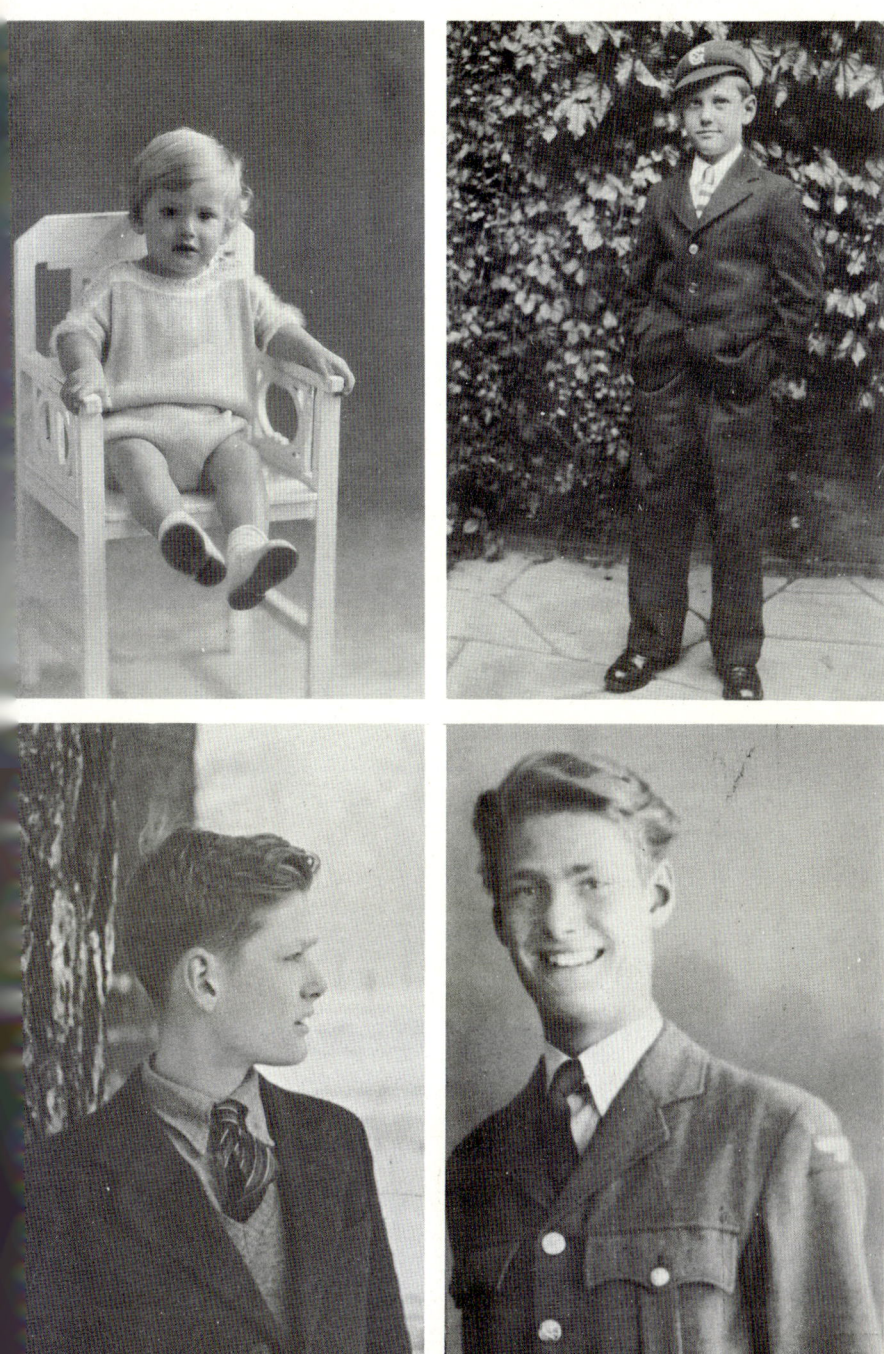

t age 1, 7, 11, and (in the RAF) 18.

Top: one of my first jobs as an extra, in 'Day Will Dawn' (1941). Hugh Williams (*far right*) was the star; somewhere in the background is Harry Walters, who was to become producer of Open House. *Left:* Me as Cliff in 'Power Without Glory' (1948) at the Booth Theatre, New York. The Boston Post said I gave "a brilliant performance". The play flopped.

PETER WOLFF

Top: With Derek Blomfield and June Thorburn in 'Escort For Hire' (1960). June died in a plane crash. Derek, o was also in my first-ever professional play, died a year after this film. *Bottom:* Me camping it up in apa' (1962), much to the amusement of shipmates (*left to right*) Edward Woodward, the late David Hughes, Timothy Grey – who later wrote 'High Spirits', the musical version of Noel Coward's 'Blithe Spirit'. *et:* my name in lights for the first time.

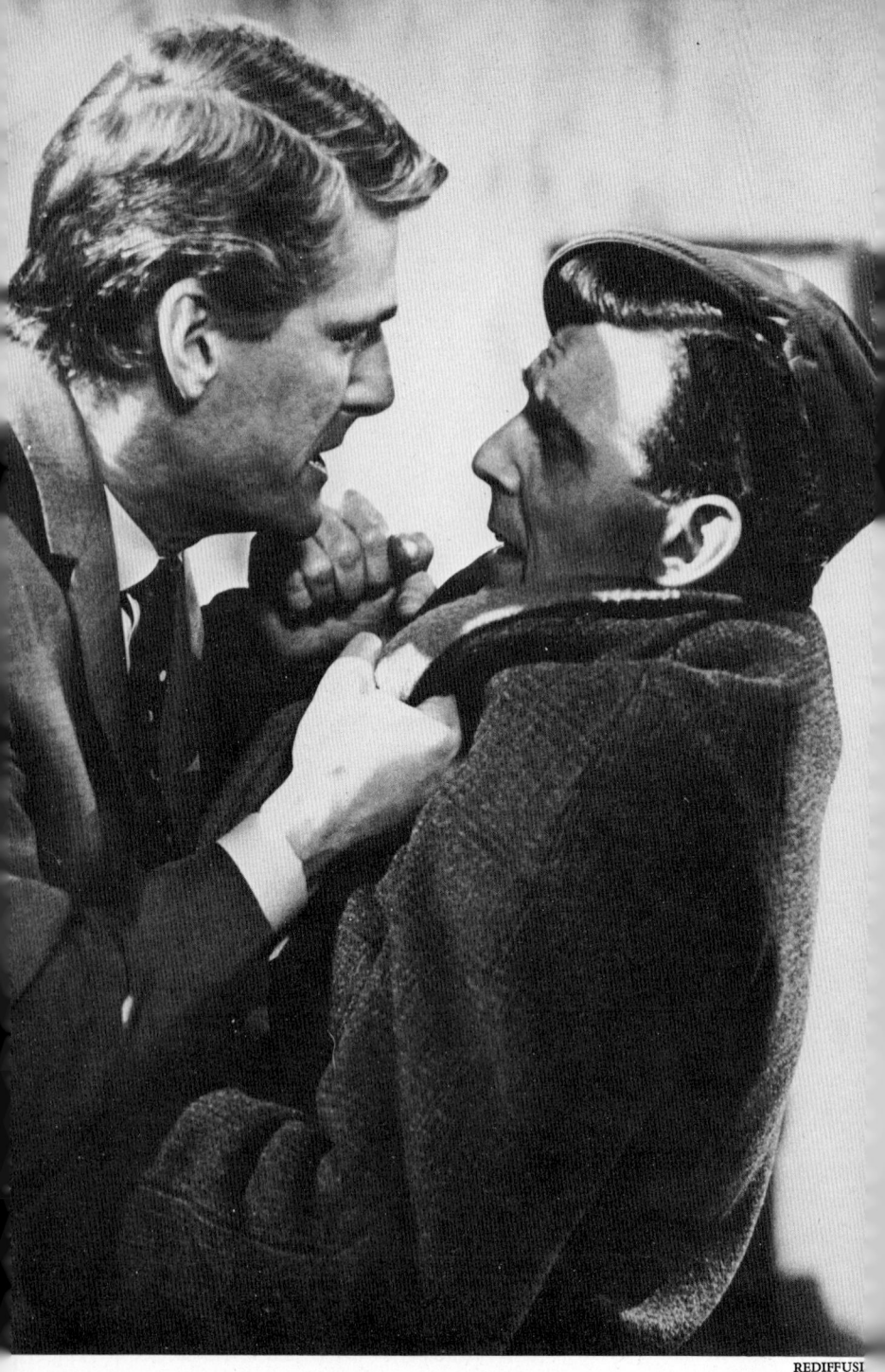

My reaction to a blackmailer (Paddy Joyce) in 'No Hiding Place' (1967).

ie Dawson's practical joke.

Above: The TV All Stars F.C. *Back row:* Bernie Winters, Jess Conrad, Larry Taylor, Ray Merrill and Peter
Thompson. *Front row:* second from left is Leslie Wise; fourth from left is Mike Winters; *far right* is Tommy
Steele. *Below:* Cup Final night 1970, after Arsenal won the Double. With Jimmy Hill and fellow-supporter
Leslie Wise.

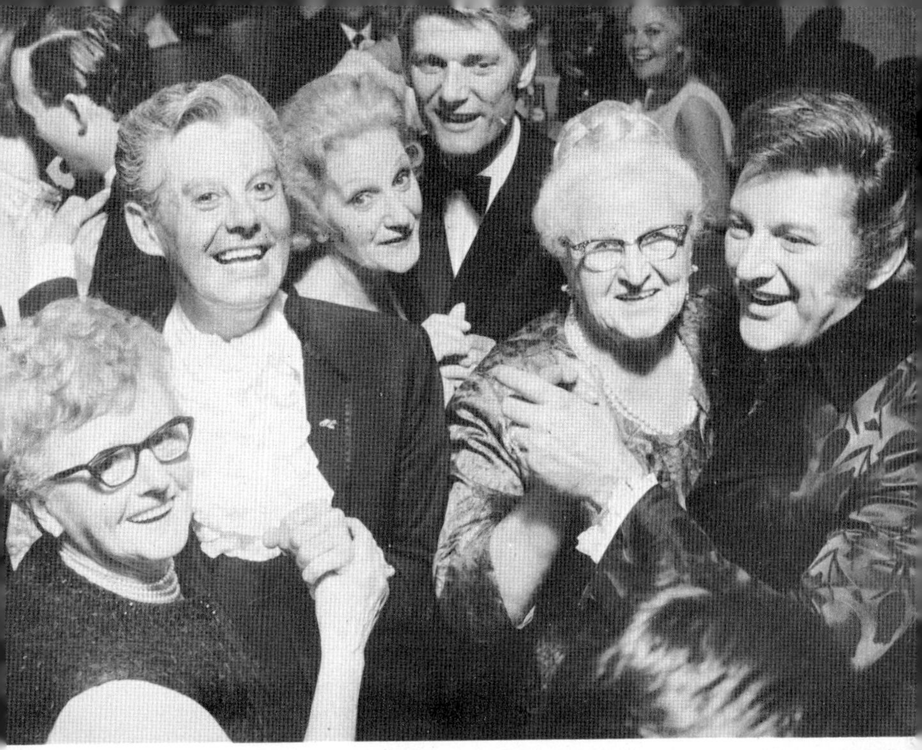

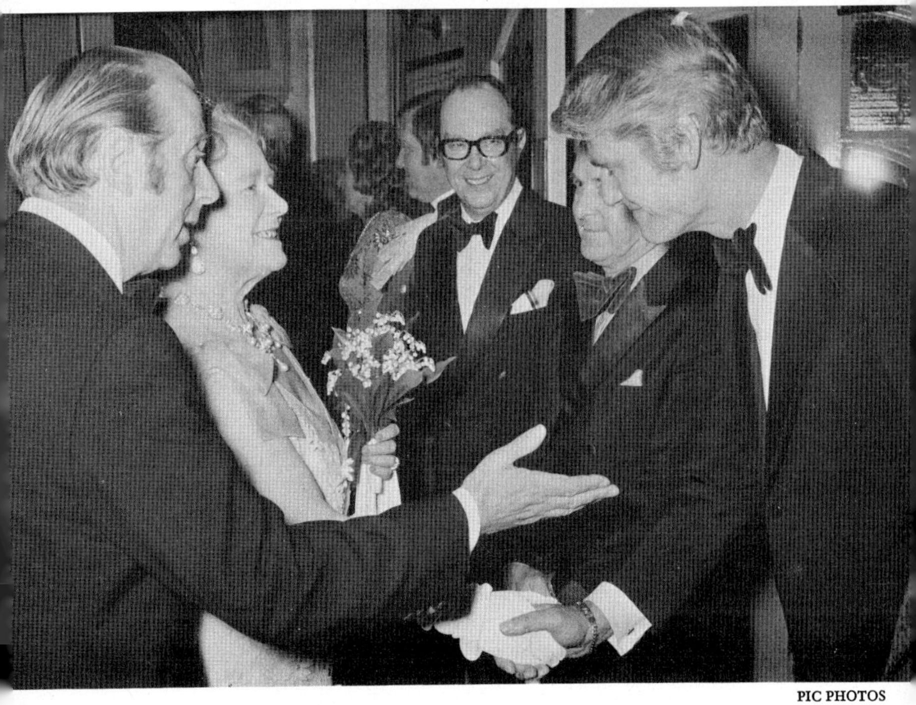

PIC PHOTOS

ove: With Danny La Rue (*left*), Liberace, and our three Mums, at Danny's club (1969). *Below:* Being
:sented to Her Majesty the Queen Mother by Leslie Grade at the Palladium in 1972. Eric Morecambe and
nie Wise are in the background.

(*Left to right*) Tony Bennet, Sacha Distel and Malcolm Roberts each challenged me to a game of tennis when they appeared on Open House; so I organised a little tournament.

Above: Les Dawson doe
strip, with my assistance
on the Open House
Roadshow at the Top
Rank Club, Sheffield
(1974). *Below:* with
Marlene Dietrich.

DOUG MCKENZIE

JOAN WILLIAMS

ove: The Morecambe and Wise Christmas Show (1972). *Below:* My first radio interview with Frankie Laine
tre) on Radio Luxembourg in 1954. Jimmy Henney is on the left, and Frankie's Dad is standing.

THAMES TV

THAMES

My son Michael: (*above*) on the beach at Cannes in 1962; and (*below*) on This Is Your Life. The inset shows m
reaction when they told me this was *my* life!

darling Tricia at home in Wimbledon.

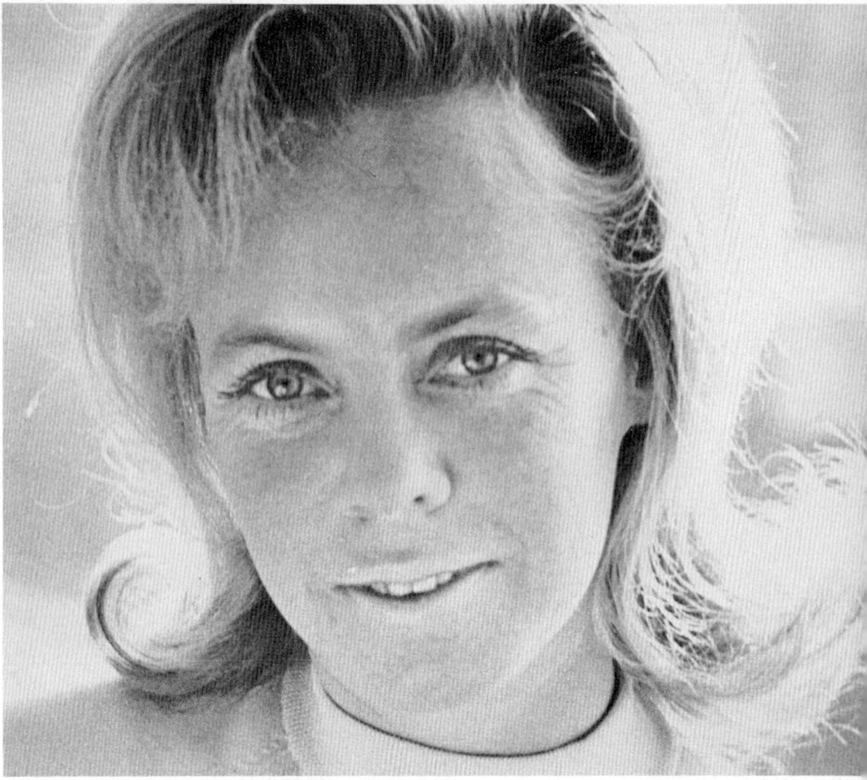

208 MAGAZINE

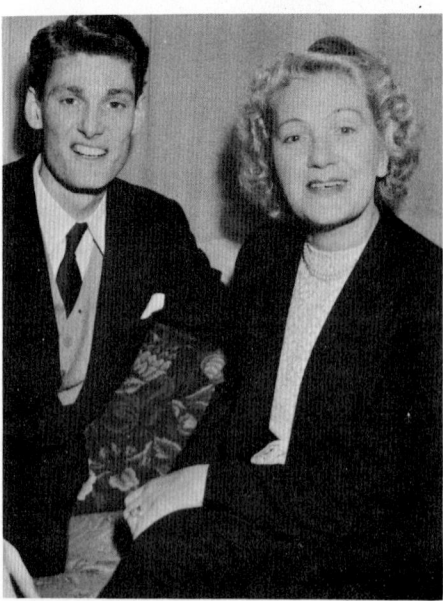

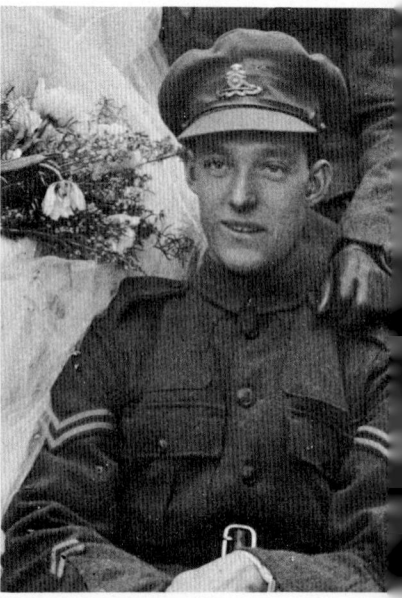

Above: Tricia. *Below left:* My Mum in 1952. *Below right:* My Dad, Harry James, during World War One.

BBC

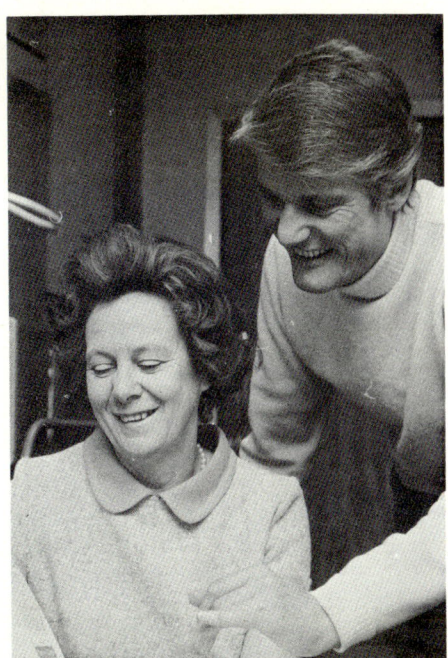

BBC

H. GOODWIN

DOUG McKENZIE

My Open House guests: *top left* – Burt Lancaster; *centre left* – George Best; *below left* – Margaret Lockwood; *top right* – Mrs Mary Wilson.

Evening Standard, Jan 2, '70

"Just a couple of appearances on 'Top of the Pops' and you could have got a bar to your DSO!"

Above: '6.5 Special' (1957). Jeremy Lloyd is in the back row at top left; Jon Pertwee is next to him; Josephine Douglas is in the striped blouse. *Below:* the cartoon which appeared in the Evening Standard wh I got my OBE.

may acquaint themselves in another chapter), this was not a hard proposition for me to imagine, although in the plot I was delighted to discover that I was an international, the nearest I ever came to *that*.

I also did a couple of episodes of an enigmatically-named series, 'The man from Room 13'. The sole reason for picking me, it appeared, was that there was a part in it of a young ne'er-do-well named Curly. And my hair, believe it or not, is tousled in the extreme. Not that you would know it from the majority of the photos in this volume. The fact was that my mother always insisted that I comb my hair when pictures were taken. It also looked darker than it really was, owing to a profligate use of photogenic Brylcream.

But on one 'Juke Box Jury' I had not had time to effect all these repairs and alterations, and my wavy locks were spotted by some keen-eyed producer.

Meanwhile, relationships with the BBC had been repaired, and I was given a programme called '12 O'clock Spin'. This was another important move for me, partly because a lunchtime BBC radio series was really IT, and partly because I was given a completely free choice of music.

Most other DJs at that time were desperately trying to be 'with-it', and 'it' was something that I could very well be without. I've always preferred good middle-of-the-road music. For example, I was the first person to play Andy Williams records, and I remember getting stacks of cards from people who had heard this unknown singer perform Irving Berlin's 'Say it isn't so.'

As a matter of fact, that would have been a good theme song for a joke I played around this time on two very good friends of mine, Peter and Cherry Barker.

I rang them one day and said: "Could I speak to the householder, please."

"Y-yes, speaking," said Peter, who is in the advertising business and stutters, which cannot be exactly helped by that nerve-devouring profession.

"You *are* number 41, Abbotsbury Road aren't you?" I said.

"Y-yeah, that's it," said Peter.

"Well I'm very sorry to disturb you," I said. "This is the Metropolitan Water Board here. We're phoning up one house in four to inform you that unfortunately we're going to have to turn the water off at the mains in the next half hour. So if it's convenient, could you please let your immediate neighbours know what we're doing, and that the water will be turned off."

"Oh, Ch-Christ, h-how long will it be off for?" asked a worried Peter.

"We're hoping it's only going to be for a day," I said, "but we do have a very serious situation, and it might last for anything up to a week."

"Oh, SH-SH-SHIT!" declared Peter.

"Yes, well *that* will be a problem" I said. "So what I advise you to do is to fill every possible receptacle you have with as much water as you can. Do you have a bath?"

"Y-yes we *do* have a b-bath," said Peter testily.

"Well, fill the bath, and every other receptacle you can think of."

Peter succumbed. "Oh, G-God, all right. I've g-got my f-father and mother-in-law staying with me as well."

Half an hour later I got my public-official voice together again and phone back. "Could I speak to the householder, please?"

"Y-yes?"

"Oh, Metropolitan Water Board here."

"Ch-Christ, what is it now?"

"We're turning off the water now, Sir."

"Oh, y-yes?" panted an exhausted Peter.

"Have you filled everything?" I asked him.

"We've f-filled every b-bloody thing we've g-got. We've filled the b-bath, and all the b-basins, and the sink. We've all had a b-bath in the last h-half hour, my w-wife and I and her p-parents, and our t-two children. And I've t-told the p-people next door and all I can say is it's a terrible b-bloody situation."

"Well, fine," I said. "Everything filled up now then, is it?"

"Y-yeah," said Peter.

"Right. Well, stay tuned to Radio Luxembourg, because it's Peter Murray here."

There was the usual pause, but a slight variation on the usual reply, once the pennies had audibly clicked into place. "You b-b-bastard."

It's a tribute to Peter and Cherry's good nature that we're still the

156

best of friends.

As indeed I have remained friends with David Jacobs, despite what various newspaper columnists, reprinting the published mistakes of other columnists, have from time to time tried to make out. It was at this time that David and I and Alan Freeman were guest artistes, for want of a better phrase, in a film called *It's Trad Dad*. The film was really made to cash in on the boom that Traditional Jazz was enjoying at that time, and it starred Helen Shapiro and Craig Douglas. Helen was becoming a very big name, and Craig was a kind of clean-cut, good-living, good-looking teenage idol.

My main memory of this not particularly exhilarating piece of cinema was of walking across the set at Shepperton with David one day.

"You know, Peter," he said in his most pin-striped voice. "I think you ought to get yourself a man."

A sort of shiver went down my spine. "David," I said, "I never realised you thought that way."

"Why, what *do* you mean?" he asked.

"Well, a man. That's what you said. I had no idea you were that way at all."

"Oh no, no, no, no," he protested, to my immediate relief. "I'm talking about a chauffeur."

He was going through a little phase of grandiosity in which he thought that the possession of a large car and a 'man' to match, would be THE thing. I think this fantasy lasted about five minutes, which was more than I got on the Jack Parr Show.

Jack Parr had the first, and the most successful, of the American late-night TV chat shows. And they decided to record four of the shows in London. To open each show, they wanted to enthral the American audience with a very English voice making the simple announcement: "Ladies and Gentlemen. The Jack Parr Show." I was chosen to fulfil this stunning role.

But it was worth it just to watch Parr working. He had a wonderful way of talking to an audience, not *at* them.

He had a very relaxed, very 'throwaway' manner, and managed to give the appearance of not really trying. I admired him a great deal, and I think he has had a great influence on me in the way that I try to

157

do my own shows now.

Now, my agent had warned me that Jack Parr was quite likely to invite me on stage without warning. "He's likely to bring anybody on," I was told. "He might well talk to you, and if he did it could be quite a big thing for you."

Sure enough, on the third show he suddenly said: "Hey, folks, I want you to meet a real live British announcer. The guy that you heard talking so beautifully at the start of the show." He turned to me, as I stood off camera. "Hey, come on. What a good-looking guy this is. And he got that suntan here in England? You haven't been away?"

"No," I said, "I got it in London, England." (Well, we'd had a good Spring.)

"Great … " said the great Jack Parr. "Great … now, eh, … hell, what's your name?"

It was possibly the worst thing he could have said. I went every colour of the rainbow and became completely tongue-tied. And my great moment of revelation to the great American TV public came to nothing. My embarrassment was their embarrassment, and they cut out the whole thing.

But the great British public were not to be let off so lightly. I had been called once again to the standard of the Danziger Brothers, with June Thorburn as my co-star once again, with appalling credits and bad lighting once again, and everything on the cheap once again. This very 'B' picture was called *Fashion for Loving*.

I played a beatnik working in a bra factory, with James Maxwell as my sidekick, if that's what beatniks have. In the story I doodle some drawings on top of a bra box, which are seen by June, one of the bra executives.

She determines to discover who has done these brilliant designs, finds this dirty monstrosity (me) with a beard and hair all over the place; she cleans me up, we have a love affair, and live happily ever after. Thus ran the gripping narrative.

At least, that was the basic plot; the dialogue, as usual, we pretty well made up as we went along, assisted by the likes of Michael Balfour, and a young girl named Angela Douglas, later Kenneth More's wife.

The highlight of the filming came when we actually shot some

158

exterior scenes in the King's Road, Chelsea. This was remarkable for the Danzigers, who in *Transatlantic* had used the studio staff canteen to portray an airport.

I was happily preparing for filming, filthy and unkempt to suit the part, in a dirty old leather jacket, and with the beard, which I was certain would make it quite sure that no-one would recognise me. But I had hardly stepped onto the pavement when some woman came up to me and said: "Hello Pete. How are you?"

Now that woman couldn't see the cameras, but she didn't say anything like "You look in a terrible state." She just took it for granted that that was how I chose to look. Some ego-trip that was!

An hour or two later I nearly ended up looking even worse. There was a bit in a scene where I had to hold up the traffic and walk across the King's Road. It was in the rush hour, but we had a 'fake' car for me to stop. We went through the performance, but, typically Danziger debacle, the shot hadn't worked. The fake car meanwhile was disappearing in the direction of Fulham, the light was going, and there wasn't enough money in the kitty to do it the following day.

"What *are* we going to do?" I asked.

"*You* will just have to walk up and stop the traffic for real," they said.

This, risking life and limb, I did.

I will never know why there was not a disastrous concertina smash that evening on the King's Road. The screeching of tyres and so on was fantastic. The nearest driver, who of course had no idea that we were filming, missed me by half an inch, and his language was so remarkable that it had to be removed from the sound-track. His reactions, though, were much better than any actor could have portrayed, and they dubbed his voice and language in afterwards. (Knowing the Danzigers, I'm pretty sure the lip movement didn't fit what he actually said.)

But it was a good film, and the only one of my Danziger epics that I ever saw. I was at a cinema in Bristol, and people actually laughed, which I found gratifying. Frankie Vaughan saw it in Liverpool, and, typically of him, actually took the trouble to write and say how much he enjoyed it. Few people bother.

It was around this time that I had a second brush with the seamier side of life. I was in the lounge of a large provincial Victorian style hotel. It was the sort of place where, if you asked for fairy cakes, no-one would bat an eyelid.

I was enveloped in one of its commodious chairs, taking tea with Victor Spinetti and the Clark Brothers, when a rather shady-looking person approached me. He was either afflicted, or had seen too many Bogart movies, because he seemed able to talk only sideways out of the corner of his mouth.

" 'Ere, you Pete Murray?" he asked, speaking at right-angles to me.

"Er, yes," I admitted.

"The boss would like to 'ave a word wiv yer."

It all seemed a bit too Raymond Chandler to be true, but I decided that it was an invitation I really shouldn't refuse. I was led past the potted palms and brought face to face with a large cigar, a very large cigar, attached to which was a man. The latter nodded to me to sit down. I sat.

"Like you to help one of the boys." It was a statement, not a request.

"Ah, yes," I said carefully. "Is he a singer?"

"No."

"Has he got a group?"

"No."

"A comedian?" I murmured, groping for conversation.

"Not so you'd notice. He's in the nick ain't 'e?"

"Is he?" I asked, superfluously.

"Yeah, and we want you to help 'im."

"How?" I asked.

The large cigar leaned forward, dragging its owner with it. Tears of compassion, or perhaps the product of the cigar smoke, poured down his cheeks.

"They won't give 'im a date."

"A date?"

"For release."

"Oh," I said, relieved that I wasn't being asked to smuggle girls into one of HM Prisons.

The cigar continued. "We thought you might 'elp."

"How?"

"Well, go 'down to the nick. Meet 'im. See what a nice feller 'e is. Then 'ave a word with the 'Ome Secretary."

160

"But I don't *know* the Home Secretary," I protested.

"Ah, but you *could* get to know 'im. Respectable bloke like you."

"Where is he?" I asked, feeling that events were overtaking me.

"At the 'Ome Office."

"No, your friend." I started to prepare myself mentally for a quick trip to Brixton, even Pentonville.

"Dartmoor," replied the Cigar.

I decided I had to pluck up courage. "Well," I said, "I'm afraid that's rather a long way. Much as I'd like to help, I'm afraid that would be impossible."

I rose, and walked back to my friends, feeling that Len Deighton might have in me the model for a new novel. But there was a postscript. Three weeks later, Big Cigar's friend was 'sprung' from Dartmoor. They never did find the body. But they did find Big Cigar. He's in the nick ain't 'e?

I *must* have a word with the Home Secretary sometime . . .

In the Spring of 1961 I had been on holiday in Spain with my mother and my son Michael, commuting every weekend to Teddington to keep up my appearances in 'Thank Your Lucky Stars'. During the second week my agent phoned me and said: "Look, they're casting *Bye Bye Birdie,* and I want you to audition for it."

"Oh my God, no!" I said.

"Yes, I want you to. If you haven't heard the score, get it."

The following weekend I mentioned this to a dancer friend who was on 'Thank Your Lucky Stars', and she lent me her LP of the show. And on the Sunday evening I met the producer, who was the husband of Chita Rivera.

"Yes," he said. "You'd be great. You look just like Dick Van Dyke. Do you sing?"

"Well, I've never actually sung in public," I replied, neatly dodging the question.

He was not to be put off. "Well, do you dance?"

"No," I admitted, "I cannot really say that I dance."

"Well, go away and think about it, and when you come back from Spain we'll do an audition," he said, relentlessly.

So, armed with my record and my fears, I returned to Spain, and spent the week learning 'Put on a happy face' and 'Talk to me'. The following Sunday, Joe Henderson was on 'Thank Your Lucky Stars,' and I confided my terror to him.

"Don't worry," said Joe. "Just sing loud. Sing out, that's all you've got to do. Don't croon, just sing out." To prove his point, he ran through the songs with me during the tea-break, and I must confess that a look of horror bordering on revulsion came over his face.

The following day I went to Her Majesty's Theatre and read the part in my practised American accent, and they all made production noises like 'Great', 'Wonderful'. Then they added: "This afternoon we'd like to do the singing."

My embarrassment that afternoon was total. I sounded like an out-of-breath Fred Astaire. But they just would not be put off. "You can work on it," they said, kindly, "and with voice production it will be fine. Great. Now for the dancing."

Well, now, I'm one of those people who can get up and dance till I'm blue in the face. Someone even alleged once that I have rhythm. But try to choreograph me, or teach me to do the quadrille, as they had done in the non-equestrian moments of *Hungry Hill,* and I'm lost. I haven't got two left feet. I have three. There occurs at these moments a total breakdown in communication between my brain and my legs.

And still they wouldn't give up. "We'll give you some simple steps to learn!" they said.

Now you might think that all this indicated that they were really interested in securing my services, and indeed were ready to mould me into a mixture of Sinatra and Victor Sylvester to achieve that end. But no. What none of us realised was that it must have been a charade for the sake of appearances. Gower Champion, the director, had apparently already cast an American named Peter Marshall to play the role.

The only person to emerge from the episode untarnished was Honor Blair of the actors' union Equity. She was supposed to be very left-wing, but if she was an example of how left-wingers work, they can't be all bad. She fought tooth and nail to get the part for me. She told them that I could do it, and that they didn't need an American in the part, and that the job had to go to an Englishman. I might have been her dearest brother, the way she fought for me. But to no avail. They had made up their minds long previously, and it was all a big waste of everyone's time.

Nor was I much luckier with my next holiday interruption. I was over in Luxembourg that summer, seeing Michael, when Germaine called me from the swimming pool to the phone. It was Rediffusion from London, asking me to do a new programme called 'Close-up', an earlier version of 'Cinema'.

I was thrilled. It seemed that for almost the first time on TV I was doing something I really wanted, interviewing well-known people in the film business. I did about six of these programmes, showing film clips, interviewing the stars of the films and so on, and all was going marvellously.

Then, disaster. A major Equity strike against ITV began. It was to fight for a decent minimum wage for actors, and I completely agreed with its aims. It never occurred to me not to obey the strike call, but when it was all over, after about a year, I shared the bitterness of many of the other strikers that members who did not strike were accepted back into the union.

I think in the end, as so often, it cost the union as much, if not more, than it won. A lot of people suffered. For instance, Keith Fordyce came off 'Lucky Stars' because he was a member.

But that didn't hurt the programme. They just hired Brian Matthew, who wasn't a member. It didn't even hurt the variety programmes, because people like Bruce Forsyth and Norman Wisdom belonged to the Variety Artists' Federation, which was then not part of Equity, so *they* could go on working.

And the crowning folly, as far as I was concerned, was revealed when the strike ended. At the time it began, I had been getting about £65 a programme for 'Close-up', which was not a fortune, but which was all right by me since I enjoyed doing the programme so much. But now, after the glorious victory of the strike, the producers told me that unfortunately they couldn't possibly offer me the job back, much as they would like to, since the minimum they were allowed to pay me was now £150.

My place was taken by a journalist called Neville Barker, and indeed the journalists moved in to a lot of other programmes once it was realised that they could do various jobs as well as Equity members, and at lower fees.

So ended Murray the militant, with another GREAT LESSON LEARNED. If you play in a team, make sure the others know which way they're supposed to be kicking the ball.

The next step in my search of an Oscar for the best supporting-supporting-supporting actor, came with an invitation from a young man called Michael Winner, now of course an internationally-famous film director.

"Pete," he said, "we've got this idea for a comedy of manners, called *Behave Yourself*. It'll only be a half-hour film, maybe a bit more, so there's only fifty quid in it for you. But it'll be a ball."

I decided to go for the ride, along with the likes of Jack Jackson, Glen Mason, Dennis Price and Harold Behrens. It was filmed at the Hampstead home of Marion Massey, a friend of Winner's who later became Lulu's manager. In those days she wasn't in the business, just a bit starry-eyed.

The theme of the film, as readers may have guessed, was a lesson in how to behave, but with jokes, rather like one of the old Pete Smith shorts. For instance, the commentary might go: "This is how you would eat spaghetti." There would be a shot of Jack struggling with it, and I would say; "No, no. You can't eat it like that. You have to know the proper way of eating spaghetti." At this, I would lean over in my immaculate dinner jacket and snip the end off with a pair of scissors.

Readers may judge just how uproarious the whole thing wasn't.

At the end of it all, my fifty quids' worth of delivery behind me, Michael Winner said: "You were sensational. I'm going to make you a star." I had heard that particular song before, and besides, at that time he wasn't really equipped to make those sort of promises. But I must admit that since then I've always wanted to ask him: "What happened?"

Anyway, what then happened to me was that in October I went to America in a major starring role ... in some commercials for Brylcream. Actually, Brylcream was rather a success story at that time. It was a British product, of the Beechams group, but had managed to become the best-selling haircream in America. It was for that reason that they thought they would use American backgrounds, in New York and Hollywood.

The commercials were for British TV, and I was accompanied by one John Abbott of ABC Films, and John Beard of Royds advertising agency, one of the twin sons of Herbert Marshall and Edna Best. I think one of the main reasons they had selected me was that, as I have mentioned, my mother's insistence on tidy hair for photos meant that I always used the said smarm to hold my hair down for photo sessions.

I stepped off the plane in New York with some trepidation, remembering that my previous trip to the States had been less than happy, and marched to the customs desks with my zip-bag in my hand. I was confronted by a typically tough nut of a New York Customs Officer, than which they do not come tougher or nuttier. But on his command to open the bag, I found that it had jammed and just wouldn't open.

"You wanna try a little Vaseline on the zip," he said, flexing his cheese-grater tonsils. "It might open a little quicker that way."

"Yes, I think that might be an idea," I said, co-operatively. "I'll try it on my flies, as well."

Now you might consider that that was hardly the quip to launch a thousand guffaws. But this guy had clearly been starved of humour, because when he finally stopped laughing, about five minutes later, he said: "Forget opening the bag. That's the first laugh I've had in a long time. You're through."

In fact, I must have created an all-time record for getting through New York customs, because when I went to the Airline desk to check if anyone was there to meet me, they just wouldn't believe I had come off the plane I said I had. I had to tell them the story to convince them.

This trip to New York was obviously going to be better than the last one, and sure enough I immediately started bumping into old friends. The very first morning at the Warwick Hotel the waiter brought me breakfast and said: "You're English ain't you? Well, you'll be delighted to know there's an English guy staying right next door." It was Al Burnett of the Stork Club, whom I had known from way back. And a couple of days later I met Peter Charlesworth, then Shirley Bassey's manager. Shirley was appearing at the Persian Room of the Plaza Hotel.

I remember going up to see her in her suite, where an American was haranguing the assembled connections. "I'm very worried about the pictures of Shirley outside here," he said. Shirley sat and said nothing, and someone asked if he thought they were too sexy.

"Hell no, they aren't too sexy, but I'll tell you something, she looks coloured."

There was a pause of disbelief, and then someone said: "What the hell are you talking about? She *is* coloured."

"Yeah," said the man. "But we don't want her to look that way."

We had no such inhibitions about the Brylcream ads. We wanted America to look like America, and we shot them on Broadway, Times Square, The Empire State Building, the lot. At one point a typically talkative American approached me and asked: "You making a motion picture?"

"Yes, we are," I told him.

"What's the picture?" he persisted.

I took pity. I couldn't say *The Brylcream Story.* It would have ruined his day. So I said: "James Bond."

"Ah, that's great," he said. "Making a movie of James Bond are they? Well, that's great. Wonderful." And he want away happy.

I had a rather different encounter the following afternoon, when I was walking down one of the sleazier little New York streets, and a girl approached me and asked: "Do you want to come in for a drink?"

"No thanks, darling. I don't want anything like that," I said.

"Come on, come in for a drink," she urged, with the manner of her kind in a hundred other cities. But I rather liked her, especially as she was smiling, a trait I hadn't noticed in too many other New Yorkers. So I went into the bar with her.

"But I want to get one thing straight," I told her. "I'm English, and I probably look like a mug, but I come from London, and I know what it's all about, I know what the game is, and I'm not going to be conned."

She laughed and said: "Hey, I like you, you're talkin' honest." She called over to the barman: "Hey, here's an honest guy," and then turned back to me and said: "I like you so much I'm gonna buy you a drink."

"That's fine by me," I said, "I'll have a Seven-Up." Of course, she thought I was kidding, but I explained my drinking habits to her, and after consuming the aforementioned fizz I made to go.

"Tell you what," she said. "Could I just have a souvenir of meeting you. Say, a piece of English money."

I pulled a ten-shilling note out of my pocket, signed it for her, as she asked, and left. It was probably the cheapest drink I had in America.

While still in New York, I ran into John Barry, whom I had known from the days of '6.5 Special'. We decided to go and see the famous Birdland, the jazz place where all the greats were supposed to have played. For some unexplained reason, the girl on the ticket desk was from Manchester.

"Ee bai gum, it's Pete Murray," she announced to me, as if I didn't know. "We'll have to get you in for nothing."

She called one of the heavies over.

"This is Pete Murray," she told him brightly.

"So?"

"Well, he's on TV."

"So?"

"He's a disc-jockey in England."

"So?"

"So can we let him in for nothing?"

"No."

It wasn't worth it anyway. The music we heard was a load of rubbish, and by comparison with Ronnie Scott's in Dean Street it looked like a doss-house. So after a while John suggested that we should go to dinner and then go to see Shirley Bassey at the Plaza. As we were going downstairs we bumped into an old actor friend of mine, with whom I played charity football, and who had been doing *Macbeth* in Canada. His name was Sean Connery, and I introduced him to John, and we all went out to dinner together.

It wasn't until a couple of years ago that I happened to mention it to John. "Do you remember us having dinner at the Plaza Hotel in New York?" I asked him. He said he did.

"And do you remember that there was an actor who had just been doing *Macbeth* in Canada?" Yes, he remembered that too.

"And do you remember who that actor was?" No, he didn't. John, whose vast success probably started with his writing the James Bond Theme, had never realised that the actor had been the one who later created Bond on the screen.

From New York we went to Hollywood. I was met at Los Angeles

Airport by the aforementioned Patrick Westwood (without dog-collar, and by no means foaming at the mouth), who had emigrated to America, and whom I had warned of my impending arrival. When he had first decided to try his luck in Hollywood, I had told him that, because of his dark hair and dark skin, "the only thing you're ever going to play is Red Indians." It turned out that the prophecy was precisely true.

Patrick bundled me into his car and drove me to my hotel, along Sunset Boulevard, the famous Hollywood Strip. I couldn't believe my eyes. It was all so tatty, like a film set with no backing to it.

"I know what you're thinking. You're thinking that this place is a dump, aren't you?" said Patrick.

"That's exactly what I'm thinking," I said.

"Well, it is," he said.

We did about a week's filming in Hollywood, one scene being shot on a flyover bridge. We soon discovered, however, that rules about filming in the film capital are stricter than anywhere. A motor-cycle cop roared up to us, looking like something from a Broderick Crawford movie. I almost shouted "Ten Four" before he'd stopped his engine.

"You guys got permission to do yer filming here?" he asked.

John Beard said that we hadn't.

"Well, what are you filming for?" asks this hunk of law officer.

"This is for Britain," said John rather lamely. Then he had a brainwave. "Would you like to be in the picture? It's an ad for Brylcream. Do you wear it?"

"No, but I'm prepared to," said the star-struck cop.

So we smothered him in Brylcream, and shot merrily away.

Another problem occurred when we did a scene at the swimming pool of the Hollywood Roosevelt Hotel, where I was staying. Because it was November, nobody had the slightest inclination to go swimming, and we needed floating bodies for the background. Just as things were getting desperate, who should happen along but Kenneth McKellar and his wife.

Actually, it wasn't such an unlikely place for Kenneth to be, since there is a big Scottish Society in America, and people like Kenneth, and Jimmy Shand, often went over there to entertain. But at that

168

moment he was a godsend, Scottish or not. I explained our predicament to him, and sure enough, he and his wife proved that the Scots really are a hardy race, by immersing themselves in the chilly waters while we did the shooting.

As he was drying himself afterwards, I asked him what he thought of the States.

"I don't like America, I don't like it at all," he said in that thick Scottish accent. "New York, for instance, everyone's so rude there. You know, Pete, I went up to a newsvendor there and I asked him which was the way to a tailor's shop I'd been told about. This fellow looks at me and says: 'Drop dead, Mac. I'm not an information bureau'. But do you know, I suppose I should be grateful. At least he knew ma name."

When our filming was finished, Dickie Dawson, who was then married to my old chum Diana Dors, and who had a house in Hollywood, persuaded me to stay on with him for a week. I found it pretty depressing. Everyone seemed so cut off from everyone else. You couldn't even take the dog for a walk. Dickie and Diana had a lovely boxer, but when I took it out one day in Beverley Hills I was stopped by a police car. "Get back inside your house," said the cop. "And take the dog with you." It seemed that anyone seen walking was regarded as either mad or a mugger.

We did go out on a couple of visits, once to James Mason's house, where I was enchanted by his daughter Portland, and once to see the comedian Jack Leonard. Apart from this, the only amusement was provided by a meeting with Vic Lewis, the former bandleader, now head of NEMS Enterprises.

Vic was there in the company of one Bill Benny, a mountainous ex-wrestler, who owned Manchester's Cabaret Club, and whom I had known for years. At least my accidental meeting with them at the Knickerbocker Hotel, where they were staying, provided a few laughs.

"I don't like this place," I said to Bill, who was sitting there stripped to the waist, brown as a berry, and sweating profusely.

"No more do I," said Bill. "I reckon it's the most unhygienic place I've ever been to in my life. And I'm bored out of my bloody mind. It drives me up the bloody wall."

Something had clearly got to Bill, and I enquired about the

particular sources of his discomfort.

"Well, you know how I love crumpet," he said. "I love it, but all the bloody birds here are hookers. They're all on the game, they're all brass, and I can't stand that sort of thing. And on top of that, staying here with Vic, that drives me up the bloody creek too. He gets into the car every day and goes forty-five miles to see a sodding game of cricket. You know what he's like about bloody cricket."

I did indeed. Vic's whole life revolves around cricket. He manages to find urgent work to do in the West Indies, when they're playing cricket there, and he treats Australia the same way. Strangely, there was a lot of cricket in California. It was started by C. Aubrey Smith, and a lot of English actors played, as well as some Americans who had caught the bug.

"I think it's disgusting," said Bill. "I went to one bloody match, and not only were they wearing shorts, but they were playing stripped to the waist. That't not the way it should be done at all."

I gave a consoling sigh as Bill summed up with his definition of Los Angeles. "All the birds are brass . . . and the bleeding cricketers are all pouffs."

Bill Benny was not happy with California.

Nor was he alone. Dickie Dawson had a barber, a real Cockney who had emigrated, and who used to come over to the house to do his cutting.

"How do you like living here?" I asked him.

"Ow, it's great," he said.

"Don't you ever get homesick?"

"Naw."

"Well, what are the things you miss?"

"Tott'nam 'Otspur. Yer know, Pete, evry Sat'day artnoon rahnd abaht free o'clock English time I fink of the boys trottin' aht at White 'Art Line. Bloody beautiful. I don't arf miss that. Then there was this lovely pub in Edmonton I used ter go to. All me mates was there. I used ter love it dahn there. Great. And we used ter go to the Palladium once a month, bloody marvellous. Yer know, if it wasn't for me bleedin' wife, I'd go strite back now."

Yes, well I gathered just how much HE loved California. He might have been a Spurs fan, but on this our feelings were mutual.

Chapter Fifteen

I am not a singer.

I have had cause to mention this failing before, but I feel that I should repeat it lest there should be any who might suspect me of false modesty. Not that this is any great loss. There are plenty of other singers around without inflicting my leathery larynx upon unguarded ears.

However, in spite of this apparent handicap, I *did* do a musical. When I returned from America, my agent Peter Pritchard asked me: "How do you fancy doing a musical?"

"Don't tell me they're going to revive *Bye Bye Birdie*," I said.

"No," he said, "they're going to do a musical version of *Seagulls Over Sorrento*, and David Hughes has already been cast as Lofty. They're interested in you as Badger, the original Ronald Shiner part."

So along I went to the home of Hugh Hastings, who had not only written the original play, but the lyrics and music for the musical. There I met David, and Timothy Gray, an American actor who later wrote the lyrics for the musical version of *Blithe Spirit*, and the other leading actor, Edward Woodward.

Hugh played us the songs and I thought they were quite good, melodic and pleasant. But I was filled with tremendous doubts. I told Peter Pritchard: "I'm very worried about this. I just don't know whether this is right for me."

"There's always a time when you've got to gamble," said Peter. "You're in the gambling business, even though you don't bet on horses. You've got to take a gamble on yourself from time to time."

So I decided to back the long-shot Murray, at odds that I reckoned at about 100-1. I remember that once I had agreed, I was asked to sit in that exalted position in the stalls and watch other actors audition for the other parts, and I remember how sorry I felt for them, especially the well-known names and faces who were obviously short of work. I had been that way so often myself.

In the January of 1962 we started rehearsals for *Scapa,* as it was to be called.

That was fun in itself, and included a number of run-throughs of what was supposed to be a camp concert (and *was,* in every sense of the word) in which I appeared in drag. We also enjoyed listening to Edward, as Haggis, doing a marvellous imitation bagpipe noise with his mouth . . . he blows a neat trumpet that way, too. Edward had just come back from doing *Rattle of a Simple Man* in South Africa, and I remember that at our first meeting he was telling me what wonderful notices he'd had out there.

That's not a knocking remark. We all do it. I've done it myself in this book. But it was a reminder of the insecurity that afflicts even actors of his huge talents.

We opened the show at the Royal Court Theatre in Liverpool, where we got very good reviews, and the audience clearly loved it, because when we went into the vast lounge of the Adelphi Hotel afterwards, about 300 people who were there got up and applauded us. I thought: "This is it. I've made it. I'm actually going to make it in show business." But in my heart of hearts I knew that we still had to face the London critics.

After two weeks in Liverpool, we went to Dublin for a fortnight, at the Olympia Theatre, and here I must pause for an ARCHITECTURAL NOTE. The Olympia has now gone. But it was not demolished. Last year, as the actors went out to take a break from rehearsals, the whole place simply collapsed. This was clearly due to my previous appearance there, and I had equal fears for the Royal Court in Liverpool. Sure enough, they announced that that too was going to be demolished to make way for a supermarket.

I started a campaign on 'Open House' to save it, and with the help of some remarkable work by Ken Dodd it remains standing. But I'm keeping an eye on the situation.

Ireland was a notable experience for me because of meeting Bridget.

The Irish girls, of course, are famous for their beauty and for their infuriating habit of saying "No."

It was either David Hughes or Edward Woodward who said to me, "The ideal thing to do ... if you can possibly find one in Southern Ireland ... is to find a Protestant nymphomaniac. And there are very few of them about."

Well, I met this receptionist from a Dublin hotel. She was 28, and a lovely-looking girl, and definitely not a Protestant, and very definitely not a nymphomaniac. We had a lot of fun together, but when it came down to the nitty-gritty it was always: "No way."

About a month later, when I was back in England, she phoned me, and said: "I'm coming to London. Can I come and stay with you?" I told her that was fine by me. Whatever else happened, or didn't, I'd have been delighted to see her anyway.

As the first evening was drawing to a close, she said: "I've made a decision."

"What's that?" I asked her.

"I've decided to give myself to you."

"Oh – thanks," I said, I was lost for words.

"Before I go to bed, there's something I must do," she said.

I was trying to puzzle out what this might be, when she went to her case, took out a crucifix and a picture of the Virgin Mary, placed them on the bed, and knelt at the foot of the bed to pray for forgiveness for her impending sin.

We remained platonic friends.

After Dublin, the show opened in London at the Adelphi Theatre. We had a storming first night, with thirteen curtain calls, but the critics, as usual, suggested that we 'had the families in'. I think they also were thrown by the fact that it was an all-male show. And as I had feared, the notices were awful.

The first four weeks were disastrous, even though the company was great fun. That was really when I first became great friends with David Hughes. He had a marvellous sense of humour, and like Robert Morley was always coming out with *sotto voce* cracks during the performance.

He had been very ill, with an early heart attack, and I persuaded him to go on a very strict diet, similar to my own. Anne, his widow, still tells me that she thinks I kept him alive longer than he would have lasted otherwise.

We had some nice visitors back-stage as well. That was when I first met Eric Robinson and his lovely wife Nicky. I'd had no idea he had been in the audience. There were also the six Argentinians who came round to meet me and said: "How very strange. We expected you to be a Cockney, but you are very big gentleman."

And there was the night we did the show for charity (we were pretty well doing that every night anyway!) and Lord Mountbatten came round afterwards. He said to me: "Absolutely splendid. I assume you were a matelot?"

"No, I wasn't," I said, refraining from any further description of my military history.

"Oh, gracious me," he said, "you talk quite posh, don't you?"

But still the public wasn't coming in. So David Hughes had a brainwave. "We're not getting enough publicity for the show," he said. "We ought to do something really daring. Why don't we do a march down Whitehall."

The whole thing, of course, was totally illegal, especially as we were wearing naval uniforms without being in the remotest way connected with Her Majesty's Forces. The whole cast donned their sailor suits, with the two 'officers', a Commander and a Lieutenant, leading the march . . . well, you could hardly call it a march. A number of the chorus boys were 'mincers', and they minced their way along the stately street.

I don't think that either of our 'officers' had ever done anything in the least bit military, but as we approached Horse Guards Parade, we got a smart salute from the Lifeguard on his big black horse. To our astonishment, our 'Commander' raised his sword, saluted, and screamed: 'Eyes, Left!''

The soldier's face bore a look of total amazement. He looked amazed. His horse looked amazed. And I'm sure they were both thinking how glad they were to be in the army.

It got us publicity, but no customers, so now Jack Hylton stepped in. It was the first time I had met him, and he had the lease of the Adelphi at that time. He loved the show, and to try to save it he gave us the theatre rent-free for the second four weeks. What's more, he persuaded Val Parnell to put an excerpt from the show on the enormously popular, and influential, 'Sunday Night at the London Palladium'.

The whole cast were going to be on the programme, and then fate stepped in in the shape of my understudy, Terence Holland, who later changed his name to Terence Frisby and wrote *Girl in my Soup*. Mr Holland/Frisby got us all into an industrial dispute, since he demanded that we should all get top money for doing the television performance.

Now the fact was that Val Parnell had nothing to gain from having us on the show. It was for our benefit, since he already had Max Bygraves booked for the second half, and that was the guarantee of an audience.

I tried to talk the cast out of the dispute. "Look," I said, "if we do the 'Sunday Night at the London Palladium' we might get a few more weeks, or months, perhaps even a year. If we don't, we come off."

Holland/Frisby wouldn't listen. He looked me straight in the eyes and said: "It's all right for you. You're still doing your Luxembourg programmes. As far as we are concerned, we want the money." On reflection, perhaps he was right.

In the end they won their fight, and we did go on at the Palladium, but despite that, and Jack Hylton's marvellous help, it was all too late, and after eight weeks the show closed.

I think I lost more by the closure than most others in the cast. Everyone else had something to go to. I had lost all my TV shows because of appearing in the theatre, and in addition I had fallen out with the BBC. When the show started I had been doing 'Pete's Party' on Tuesday nights. The Press interviewed me and asked what would happen to the programme. I said: "The BBC have agreed that I can record them." In fact they hadn't. They had merely agreed that if there were odd occasions when I couldn't do the programme live, they would let me record it, a very different thing from a regular arrangement. They took a dim view of it, and I lost the programme.

Most important of all, I had lost my personal gamble, my chance to get out of the rut, and away from the 'Disc-Jockey Pete Murray' image. I have always hated being described as a DJ, and I really believe that as far as show business is concerned, it's the lowest common denominator.

I had had a salutary reminder of this shortly after I came back from America, when I went over to Paris to see a play. I was sitting in a boulevard café, and English people kept coming up and asking for my autograph.

A French waiter asked some English people at a nearby table: "Er, excuse me, but could you tell me what this gentleman does for a living? Is 'e very famous?"

"It's Pete Murray," they said.

"Oo is 'e? What does 'e do? Is 'e a singer? Is 'e an actor?"

"He's a disc jockey," they told him.

"A disc jockey? What is a disc jockey?"

"Well, he plays records on the radio," they explained.

His face was a picture. That anyone should want the autograph of a man who played records on radio was totally beyond his comprehension. He wandered off shaking his head and muttering: "Les Anglais ... les Anglais." And I didn't really blame him.

In an attempt to patch up the pieces of my meandering career, Peter Pritchard now told me that they were going to do a musical version of *Pickwick,* and that he thought I would be right for the part of Mr Jingle. Musicals hadn't exactly been a roaring success for me so far, but it was work, and I went for an audition in front of the producer, Peter Coe.

I did a Paddy Roberts number, and when I had finished he said: "That was fantastic. Wonderful. I've never heard anything better." For one blissful moment I though he was referring to my performance. But no. It was the Paddy Roberts song he loved. As to my performance, let's just say that I didn't get the part.

But I did get a part in another Michael Winner film, *The Cool Mikado,* a modern adaptation of the Gilbert and Sullivan piece. I only had a small part, and remember little of what it was about, except for the leopard.

The leopard was name Chiefy, and he was somehow involved with a lady named Jacqueline Jones. The leopard was in a cage, and the technicians were standing round about the cage, and Michael informed me that the leopard was tame, and, knowing I like animals, invited me to go into the cage with the leopard.

The leopard was lying on its back. "Go on, stroke its tummy," said Michael Winner. "Don't worry, it's tame." I advanced towards the recumbent leopard and gingerly ran a hand along the said tummy. The leopard looked at me, looked at my hand, roared, and bit me. I bled.

176

I was not happy with this leopard.

Nor was I happy with Michael Winner. He had become rather brittle, hard, and temperamental, and by the time the shooting of this terrible film was completed, the crew weren't all that happy with him either.

During the party at the end, they arranged for him to be manoeuvred into a certain spot where a bucket of water was emptied over him and his new mohair suit. I think he took it quite well, but I was never invited to work for him again.

I did however get back on to television in a programme for Granada called 'Spot the Tune'. It had been going for about seven years, with a number of different compères, and was produced by Johnny Hamp, an enormously talented character who was later to be the originator of 'The Comedians' and 'The Wheeltappers and Shunters Social Club'. It was a musical quiz programme with a great deal of involvement with members of the public, and I loved it. It was one of the very few programmes where I have been able to be myself.

In fact, the only thing that ever went wrong, as far as I was concerned, was when Johnny Hamp passed on a note he had had from Sidney Bernstein, the head of Granada. It said: "Murray was wearing a handkerchief in his top pocket on the show tonight. Will you please tell him not to do this again, as this is now decidedly non-U. Handkerchiefs are no longer being worn in top pockets."

Well, who was I to argue with Mr Bernstein's little sartorial tips? The handkerchief disappeared thenceforward. If it seemed a bit pernicketty, there was another side to the man. He has a private plane which he uses to commute between London and Manchester. And if the plane happens to be going, and there's a spare seat, he lets anybody use it ... plumber, carpenter, secretary or star.

Sadly, 'Spot the Tune' was to be yet another instance in my life where I've felt really happy doing something, only to have it pulled from under my feet. I didn't realise it when I took it on, but it was already in its death throes. The Government and the ITA had decided that give-away programmes were immoral, and that the winning of a few pounds on quiz programmes would corrupt the nation in a way that pools wins of hundreds of thousands would not.

So, after a run of nine weeks, I escorted 'Spot the Tune' to the demolition site. And the Chelsea Palace, from where it went out ... well, need I say?

It was, one way and another, time for a rest, and I took Michael down to Cannes, in the South of France, to stay at the Bleu Rivage, our favourite haunt. It was to be one of my more fateful decisions, but I had had the offer to take over from Bob Monkhouse in Neil Simon's *Come Blow Your Horn,* and I wanted the chance to read the part in peace.

One of the other guests at the Bleu Rivage was a vivacious and dark-haired beauty from Marseilles, whose name, I was to discover, was Michelle. She was also staying there with her son. I remember noticing these flashing eyes, the first night we dined there, and I remarked to Michael that I thought she was rather lovely.

"Yes," he said, with the private perception unique in ten year-olds, "and I think she's flashing her eyes at you, Dad."

"Oh no, I'm sure she's not," I said, unconvinced, and unconvincing. The fact was that she was a stunner, and that I felt overwhelmed by her personality. Yet there was something not quite right about her.

"She's nice," I said to Michael by way of voicing my thoughts aloud, "but I think she's a bit potty."

"You could be right," he said, with the air of a man who knows all about these things.

Now one of my rules when taking Michael on holiday had always been not to get involved in any heavy flirtations. Apart from anything else, I didn't want him to get complexes about Germaine and me, though of course he knew we were living apart, and in fact our divorce was in the legal pipe-line.

But I couldn't help thinking about this lady. To cap it all, it was a question of 'love her dog, love her,' because she had this Alsatian called Ula, who was so gentle that once, when I saw her attacked by a couple of wild cats, she simply lifted her head and walked away. I was mad about that dog.

Getting to talk to Michelle was another thing. I have never been the type of man who could go up to a girl and say: "I fancy you," or: "You're lovely". I'm always terrified I'm going to be turned down. But help was at hand.

A few months earlier I had been interviewed, for the Daily Express, by a young journalist called Jeremy Hornsby. We had become friends, and as it happened that he too had planned his holiday in the South of France, we had arranged to meet.

One afternoon I was lying on the beach gazing across far too much sand at the lovely Michelle, when Jeremy appeared. After the usual salutations, I told him the situation.

"Hang on," he said, "I'll see what I can do."

Thereupon he got up, walked across the beach to the lady in question, and without any unnecessary formalities declared: "Mon ami vous aime." I felt it was a remarkably frank speech on my behalf.

"Oh," said Michelle. What else could she say? And we met. In view of what happened subsequently, I think it is a testimony to my forgiving nature that I invited Jeremy to help me with this book. I was never done a worse turn than that introduction.

For the rest of that holiday, Michelle and I spent a great deal of time together, albeit platonically. Apart from Michael's presence, the South of France always makes me very sleepy anyway. But we had a great time, at the Sporting Club in Monte Carlo, at little intimate cafés, and on the beach. Michelle owned a restaurant in Paris, and was also an aspiring singer, and it seemed that she knew, and was respected by, everyone that we met in the South of France.

When the time came for us to leave, she drove us to the airport at Nice, and as we were waving goodbye Michael turned to me and made another of his unnervingly precocious prophecies: "I don't think that's the last you're going to hear of her."

Two days later, she phoned me from Marseilles, to say that she was coming to Paris in a week's time, and why didn't I join her? I thought this was a rather romantic idea, so I agreed, and the following weekend she met me at Le Bourget, looking stunning, and kissed me on the cheek, which nearly made me faint, not from ardour but from odour … she had consumed a vast quantity of garlic.

She had a very pleasant flat, furnished heavily in the style of Louis-I-can't-remember-which-number-it-was. I sat down and found myself wondering what on earth I was doing there, with this woman whom I liked but didn't really fancy. As this was going through my mind, she put a record on the gramophone. It was David Hughes singing 'True Love', and I chuckled to myself at what David would have said, had he known.

Whether it was the influence of the Hughes tenor tonsils I don't know, but from that moment the relationship blossomed, and we started seeing each other every weekend, either in London or Paris. On top of that, I was invited back into the bosom of the BBC, doing an evening programme called 'Pop to Bed with Pete Murray'. In those non-permissive days, I had to give Michelle a rather detailed explanation of why it was called that.

I remember taking the chance to play a request on my own account. I told Michelle over the air: "Si tu écoute en Paris, chérie, c'est pour toi." The record was Tony Bennett's 'I left my heart in San Francisco', the first time I had ever played it, and whenever I play it now I can't help thinking of that first time.

That Christmas, I got the offer of presenting a programme called 'London Lights', a radio variety programme in which I did a regular sketch with Joan Sims. Michelle would often come over and sit in while we were doing the show, and everyone concerned with it thought she was enchanting. I seemed to spend all my time translating for her, and especially when there was a film on TV. That was the most exhausting TV watching I ever had in my life. But I had equally to thank her, because she taught me to speak French fluently in a way that Buster Reed, and later the tutorial discs of Assimil, had singularly failed to do.

We had a lot of stars on the programme, and I remember one occasion when Lita Roza turned up in the company of a young man whom I took to be her boy friend. In fact, he was a comedian who had been booked for the show.

He was so good and so funny, that they booked him for a second week, and I got on to the Grade Organisation straight away. "You've just got to come and see him," I told them. "He is going to be a star, no doubt about it." They promised to come along the following week.

The morning after they had been, I phoned them. "Did you see him?" I asked.

"Yes, but he'll never be anything," they said.

"You're joking. He's going to be a star," I insisted.

"Pete, forget it. We're agents. We know the business," they said.

The name of that young comedian was Dave Allen.

180

That was a hard and wicked winter in every way. The weather was bitter, which meant that instead of getting audiences of 400, as we should have done, only about 25 struggled through the rain and snow to get to the studio.

Any comedian will tell you that comedy is amost impossible without a good audience to react with. And if you have only a handful, even they are self-conscious about laughing. My big comedy chance with 'London Lights' went down the drain with the flood waters.

And the romance started to go the same way. One day I came home to the flat unexpectedly early. Michelle, who was staying with me, had gone out to the shops or somewhere, and on the table was a letter she was writing to someone in France. I suppose I should have ignored it, but there it was, and I read it. It was to a man, and it was all about how she had met this nice English boy, and that there was a possibility of marriage, but that he shouldn't worry, because things would still be the same between them. It was quite clearly a letter to a sugar-daddy.

I said nothing, and soon after this we went to the Spastics Ball at Grosvenor House, taking Jeremy Hornsby and his girl-friend as our guests. Half-way through the evening, I went over and asked Jill Browne, a very old friend, for a dance, in the middle of which, right in front of everyone and with no secrecy about it, I gave a her a friendly kiss.

When I got back to our table, Michelle was gone. "Where's she disappeared to?" I asked Jeremy.

"I don't know," he said. "She suddenly took off without any explanation. I thought you would know."

Well I didn't, but I soon found out. She had gone home in an insane fit of jealousy, and when I came in she threw four pairs of shoes, a standard lamp, and various other items in my direction, following which she collapsed on to the floor and frothed at the mouth.

I now realised that I had a problem. She had previously started to display elements of jealousy, and had once told me: "If ever you treat me badly, I'll ruin your career." The many good times we had had were starting to get more and more clouded by possessiveness. Every time the phone rang, even if it was only my agent, she though I was making an assignation with another woman.

I decided to try to cool things off, but I was still seeing her, and

181

things were getting more and more sticky when, early in May, it all came to a horrible head.

I was again due to take over from Bob Monkhouse in the play *Come Blow Your Horn,* and was busy rehearsing with the rest of the cast, Michael Crawford, David Kossoff, Shirley Eaton and Libby Morris. Michelle had been getting more and more impossible, hovering over my phone calls, reading all my mail and so on, and finally, early in the afternoon of the Friday on which I was due to take over, I said: "Michelle, it just can't go on like this."

"You mean you want us to finish?" she asked.

"I've got to be honest with you," I said, "but I just can't go on. I'm a living wreck. I can't take it."

"Very well, c'est bien." she said, and walked into the kitchen.

Suddenly I heard the words: "Ça y est. C'est fait." There was something about the way she had said them, and I got up and hurried to the kitchen door to meet her coming back into the living room, laughing maniacally, with blood pouring in all directions from the two great slits she had made in her wrists with a kitchen knife.

Total terror overtook me. I had no idea how long it would take for someone to die after cutting their wrists. It could have been straight away for all I knew. At the back of my mind was the sudden realisation that it was three o'clock and that my first night at the theatre was in four hours time. And at the front of my mind, ludicrously, was the question of how I was going to get the bloodstains out of the carpet.

As the antidote to all these problems I dialled 999. A girl answered.

"I want an ambulance quickly," I said, "My address is 31, Montagu Mansions, London, W.1." Formal, but efficient, I thought.

"What is the nature of your enquiry?" asked the girl.

"Look darling," I pleaded, "this is a matter of life and death. For Christ's sake get me an ambulance."

"I must know the reason for it, and what it's all about," said this 'emergency' operator. I was surprised she didn't ask for my reply in triplicate.

"Somebody's dying," I shouted. "For God's sake, get an ambulance."

"I'm sorry, I can't unless ... " I slammed the phone down.

Michelle was laughing hysterically, and I thought she was about to die on the spot. I forced her out of the flat, and down to the hall floor, where I knew a woman who was a beautician. I thought somehow that she might have some medical knowledge. She came to the door, took one look at Michelle, who was lying bleeding all over the hallway, and screamed.

At this all the ladies who were in the process of beautification came rushing out. "Help me. Help me. Help me," I shouted, illogically. What I meant was "Help Michelle". They got the message and bandaged her up, and in the middle of this utter confusion who should turn up to see me but my old friend Leslie Conn. Poor, dear, innocent Leslie Conn.

"Hello Pete . . . oh my God, what's happened?"

"We've got to get her to hospital, Leslie." It was no time for formal explanation.

"I've got a car outside," he said. "I'll see if I can find a policeman."

In about ninety seconds flat he returned, with a bobby in tow. We got her into the car, a convertible, and the policeman said he would have to come with us, so we pushed back the hood, upon which he sat, promptly breaking it. I jumped in on the outside of Michelle, who was still laughing in this terrifying way, and Leslie jumped into the driver's seat and roared away down Marylebone High Street at about 60 mph, on the wrong side of the road. The fierce acceleration briskly removed the policeman's helmet, which was lost beneath the wheels of oncoming traffic.

We skidded up to the front door of the London Clinic, and I dragged Michelle out of the car and up the steps. She was a handful. I turned to look for help from Leslie, but what was he doing? Buying a bunch of flowers.

"What on earth are you doing?" I shouted down to him.

"I'm buying some flowers for her," said the thoughtful Leslie.

"You've got to be raving mad," I yelled. "If you're going to get anything it'll have to be a wreath. Help me get her in."

Together we struggled with the berserk and bleeding Michelle into the wealthy portals of the London Clinic. "We don't take casualties. You'll have to take her to the Middlesex Hospital," they said.

So we leapt back down to the car, which by now had attracted a convoy of not one but two ambulances. It later turned out that my 999 call had had some effect, but that the two drivers had had an argument about who was going to come, so they both came. Now a further argument began on the pavement, upon which Michelle was bleeding what, as far as I was concerned, were the last drops in her body.

"For Christ's sake don't argue about who's going to take her," I snapped at them. "Just put her in one and get her down there straight away. I'll follow in the car." So off we rushed, like the Keystone Cops, to the Middlesex, where she was admitted.

Leslie, the policeman, and I were put into a quiet waiting room, while the doctors set about repairing Michelle's gaping wrists. Then a nurse came in and told us she was going to be all right, whereupon the policeman decided that that would be a suitable moment for him to adopt his official posture. Out came his book.

"Now sir, I think I'd better make a few notes. Could I have your name please ... "

After I had given him the details of the preceding events, he said: "You think you've got troubles?"

"What do you mean?" I asked him.

"Troubles," he said. "It's me that's got troubles. I'll tell you something. I was just going for a quiet cuppa when your friend rushed up and said: 'There's a woman dying,' so of course I automatically rushed back with him."

"So what's the problem about that?" I asked.

"It's not my area, is it? It's not my manor. I was going for my nice cuppa in a place I wasn't supposed to be." At this, he seemed to be on the point of tears. "And what's more," he added, "I've lost me 'elmet."

I started to commiserate with him. I mean, what was a dying woman compared with these disasters? Then he turned to Leslie. "May I have your name too, please sir." Leslie gave it to him.

"I'm very sorry sir," said this tragic copper, "but I'm going to have to have you up for dangerous driving."

Looking back, it was the final element of total farce, but at the time my legs and arms were like jelly. Peter Pritchard came to the hospital and sat with Michelle for a while, then took me to the theatre. Somehow he managed to get me sufficiently together to do the show, and afterwards smuggled me out past an army of pressmen waiting outside. I stayed the night with Uncle Bill in Chelsea.

The following morning, David Hughes rang me.

"'Pete, you must be going through absolute hell,'' he said. "We've seen the papers. Why don't you come and stay with Anne and me out at Elstree tonight?" I was very grateful. I knew Michelle was all right, and I had no desire to see her or have anything to do with her.

That evening, David picked me up after the show. An ex-music publisher I knew was sitting in the front of the car, and in the back, next to me, was a man who was fidgetting like mad. I thought there was something a bit peculiar about him.

We dropped them both off on the way, and when we got to Elstree, David said: "I don't know, you'll probably think I'm mad, but what do you feel about clairvoyance?"

"Well, I don't sneer at anything," I said. "But I've never had any particular dealings with it."

"Well," said David, "the fellow who was sitting next to you works for a branch of the police force. He's also a clairvoyant. He was watching you on television a few weeks ago, and said that he thought something terrible was going to happen to you, and that he wanted to help when it did happen. Would you be interested in talking to him?"

"Sure," I said. "I'll ring him next week."

I stayed the weekend with David and Anne, and arranged over the phone for Michelle to be moved to the Harley Street Nursing Home. On the Monday I visited her, and felt full of remorse, and sorry for her, looking so terribly weak in bed there. Luckily, I had Peter Pritchard, who is tougher and more logical than I am, to remind me of what had happened. "If you ever go back to that woman after what she's tried to do to you, as far as I'm concerned I don't want to handle you any more." It was a very serious thing for him to say, and it brought me up sharp.

The following weekend I got a friend of mine to pick up Michelle from the nursing home, and we drove her to the house of a girl she had once helped, when she was in Marseilles, and who was now living on the outskirts of London. Michelle was in a very strange mood, and when the woman went out, saying she was going to get some food, Michelle said: "You don't love me any more, do you?"

My silence spoke for itself.

185

"Well, obviously there is no future for us," she went on, "so I think we ought to come to a business arrangement."

"What on earth do you mean by that?" I asked.

"I mean that we either go on, or I want two million new francs in compensation."

"You've got to be joking," I said. "Where would I find that kind of money?"

"You've got friends. You can find it."

"My friends aren't *that* friendly," I said, shaken.

"If you don't," she said, "I will make a scandal."

"What do you have in the way of making a scandal?" I asked.

"I will give my story to the newspapers."

At this point her friend came back and made lunch. I had an early evening matinée, and a late evening performance to do that night, and I felt sick to the bottom of my stomach. But I ate an enormous meal, not through hunger, but to give the impression that I wasn't worried. But I was.

On the one hand, I reckoned that she had no real claim for 'compensation', since we had never lived together. She had mentioned 'loss of face', and the fact that she had been neglecting her Paris business because of me, but I knew that it was only a very small restaurant, and she had managers in anyway. Against all this I had to balance the fact that she was appearing to be a totally unreasonable woman.

Michelle watched me eating. "You don't seem to be very worried by all this," she said.

"What should I worry about?" I asked.

"I'll give you plenty to worry about," she said.

I decided to phone David's clairvoyant friend for help, but the phone was answered by the ex-music publisher, who shared a flat with him.

"Look, I've got a bit of a problem," I said. "Can I speak to your friend?"

"No, Pete, I'm afraid he's away on a case at the moment," he said. "But I'll come round and see you this evening, because he foresaw all this."

Between the two shows that evening he came to my dressing room. "Don't tell me what's happened. I'll tell you," he said.

"How do you mean?" I asked.

"Well last week, after we were in that car and he was sitting next to you, when we got out he said: 'If you think Pete Murray's got problems now, it's nothing to what he'll be having this time next week. And I'll be hearing from him.'"

"Well, what else did say?" I asked.

"He just used one word ... 'blackmail'."

Of course, it wasn't blackmail. Michelle had been in a vengeful mood, and was after what she thought at the time were her rights. But it was so close to what had happened that I made an appointment to see the clairvoyant the following day.

"Your immediate reaction is to give this woman money because you feel sorry for her," he told me. "But whatever you do, you must not give her anything at all. I see a warning about this quite clearly."

I took his advice. Shortly afterwards, I was watching the 1963 Cup Final on TV when I had a call from a reporter on The People.

"Oh, sorry to trouble you this afternoon, Mr Murray," he said, "but we have an article from a lady who purports to be a friend of yours. It's the lady who attempted suicide in your flat, named Michelle. She has written an article about you. Would you like to comment on it?"

"I have no comment, no comment whatsoever, nothing that I wish to say," I told him.

It really wasn't as bad as it might have been, when it came out. She was quoted as saying: "I was in love with Peter. I thought he loved me. I hoped that he would marry me when he is free (my divorce from Germaine still wasn't finalised). I wouldn't have given up so much in France, if I hadn't believed that.

"But when one day I realised he didn't want me, all my illusions were shattered. A couple of days later I picked up a kitchen knife and cut my wrists. I don't know why I did it. It certainly wasn't for love of Peter. Not any more."

Well, that was her side of it. Now I have told mine. After the article appeared I never saw her again, but had one vitriolic letter in which she virtually wished me and my family to hell, a letter of damnation for me, my son, my mother, the lot. Very unpleasant.

I went to a solicitor and put the whole matter in his hands, and Michelle was advised to leave the country quietly, which she did.

I was not happy about this episode in my life, in spite of its funny moments. But it taught me enough GREAT LESSONS to last for years.

Chapter Sixteen

I am not a sex-maniac.

I thought that I should make this plain lest my clear preference for 'Yes' rather than 'No', and the occasional little anecdotes which have crept into this narrative, should make readers think otherwise.

On the other hand, my parents could have been forgiven, when I was still very young, for having their suspicions.

I was six. Pamela was blonde, and beautiful, and four. We used to go for family outings to Bournemouth, five or six families and all the relatives, piled into convoys of cars to descend upon the defenceless beaches.

One evening, on the return to London, the leaders of the convoy decided to stop for a drink and a bite to eat at some wayside pub, and Pamela and I were left outside, in her family's car, and to our own devices.

I remember it like yesterday. She started talking about her cousin. This made me very jealous, even though the cousin in question was a mere six months old. And my reaction was to initiate an immediate and involved session of kissing and cuddling with the adorable Pamela. I was very sorry when the family hordes returned from the pub.

It was time to go. My mother, as she always did, to my infuriation insisted that I kiss Pamela goodbye. Now, public displays were not my idea of a good thing. I was very much a consenting infant in private. So I protested.

"Well, why not?" demanded my little blonde bombshell. "After all, you've been kissing me in the car all the time they were gone."

My humiliation was absolute.

Thirty years later, the early suspicions of all things feminine, thus-founded, were confirmed by the Michelle affair, I had no desire at all to adopt the usually-prescribed antidote of rushing out and finding another woman to console me for love lost. Instead, I did a play for ABC TV, with the incredibly apt title, *Jezebel. Ex-UK.*

In this I played an Australian con-man, the husband of Heather Sears, but I attracted less attention for my portrayal of the role than for the question of what I was to be called. The play's producer considered that I should be Peter Murray, rather than Pete. I thought about this, and knowing that 'Lucky Stars' was shortly going to begin, I thought it would be ridiculous to be Peter for one and Pete for the other – not that I cared what I was called.

Finally I agreed to revert to my mother's original choice, but by then the producer had sent the billing to the TV Times, and I appeared in that as Pete, whereas 'Lucky Stars', where Pete was much more suitable, had heard of my reversion and called me Peter. It couldn't have been more of a mix-up.

This piece of nonsense seemed to attract more interest in the press than any of my more serious activities. Douglas Marlborough of the Daily Mail rang up and asked me why I had changed my name. "What *do* you mean?" I asked him.

"Well, why do you call yourself Peter after all these years?"

I explained, but I think the impression still got out that I was being rather snooty, though Peter Chambers, of the Daily Express, wrote one of his typically funny pieces in which he referred to Dick Dimbleby and so on. He signed it Pete Chambers, I remember.

Tony Newley became Anthony Newley. Johnny Dankworth went back to John Dankworth. Nobody minded. But poor old Pete Murray went back to Peter and it was a national crisis! It all got very complicated, and I even turned down a commercial because they insisted I should be Pete Murray. Peter Pritchard said I was raving mad. But I said: "Look, I've just made a statement about this silly business, and I'll look a complete idiot if I go back to Pete just because I'm recommending some gramophone. I'd look a total phoney." Eric Robinson got that job.

But it was a losing battle, as Anna Instone pointed out to me when the BBC brought back 'Pete's Party'. "We can't call it Peter's Party, *can* we," she said. In the end I just settled for Pete . . . permanently.

My other memory of that play was a little matter of manipulation. During my stay at Towerleaze, in the early throes of hepatitis, I had become interested in osteopathy, and I had discovered that I had a certain aptitude in that direction.

One afternoon, I noticed that the actor Emrys Jones, who was also in the play, was holding his neck to one side and was clearly in pain... I could not resist the challenge.

"Emrys," I said, "I'm just going to have to do it for you."

"Do what?" he asked, in some alarm.

I explained, and he succumbed to some gentle massage around the offending neck, at which he murmured:

"Lovely. That's lovely." At that moment I clicked the neck back into place, there was a loud crack which must have been audible half-way across the set, and everybody in the dressing room went rigid.

The reason they went rigid was the scream which Emrys uttered, a scream so diabolical that the Teddington Studios security men came rushing in, under the certain assumption that some one had been murdered, for real. After about half an hour of some discomfort, he told me happily − and I was happy to hear it − that all the pain had gone.

There were a couple of other notable occasions when I performed this little piece of manipulative magic. One was in a tube train. I saw this man in obvious pain − on the Piccadilly Line, as it happens − and offered him my help.

"Where would you do it?" he asked.

"Well," I said, "Covent Garden Station is very quiet. Why don't we get off there?"

He had no idea who I was, but he must have been a very trusting soul, because sure enough he got off at Covent Garden, where I did the next trick. The cry that echoed down the tunnel is still ringing down to Hounslow West, I reckon.

The other scream occurred at a Royal Film Premiere. June Thorburn, who was sitting just in front of me, was in obvious discomfort, and just as I was putting the rick to rights, the Queen entered, to be greeted by the scream. I swear the royal tiara trembled just a touch.

It was soon after the Michelle debacle that I acquired myself a personal manager to supplement the services of my agent. I had managed to get the bloodstains out of the carpet, and a month or so later my divorce from Germaine was finalised. Now I really wanted to see if my emancipation, together with the restoration of my proper name, could bring me some work in the theatre.

The man chosen to help me in this task was Clive Sharp, an old friend of mine, and it was to him that I turned for advice when Johnny Stewart of the BBC, with whom I had worked ten years earlier, came to me in 1964 with an idea for a new pop programme to be called 'Top of the Pops'.

Clive was in Rome at the time, and I called him there.

"What do you think, Clive?" I asked. "Do you think this is going to be the nail in the coffin of my acting career?"

He was inclined to think that it might be, but was not prepared to advise me one way or the other.

"You should really turn it down," he said, "but in the end it's up to you."

So I took it, not without considerable misgivings. But then, I had to live, and fancy ambitions don't pay the gas bills. I kept thinking of a conversation I had had when I sat next to film-director Ken Annakin at a dinner.

"I read in the papers that you want to act, and that you don't want to go on doing what you are doing at the moment," he said.

"That's quite right," I said.

"Well then, you must give it all up," he said calmly.

I told him that I would like to, and he then went on to say that he had seen me in *The Last Enemy*. "I'm amazed you're not acting now," he said. "You must give everything else up, because people won't take you seriously while you're doing these other things."

"That's all very well," I told him, "but I was out of work for ten months trying not to spoil the image of *The Last Enemy*. How many films have you made since that came out?"

"Oh, about eight or nine," he replied.

"And you liked my performance in *The Last Enemy*?"

"Yes, I did. That was why I asked to sit next to you at this dinner."

"So," I said, "you've made eight or nine films in that time, Ken, and you've been kind enough to say that you liked my performance as Richard Hillary. So you respect me as an actor, apparently. But you never asked me to appear in any of those eight or nine films, did you?"

To that, as Morecambe and Wise would say, there was no answer. The whole business was giving me a gigantic chip on my shoulder.

But I was saved from total inundation in pop. After I had agreed to do 'Top of the Pops', they told me that they were going to switch from the original plan of having me every week, and that instead I would alternate with David Jacobs, Alan Freeman, and Jimmy Savile. I don't know if they thought I would be disappointed, but I was really quite relieved.

The relief was short-lived. I was promptly booked to do a sort of magazine rock-and-roll show for Scottish TV. Together with 'Top of the Pops', and my Luxembourg programmes for Decca and Clark's Shoes, this was starting to mean a good deal of travelling. To cap it all, Grundig came up with the German connection.

They wanted me to do a show for them for Luxembourg. But for some reason, it was to be recorded at the Star Club in Hamburg. Life became one long travelogue. I would finish 'Twelve O'Clock Spin' for the BBC at 12.30, catch a plane at 1.30 for Amsterdam, change there for Hamburg, and get to the Star Club at about 5.0.

There the problems started. We would have to record various groups for the show and speak to them in German, a facility I lacked. I made up my mind to repair this deficiency, and turned to my old friends, the Assimil organisation. This time, all I achieved was derisive laughter at my guttural grunts.

I think everyone has some pet phrase from their early attempts to learn languages. My first gem from my grappling with the tongue Teutonic was: "Otto Schmidt soll sein gramophon bringen, und Ich habe meine Flöte." This, roughly translated, means that Otto Smith will bring his gramophone and I have my flute.

The Germans are a musical nation, of course, and doubtless this had been designed by the linguists as a typical introduction to a gay evening of operatic highlights. But it wasn't quite right for the Grundig show.

(It is quite irrelevant, but I have to add that the equivalent phrase I learned in my attempts at Spanish was: "The Spanish railway tracks are much wider than the French." At least, that was what I was *told* the phrase meant. I tried it out one day on a girl in order to impress her with my command of her language, and her reply was to slap my face.)

To continue the travelogue, these awful programmes, done under appalling conditions and against the noisy onslaughts of a mass of yobby German kids, would end at two in the morning, and I would gratefully sink into my hotel bed. I mention this only because Hamburg is noted for more convivial delights, such as the Winkelstrasse, where all the girls sit in the windows advertising their wares. I had walked down there on one of my first visits, and thought that the whole place, blocked off from traffic, looked rather like a giant toilet.

I was with friends, and had no desire to experience the above-mentioned delights, but I must admit to some chagrin that not once was I accosted. I was rather insulted. I thought that at least out of courtesy someone would accost me. Not a one. I obviously looked the mean type.

So at ten the following morning, my sleep uncluttered by Rhine-maidens, I would leap aboard the plane for London, change at the airport, and get another plane to Glasgow, where I would do the Scottish rock-and-roll fiesta, then hop another plane to Manchester for 'Top of the Pops', which went out at the same time. In between whiles, I had to record the Luxembourg programmes. Seldom in the field of broadcasting has one man rushed around so much to achieve so little!

But it did look as though I was going to achieve one life-long ambition. I'd always had this great longing to be a cowboy and act in a Western, and suddenly, out of the blue, I got this letter from MGM in Hollywood, on their splendidly-headed notepaper.

"Dear Mr Murray," they wrote. "We have seen shots of you in one of your television programmes, and we think that you have the sort of face we would like to use. In fact, you are just right for a particular Western we are planning to make, which has the part of an Englishman in it.

"If it would be convenient to you, we would be most grateful if you could get fitted out in a cowboy outfit from one of the London theatrical costumiers and have pictures taken and sent to us, preferably

194

on a horse, if that would be possible."

If that would be possible! My wildest wild western dreams about to materialise, I went hot-foot to Berman's for the gear, and took it out to Stanmore, where I had some photos taken aboard some prancing palfrey from the stables.

The pictures I immediately despatched to the celluloid city. The reply came back a few days later – "You'll never make it, kid. Love, Dickie." It was Dickie Dawson, in whom I had confided my secret longing. For once, it was I who had been well and truly had.

On the other hand, I really did get into Madame Tussauds that year. They were doing a mock-up of 'Juke Box Jury', with David Jacobs, Arthur Askey, Cilla Black and one other.

The modelling was quite fun, but I never had the nerve to go and see my effigy. And now I never will. Madame Tussauds remains; the Murray model has been demolished, melted down a couple of years later at the same time as Harold Wilson, who had, I think, fallen from power. Fame, brief fame, and at last I knew the meaning of the phrase "waxing and waning".

My appearance in wax caused rather less comment than my appearance at that time in a commercial for the aperitif Noilly Prat, a name which carried its own problems. The advertisers insisted that I pronounce it "Noily" rather than, as the French would do, "Noyi". They said that they thought the British public would not understand it the proper way. So I suggested that they should go the whole hog and call it "Noily Pratt".

They did not take kindly to my suggestion.

The commotion, however, occurred because I had done it at all. A Sunday paper's newshound, convinced that he had found the scoop of the sixties, rang me up.

"You don't drink," he informed me.

"I am grateful for the information, but I am aware of that fact," I said.

"Well, why then have you done a drinks commercial?" he demanded triumphantly, pinioning my ear to the phone.

I tried patience. "If you care to listen to the jingle," I told him, "you will hear that it says, 'When Pete meets his friends, he offers them a Noilly Prat'."

"Yes," he persisted, "but you don't drink."

"For the second time, you are correct," I said. "But does it not cross your mind that I am not saying that I do drink it? Nor do I. But I am teetotal, not temperance. And I always offer people a drink, whether it be Dubonnet, or Scotch, or Noilly Prat."

The telephonic sleuth slunk from the line, but of course a story still appeared, twisted as far as the laws of libel would allow. It was a very silly fuss, though as a matter of interest, I should add that there are many commercials I would *not* do. And I have missed out on a lot because of it. I wouldn't do aspirins, for example, and I have refused beer ads. That's mainly because I won't have anything to do with a commercial where I was involved in being seen to drink. Except for lemonade. I am, I can now reveal, a secret lemonade drinker.

So that it was in lemonade that I toasted the New Year of 1965 in Norman Newell's flat at Montagu Mansions. His flat was bigger than mine so we always used to have parties there, and he certainly did us proud. The situation suited me well, because, having no desire to greet the New Year in total intoxication, I could slop along there in my carpet slippers, see the New Year in, and pop back to bed. Very convenient.

The first thing to celebrate that year was a guest spot in the Arthur Haynes Show. I liked Arthur very much, and I enjoyed the show especially, because it was written by Johnny Speight, the creator of Alf Garnett. I had a straight part, as a doctor, but still got a lot of laughs because of the brilliance of Speight's scripts. I think that a lot of British comedy is an insult to the public, because the laughs depend on the removal of trousers, or jokes about lavatories. We need more of Speight's type of straight comedy.

In fact, Johnny Speight might well have written the saga of Leslie Conn's nose.

Leslie Conn, my dear friend Leslie Conn, he of the bouquet and the dangerous driving (he got off with a warning, by the way) has what you might call a rather large hooter, an extremely preponderant proboscis.

I was having lunch with Leslie one day when, merely upon some mischievous impulse, I said: "Leslie, you look upon me as a friend, don't you?"

"Yes, indeed I do, Peter," he said.

"Well, would you mind if I were terribly personal?" I said.

"No, not at all."

"You would take it from me?" I persisted.

"Yes, of course I would. Now, what is it?" he asked.

"Leslie," I said, "it's your nose."

"My nose?"

"Yes," I said. "Your nose."

"What's wrong with my nose?" demanded Leslie, waving the fearsome feature in my direction. "It's the only nose where you can smoke a cigarette, go under the shower, and come out with the cigarette still dry."

"That's as may be," I said, "but you can't go around with a nose like that for the rest of your life. It gives you a terrible complex. You walk around with your nose in your hand all the time."

"I do not," he said in an aggrieved tone. "And there's nothing wrong with my nose."

"Now, I'm only speaking as a friend," I said. "It's just that I think that you ought to have your nose done."

I was joking, of course, and there I thought the matter of this brontosaurian breather would drop. I was wrong. Three days later I got a phone call from him.

"Pete?" Leslie talks in this very brisk manner.

"Yes, who's that?"

"Leslie."

"Oh, hello Leslie, how are you?"

"I'm going in, you know," he said.

"I beg your pardon," I said, having no idea what he was talking about.

"I'm going in," he repeated,

"Into what are you going?"

"Into hospital, of course."

"What's the matter?" I asked, starting to worry for the health of my old chum.

"There's nothing wrong with *me*," he said proudly.

"Well what on earth are you going into hospital for?"

"I'm going to have my nose done."

The penny dropped the proverbial clang. "Oh my God, are you really?" I said, horrified by this development.

"Yes," said Leslie cheerfully. "And you know what?"

"What?" I asked, in dread.

"Well, I've had a word with my sister, and she's going to have hers done as well."

"Well, congratulations" I said, somewhat inadequately.

Two or three weeks later, I had been abroad, and as I arrived back at Heathrow I happened to bump into a friend of mine.

"Here, have you heard about Leslie Conn?" he asked me.

"What about him?" I said.

"He's in hospital."

"Yes, I know," I said, "he's been in there to have his nose done."

"But haven't you heard what's happened?"

"No, what is it?" I asked, with foreboding.

"They've found out he's got haemophilia."

"Oh my God," I said, aware that the situation had escalated beyond reason. I hurried home and phoned the hospital, who told me that he was under sedation. But first thing the following morning I was woken by the phone. A sort of muffled moan came down the line.

"Pete? Hello, Pete?"

"Yeah, speaking."

"Pete, this is Leslie," the murmur identified itself.

"Leslie, I'm terribly sorry, what awful news," I said.

"Oh God, I've been so ill. They thought I was going to die."

"Oh, Leslie, I'm so sorry," I said. "I feel responsible."

"Don't feel that, just come and see me," murmured the moan. "Frankie Vaughan's been in, and David Jacobs, but you put me here. Can you come round and see me?"

"Of course I can," I said, and throwing on some clothes I dashed down to the Harley Street Nursing Home. There I discovered the suffering nose all done up in bandages, with all sorts of tube meandering their way to and from the afflicted area. Somewhere beneath this concoction lay Leslie.

"Here, I've got a bird coming in a minute," said Leslie, who was on the way to divorce from his wife. "And my wife's coming a bit later on. If the bird's still here, and you're here, and the wife arrives, say the bird is with you."

So the girl arrived, and the wife arrived, and soon afterwards the doctor arrived and said in the tone of a mayor about to declare open the extension to the town hall: "I am now going to remove the bandages. And I am going to look at the nose here."

Which he did, revealing the rehabilitated nostrils to a waiting world. The girl looked at him. His wife looked at him. The doctor looked at him. I looked at him. And Leslie, poor Leslie, looked up at me and asked: "Well? What do you think?"

There was an agonising pause while I wrestled between tact and truth. But for a friend only the truth will do, and I looked down at him with all the consolation I could muster and said: "Leslie. It grieves me to have to tell you. I cannot tell the difference."

But at least they found out about the haemophilia, so I keep telling myself I did him a good turn. Of sorts.

And I was done a good turn by the BBC that year, when they gave me 'Late Night Saturday', a record and interview programme which was really to be the forerunner of 'Open House'. It started at 11.0 pm and went through till two in the morning, the first BBC programme to go past midnight.

I remember the first night we had a quite extraordinary line-up of guests – Bob Monkhouse, Lionel Bart – who was a very hot property just then because of 'Oliver' – and the one and only Judy Garland. Judy managed to make her typically early mark with her opening sentence which was: "OK. When do I get paid?" Knowing the sort of fees the BBC were paying then, I assumed she was joking.

Soon after that we had the incredible Marlene Dietrich. It was the first time that I had met her, and it had not been at all easy to persuade her to come on a live programme, so we were all a bit apprehensive. She is one of the few people of whom the 'legend in her own lifetime' phrase is actually true.

But I find with superstars that they are like horses. If they know that you're scared of them, they'll play you up. You have to be courteous, and at the same time treat them as if they were anybody else, which of course is what they are.

Anyway, I started off calling her "Miss Dietrich", and after a couple of records she said: "Please don't call me Miss Dietrich any more. I don't like that. Please call me Marlene." Of course, if I had called her Marlene in the first place, it would have been: "Call me Miss Dietrich" pretty damn quick. You have to use psychology in these matters!

That night we also had on the programme a man named Helmut Zacharias, a German violinist of some note. When he came into the studio I was horrified to discover that he didn't speak a single word of English, and it wouldn't do much good for me to tell him that Otto Smith was going to bring his gramophone, nor that I had my flute.

So an announcer called Paul Hollingdale, an old Luxembourg hand, came in and said that he would do the interpreting. Five minutes later, Marlene Dietrich, who had already done her bit on the programme, came back into the studio, having poured out coffee and drinks for everyone. It was then that I first discovered how much she likes looking after people.

She might just as easily have gone home to a comfortable bed, but instead she offered to take over from Paul and do all the interpreting for the voluble violinist. That's what she is really like.

I know she has the reputation of sometimes being a little difficult. Indeed, at times I have tried to contact her and have discovered that she has this knack, if she feels like being a recluse, of picking up the phone and saying: "Miss Dietrich iss not here. Ziss iss der cleaner." You know perfectly well that it's actually Marlene, because she loves looking after her own place, and wouldn't have a cleaner in to save her life. But if that's how she's feeling that day, that's her privilege.

Another early guest was Sammy Davis. Now I was rather apprehensive about this, because about a year earlier, when I was on 'Juke Box Jury' with Andy Williams and his wife, a Sammy Davis record was played. And I remarked that although he had made some good records, he wasn't really a top recording artist but a top live entertainer whom you needed to go to see.

Andy Williams agreed with me about this, but at dinner that evening Alan Freeman (not the DJ, but a man in the record business) said: "You've upset Sammy Davis. He asked me who is this guy Pete Murray."

"That's a question I often ask myself," I said. "But when you see him next, tell him that those were genuine views. And although I don't

200

think he's a great recording artist, I think he's a marvellous entertainer."

So, about a year later, Sammy Davis finds himself pretty well forced into the studio by his management. He was in a black mood. He didn't like the look of me, and he didn't know what he was doing there. I could see him thinking: "I need a plug like I need a hole in the head. Who needs my record playing?" It was about 11.30 pm.

Luckily, inspiration came. While the first record was playing, I said: "I believe we have a mutual friend."

"Who's that?" he asked, grumpily.

"Well, one of my very best friends is Tony Newley."

He lit up like a flaring candle. "You know Tony Newley?"

"Sure," I said. "We play football together, and we've known each other for years."

"Ah," he said, enigmatically.

The record ended, and I said: "Our guest tonight is Sammy Davis." There was just the slightest pause, and then he said: "Hiya Pete. Great to be here."

I've seldom seen such a total change in a man, but I understood why Americans tend to be a bit wary. In America, interviewing is mostly a snide business, trying to delve into your worst aspects, or how your latest divorce is going. Those are areas I just don't get into.

At the end of the programme, Sammy Davis asked me: "Have you ever had Frank on the show?"

"Frank who?" I asked.

"Frank Sinatra," he said.

"No," I said. "A few weeks ago on his birthday it was arranged that we could speak to him, and we did try to get through, but although we got his number they said he wasn't there."

"I'll talk to him," he said. "I'm going to tell him all about you. He'll do the show. I'm sure he's going to do the show. He'd dig you."

"Well, the feeling would be mutual," I said, "because I think he's absolutely great, and I'd love to have him on."

Some time later Sinatra was over in England, and was with his great English friend Harold Davidson, the impresario, when he heard us play one of his records. On the following Monday Harold told me: "Hey, Frank nearly called you on the phone on Saturday night."

201

"Well, I wish he had," I said.

"Well," he said, "Frank is doing some concerts here, and we're using Peter Sellers to compère the Leicester Square Odeon, David Jacobs for the Festival Hall TV show, and we have one more at the Gaumont Hammersmith (now the Odeon). How about it?"

I accepted, of course, and loved every minute of it, especially the discovery about his trousers. He's such a perfectionist, and so immaculate, that he never puts his trousers on until just before he's due to go on stage, and will never sit down in them in case there should be the slightest crease.

Howard Koch, his producer, and I got on very well together, and after the first house he said: "Pete, you haven't met Frank yet, have you? You've got to meet him. You'll meet him during the second house."

That evening I was standing in the wings when Sinatra appeared. Howard said: ":Oh Frank, there's a guy I want you to meet. This is Pete Murray, who introduces you here."

Sinatra turned to me with the bluest of blue eyes I've ever seen in my life and said: "I wanna thank you sincerely for all you're doing towards helping us with this charity." Then he turned on his heel and left me clutching the handful of the only words Sinatra ever spoke to me.

I'd have loved to ask him to do the radio show, but it wouldn't have been fair at that moment. I would have preferred to do it over a cup of coffee, but he's always surrounded by so many people that one thing you do not do is to get to have a cup of coffee with him.

Instead, I got together with Jo Douglas again, for the first time since '6.5 Special', in a TV play she was producing called It's sad about Eddie. It starred Max Bygraves as a run-down former star working in a night-club. I was given the difficult part of playing myself, listening to him telling his story in a bar. I obviously managed it all right, because one critic wrote: "Max Bygraves had trouble with his part, but Pete Murray managed to get into the skin of Pete Murray quite well." That's what dramatic training does for you.

Rather less dramatic was a series I did for Anglia TV that summer, called 'Glamour 65'. It was really just another beauty competition, ranging over the Anglia area, which in those days stretched from about

Hull to Southend, thus enlarging the Murray travelogue. The one highlight or actually rather lowlight, came when we did it from the Corn Exchange at March, in Cambridgeshire.

Now March happens to be rather a raving place, against all the odds. It has a very wide high street, like something out of the Middle-West of America, and the farmers all come in there to have a good time, with the result that there are quite a number of clubs. On this occasion, Kenny Lynch was singing on the show, and afterwards we went to one of these clubs, where there was a stripper who was also, by way of diversion, a flame-swallower.

I was sitting quietly enjoying myself, and talking to some of the Anglia TV people, when one of the club heavies came over.

"Pete?"

"Yes?" I said.

"The strippa wants to 'ave a word wiv yer," said this worthy.

"Really," I said. "Where do I find her?"

"She's up there on the stairs, waitin' to go on."

I went over to the trysting place, and discovered the Liverpudlian lady in her bathrobe.

"You goin' 'ome tonight?" she asked, without preamble.

"Er, no, I'm staying here tonight," I said.

"Oi'd like to give yer one," she said.

"I beg your pardon" I said, wondering whether the noise in the club had made me mis-hear.

"Oi'd like to give yer one," she said, more distinctly.

"Oh no, I really couldn't do that," I said.

"Why not?"

"Well, I have to tell you this; Kenny Lynch happens to have fallen madly in love with you, and there's an unwritten code between me and my friends that we never interefere with – "

"You're givin' me the business."

"No," I assured her. "It's absolutely true."

"Anyway, 'e's goin' back ter London. Oi found that out."

"You see," I said, "you did know that Kenny – "

"Ow no Oi didn't. Not at all. Oi'd like ter 'ave it off with you."

"No, I'm terribly sorry," I protested, "but I'm terribly straight, and I don't want to know about anything like that."

I retired to the table to watch her strip routine, which was somewhat uninspiring, after which, re-clothed I'm happy to say, she came and joined us at the table. She then launched another series of invitations to partake of her person, which finally drove me potty, so I bade everybody goodnight and went to my hotel and to bed.

About an hour later I was woken by a knock at the door.

"Who's that?" I called, sleepily.

"It's the strippa," said a voice. "Can Oi come in?"

"No, you can't," I shouted, fully awake by now.

"Well Oi wanna come in," said the voice defiantly. "And if yer don't let me in Oi'll mike a noise."

To avoid embarrassment I opened the door.

"Oi wanna mike love to yer," came the refrain.

"Look here," I said, "I've already explained that Kenny Lynch –"

"Ow, don't give me all that rubbish. 'E's gone back ter London anyway." With that she made ominous moves towards removing her clothing for the second time that night.

"Now look here," I said, in my most schoolmasterly tone. "Quite honestly I don't wish to make love to you."

The message finally sank home. I could almost hear her mind groping for some explanation for this incomprehensible refusal of her charms. Then it came.

"You're a bloody queer, ain't yer?"

Clutching at straws is one thing, but here I had suddenly been offered a haystack. I thought back to the landlady in Grimsby, heaved a sigh of relief which she probably took as melancholy at her discovery, and said: "Yes. You're absolutely right."

From pretending to be queer, which I wasn't. I went on to acting an alcoholic, which I wasn't. It was a part in a 'No Hiding Place', directed by Christopher Hodgson, a great friend of Derek Chinnery, who had given me my first break on BBC radio. I was supposed to be not only alcoholic, but neurotic to boot.

Now I felt quite happy in that part. In fact, a lot of the best stage drunks are people who don't drink, like Jimmy James and Freddie Frinton. And as a kid I always used to play a drunk, with a glass of water as a prop. But Peter Willis, a very smart man, now head of Drama at Yorkshire TV, saw me and was clearly horrified by my appearance.

"You haven't shaved for a couple of days," he said.

"I know," I told him, "but I'm playing an alcoholic and that's what alcoholics are like. They don't bother. They get seedy, and don't do their ties up properly."

"I still think you should have a shave," he said, eyeing me with considerable distaste.

As they say, you can't please everybody, and that was certainly the case with students. It was about this time that I started being invited to lecture on various matters, sometimes specific, as on the occasion when I went to a vegetarian youth camp in Chingford (truly!), and sometimes more general, an invitation to air my views on life.

I soon discovered that such views, enthralling though they might be to me, held less than total fascination for others. So I developed a technique of talking for above five minutes and then throwing the floor open to questions. Nowadays I just won't do the student circuit, because while I don't mind people hating me, I do think they should be able to hear what I'm saying, and the Marxists, of whom there are many around, seem disinclined to allow this to happen.

But in those days it was good fun, with a lot of give and take, and I remember one particular visit to London University. There were about 3,000 students in this hall, and they threw questions at me from all sides, even about things I'd said as far back as 1945. They were so sharp it wasn't true, but I really enjoyed it.

Now on these occasions there is always this one guy, this one fellow who's going to get you. On the other hand, if the students think his question is a good one, they'll applaud, and this gives you a moment to think.

Sure enough, towards the end of the session this student shouts down from the top of the gallery: "Mr Murray. I've been observing you on the stage for the past forty-five minutes. I have observed that your legs have been crossed. And it is pretty evident to myself and to the whole assembly here that you have knobbly knees."

This was hardly what I would call a rapier-thrust of repartee, but for some reason it brought the house down. There were roars of laughter, hurrahs, and applause. I just stood there, leaning against the lecture table, and waited till it subsided. Then I looked up at him and said:

"Sir, I am not a man given to boasting, but *that* is not my knee."

Collapse of stout student.

But even when people did like me it didn't necessarily work in my favour. Early in 1966 there was a nice letter in the now-demolished Daily Sketch from one R. Peacock of Bishop Auckland. Mr Peacock wrote that Pete Murray's 'Late Night Saturday' was the best thing the BBC had ever produced. (An exaggeration, I'll admit.) He went on to ask whether it couldn't be put on TV.

Now the BBC are very serious about correspondence. You get a thousand letters, and if one of them happens to be rude they hold a meeting about it. But now that someone had actually written in praise, a staff member was quoted as saying "Oh yes, well he's obviously got someone to write in about that." Not true.

I was unhappy about this quote.

I must admit, however, that there were times when I *did* fix the applause. I refer to a small episode with Frank Barnes, who managed my Luxembourg programmes for Decca. Frank was a marvellous help and encouragement. He was full of bonhomie, but he had one minor defect – he was a hypochondriac. We used to pander to this by taking turns to ask him how he felt.

Well, on one particular occasion around this time, he really wasn't so good, and had to take some days off. Someone else handled the show. On the day of Frank's return, I made some prior arrangement with the Radio Luxembourg boys, and with the landlord's wife at the Mayfair, the pub where we all used to have lunch.

When Frank came in to join us, the boys started. "Super programme last night, Pete." "God, Pete, didn't that go well last night."

Frank started to get a bit hurt. "Quite obviously you don't need me," he said. "Apparently your programme was marvellous last night."

"Well, it was one of the better ones, Frank," I said, with appropriate modesty. At this, the landlady came over. "I'm sorry, gentlemen," she said, "I don't want to interrupt you, but I felt I just had to say how much I enjoyed the show last night. It was really wonderful."

Frank stood up, a look of utter despondency cascading down his freshly-recovered features. "I've had enough of this," he said. "I'm going home. I don't feel well."

To this day he doesn't know that we were putting him on. But, like Shaw Taylor, he will now.

In the Spring of 1966 Curry's, the cycle shops, for whom I was doing the Luxembourg programme, said they wanted a different sort of show. I suppose in a way it was to be the forerunner of the 'Open House' road shows, because we used to go round to all the Curry's shops, having announced our arrival in the local press, and give out records to kids, taping the proceedings for the programme.

But in the end they had to abandon the project. One day we arrived in Brighton, at a little shop opposite Preston park, and instead of the few dozen kids they expected, some 600 turned up. Curry's decided that the number of television sets that were ruined in the ensuing chaos wasn't really justified by the publicity.

So now they had a different idea. The pirate radio stations had started up, and Curry's decided they would have the only networked programme on the pirate stations. "It'll be heard from Radio London right up to Radio Scotland," they said. "We'll go to various night clubs, mainly in the North of England, and record mixed shows, with jazz, groups, and solo singers."

I thought about the proposition, and decided that, since the BBC were happy with me doing Luxembourg (and therefore accepted the commercial principle), the only duty I had was to go to Luxembourg and see it it was all right with them.

Geoffrey Everitt, my old colleague, now boss of the outfit, said: "As far as I'm concerned, you're freelance. If you want to work for the pirates, then by all means you have my blessing."

So I started the series, and the Wrath of God descended on my head. The BBC were aghast. I had a contract with them so they couldn't do much about it, but they asked me to withdraw.

But withdraw I couldn't. Curry's wouldn't hear of it. Decca then joined the fun and, adopting a very high, mighty and righteous attitude, threatened to take me off Luxembourg. There was talk of taking me off not only 'Juke Box Jury' but 'Top of the Pops' as well.

I was not happy with this furore. To put it another way, I was miserable, though I thought there was a lot of hypocrisy in the outraged screams. The Daily Mirror thought so too, because they ran a leader article defending me and referring to the BBC as the British

Blackmail Corporation. That made matters worse, since the BBC were clearly not happy with this article.

The whole affair finally blew up in our faces in Bradford. We were due to record the show at a club there, with Kenny Ball. The Four Pennies, the Swinging Blue Jeans, and Pinkerton's Assorted Colours. A delegation arrived from the Musicians' Union, and instructed their members not to play for the show. The head of the delegation was very polite and apologetic, but he said that as far as the union was concerned, the pirates were persona non grata. The irony of this was that the union's great battle at that time was to get the broadcasting media to use live musicians, and we were one of the few programmes to use nothing *but* live musicians.

Kenny Ball stayed on and played for fun and for all the members of the public who had turned up. But that was the end of my buccaneer broadcasting, and the Jolly Roger was hauled down from the Murray mast-head.

But I *had* established one record that can never now be broken, now that the pirates have gone. I was the only person to have worked for BBC Radio, BBC TV, Independent Television, Radio Luxembourg, AND the pirates all at the same time.

It was all, you might say, a part of broadcasting's rich pattern. But it wasn't getting me any nearer playing Hamlet.

Chapter Seventeen

I am not a good cook.

Let's face it, I'm not a cook at all. A cup of tea and a boiled egg and that's it.

The discovery that this was so came at an early age, when I went to one of the summer camps with the City of London Boy Scouts. Cooking was one of the tests we had to pass, and I was required to prepare some sausages.

When I had finished, the Scout Master told me: "I am prepared to pass you on two conditions. One is that you should be bold enough to eat that ..." he paused for the right word, but could not find one to match the sticky mess. "Well, to eat THAT. The second condition is that you pay for the replacement of the tent which you have burned down in the process."

I was clearly not destined to be another Fanny Cradock.

Luckily for me, this deficiency was made good by a liaison I had started in 1965 with a girl whom I must call Miss X. She is now happily married, but even if she weren't she would have to remain Miss X, because that was the way she wanted it.

She worked for a record company, and was about 19 when I first met her. She was attractive, without being beautiful, but was in all sorts of ways a very exciting girl to know. But throughout our relationship which lasted about three years, there was one thing upon which she insisted. She would not let anyone know that I was her boyfriend.

I thought at the start that she was ashamed of admitting it, but in fact I believe she was afraid of being hurt. She was frightened of the publicity if we broke up, and what she thought would be the resulting humiliation. She went to parties on her own, and she would never be seen with me in public, which in the end rather got me down. But I respected her wishes, and no-one ever knew. And although she was much younger than myself, she was tough. Several times I offered to pay for taxis to take her home to South London, but she always quite rightly insisted: "You've spent the evening with me. You take me home."

That year, 1966, I met up again with John Irwin, a producer by now, whom I had known a couple of decades before when I did some shows called 'Kaleidoscope' from the Alexandra Palace. John now came to me with an idea for a children's TV series to oppose the BBC's 'Blue Peter', which was to be called 'Action'.

'Action' was fun all the way, and within the confines of any one situation I was given what you might call total ad-liberty. It was often necessary. I remember we had the James Bond car on the show and absolutely nothing about it would work.

We also tended to have quantities of animals in the studio, which suited me fine, except for one rodent-like creature which darted all over the place and clawed and scratched me. Ever since, as a child, I had put on a wellington boot and stood on a dead mouse at the bottom of it, I had been terrified of mice running up my leg. This creature, whatever it was, looked ominously likely to do exactly that, and I stood there petrified while everyone roared their heads off.

Then there was Jamie. Jamie was a chimpanzee, from the London Zoo, and the first time we met we got on fine. But Jamie returned, by popular request some weeks later, and was at a chimpanzee's 'difficult' stage. He was very possessive about his keeper, utterly rejected advances, and bit me on the lip, necessitating my immediate removal to a doctor for anti-tetanus injections. What with Jamie and the leopard, I was apparently not destined to be a second David Attenborough.

But I did know about music, and John Irwin, who didn't, left most of the musical decisions to me. Then one day he came to me and said: "I haven't asked your advice about the music this week because I heard a group the other night and I've booked them."

I thought to myself: "Oh Lord, what *has* he done?" They turned out to be a group I had never heard, called the Peddlers, and I thought they were nothing less than sensational.

Now I have always been a going-home, never a night-club, man, but when I found out that they were working at the Pickwick Club I went to see them there and, for probably the first time in my life, I became a fan. The place was always packed out while they were there. Mick Jagger and Charlie Wyman of the Stones, old Billy Cotton, Milton Shulman apparently every night, and even Frank Sinatra, were just a few of the people they attracted. They were unique, taking standards and giving them their own special style.

They made a record playing live from the Pickwick, and asked me to introduce it. I did, and wrote the sleeve notes, and all for no payment because I thought so highly of them, though I'm sure that people believed I had money in them, so often did I play their records.

That summer, I went with Michael and my friend Tony Lewis on holiday to Cannes, where we spent a great deal of time on the yacht of some Australian millionaires. This satisfied my lifelong ambition of steaming grandly into port and having all the people on the quay looking at you enviously. After a lifetime of doing the quay bit, I figured it was about my turn. It also taught Michael what an idiot he has for a father, since I am by no means nautical, and my whole time seemed to be spent in trying to step into small boats, failing, and falling into the water instead, or alternatively dangling in mid-air from ropes in attempts not to drown.

But at least Tony Lewis kept me laughing. We tended to be like a couple of naughty schoolboys together, and one of the regular stunts we pulled went like this. We would be sitting in a restaurant with a girl, and I would ask Tony: "How's the book going?"

"What book's that?" the girl would ask.

"I don't wish to discuss my book," Tony would declare.

"He's a funny man, you know," I would say. "He's not only in the theatrical business, but he is by profession a psychiatrist."

Tony would protest a bit more, and we would then launch into a conversational review of his views on sex. Invariably, the girl or girls present would leap in with astonishing revelations about their private past and ask Tony for his advice and diagnosis. We mostly did it with girls, but it worked with anybody.

Once when we were up in Manchester we were telling some TV

people about this, and one of the girl Producer Assistants thought the whole thing was very funny. She asked if she could be present when we did it next. So later that day we performed for her benefit, and sure enough the girls we talked to poured out volumes of amazing details about themselves.

But the unbelievable thing was still to come. As part of the build-up, Tony had referred to some lectures he said he was due to give at the Salford Infirmary. When we got back to London we had a phone call from the boss of the PA girl who had been in on the joke. He told us that she had found Tony Lewis a fascinating man, and wanted to go to listen to him lecture at the Infirmary, and could she have the time off!

It was with such trifling successes behind us that Tony and I set off one evening for the huge Whisky A Gogo discotheque in Cannes. I have to say that Tony, who is very Jewish, goes very dark in the sun and passes very well for an Arab.

So it was not surprising when we sat down next to a couple of Australian girls, that he should launch into a patter that went: "Shallachalollomischchallala" – or something to that effect. I answered briskly in similar gibberish of an Arabic nature. We kept this up for a few minutes, raising the eyebrows and provoking interchanges of surprised looks from the two girls.

After a while I turned to them and said: "I am terribly sorry to disturb you, but this is Sheik Abdul Lou Levison from Beirut, and he has taken a distinct liking to you two girls."

"Aw reely?"

"Yes," I said, "I have the honour to be his Excellency's interpreter, and only the other day he was up in the Casino and gave a girl ten thousand francs just because he liked the look of her."

"Aw, grite."

Tony now weighed in with a further basinful of gibberish, which I translated. "The sheik [who was actually staying, as I was, in a doss house up in the hills] would like you to come back to the suite at the Carlton Hotel, where we are staying."

"Aw, dunno about thet."

More gibberish from Tony. A quick piece of balderdash in reply from me. Then: "Well, this is what he would like you to do. As you know, Britain is going through a severe economic crisis at the moment, and Sheik Abdul is flying to London tomorrow to see the Prime Minister and find out if there is any way in which he can help."

"Aw, strite up?"

"Yes," I said, "and when he flies back he would like you to join us in Sardinia. We're going on a cruise of the Greek Islands, and he will give you each five hundred dollars a week and all your keep. I should add, if I might, that there is nothing to worry about, since he is totally impotent."

Tony gave me a glare and spoke some sharp gibberish to me, and I looked suitably crestfallen.

"Well, what about me dawg?" asked one of the girls. Gibberish from me to Tony. Gibberish in reply. "He says, bring the dog with you."

This performance continued from 11.0 pm, when we had entered, until 3.0 in the morning, by which time the discotheque, which had been packed, was empty save for the four of us. The girls by now had accepted all sorts of weird suggestions from the 'Sheik', and true to my instructions they stood and bowed every time Tony went to the toilet, and the same every time he came back.

Then right at the end of the evening, Tony, who had spoken not a word of anything but gibberish all the time, stood up very erect and said: "It is most evident to me, Peter, that these two young ladies are virgins. I think we are wasting my time."

I stood up, the girls stood up, and both proceeded to deliver me the most enormous slap across the face. And Tony? He turned on his imperious heel to walk out, and as he did so, both girls bowed low.

A few months later, in London, we were going up in the lift at the Hilton with a lot of Arabs, and Tony threw me a line of 'Arabic' to which I replied in kind. At this, all the real Arabs started laughing. Perhaps it wasn't gibberish after all!

On a more sober note, on my return to England I did a commercial for the Milk Marketing Board, than which they come no more sober. I think it was probably the best commercial I've ever done, and it had the added advantage that Fleet Street was not agog to know whether or not I actually drank milk. (I do)

The director was a marvellous man called Joe McGrath who told me: "Pete, this is what you're going to do on film. You'll be driving home after a programme, tired, and dying for a nice drink. You get home, throw your coat on the chair, go to the drinks cupboard, get a glass, go to the kitchen, and pour yourself a glass of milk. Just that.

"Now I want you to sit down and write out for me just what you might say naturally as you're coming home in the car."

For once, there was not the crowd of hangers-on, clients, ad-men, con-men, yes-men, who cluster round the making of commercials. There was just him and me. He recorded what I said on the spot, and used it as it was, without any changes, over the film.

What was sad, was that the commercial won an award in Venice, and an award at Cannes for the best film commercial of the year, and both Joe and I had to read about it in the newspapers. Nobody told us! It was as if the advertising agency were frightened that, if we knew we'd won an award, we'd ask for more money!

Towards the end of 1966 the BBC decided that there should be more pundits on 'Juke Box Jury'. So the pundits were assembled . . . Alan Freeman, Jimmy Savile, Simon Dee, and myself, with David Jacobs (whom I love) in the chair.

We fooled around a lot, as well as giving the viewers the benefit of our incomparable expertise and punditry, and Alan Freeman became the butt of most of the jokes, because that's the way he likes it. He loves being sent up, and is a great straight man. This upset quite a number of viewers, including Liz Fraser, as she told me later, who thought that we were being unfair to Fluff.

And one critic wrote: "There is an aspect of the blackboard jungle about the set-up. Murray is obviously the leader of the gang, with Savile his henchman, deferring to him slightly. Simon Dee comes over as the careful young hanger-on, with status only to dig occasionally at Freeman, the butt. Jacobs schoolmasters it over the lot of them, hesitating to clash too much with the two tough guys, but laying into Freeman and Dee now and then to teach the others a lesson. Curious business!"

But the truth of the matter was that we only did it because Alan went along with it, and in fact encouraged it. More important, we knew he could cope with it. Simon Dee, on the other hand, might not have managed. I always felt he would be at a loss for words, which could lead to embarrassment.

We had warning of this quite early on. We were going off somewhere after the show, and Simon said: "Oh well, I'll follow you in my mini."

"No, no, no," I said, "Don't bother about that. Just wear your trousers." Everyone laughed except Simon, who just didn't get it.

I think Simon Dee was one of the classic tragedies of what the media can do, and undo, to a person. He could have had a great future, but he was a silly boy. He took himself too seriously, and he said a lot of unnecessary things, and behaved tactlessly toward many people, including those who had been good to him, kind to him, and those who had helped him. He came, and thanks to himself he went.

That October, I became persona grata with the BBC again. During the piracy problems the Beeb had not renewed my thirteen-week contract. I was freelance. Very freelance. And I believed the pirates provided a long-felt want. If commercial TV, why not radio? At least they made everyone sit up and take notice, and realise that there was more to radio than just the BBC.

Anyway, Auntie now gave me my late-night Saturday programme back, this time called 'Pete's Party'. We used Count Basie's 'This could be the start of something big' as a signature tune, and there's no doubt that for me that's exactly what it was, because it was to lead directly to 'Open House'.

Then in 1967, came the big re-organisation of BBC Radio, and the show became 'Pete Murray meets Pete's People'. The main change was that instead of playing only records, we now had to use a great number of tapes, of groups and orchestras. And the complaints started to flood in, because they had designated the show as what the BBC called "the sharp end", which meant playing the music of people like Marmalade and Geno Washington, which wasn't my style at all.

So after a few months I went to Robin Scott, the Head of Radio One, and said: "Look, this is the wrong format for that time of night. I know we have to use tapes, but couldn't we have something on a more melodic line?" I was acutely conscious that most of the modern groups do not have melody uppermost in their minds.

"Well," said Robin Scott somewhat surprised, "I never intended that yours should be a sharp programme anyway."

To the delight of the producer John Hooper and myself, he agreed to let us do our own thing. And the words and the music reverted to that old-fashioned characteristic of being audible.

I often, in those days, would put on the sexy girl's voice, phone up some music-publisher or other, and say: "Oh darling, I've heard about you, you know, and I've been told to give you a call to see if you could possibly help me in my singing career. I mean, here I am all alone in my negligee . . . Stop it, Poodles . . . sorry, that's my little dog Poodles . . . and I mean I wondered whether you might like to come round for a little drinkee . . . or something." That would usually get them hurtling out of the house.

On one occasion about this time I phoned a good friend of mine in the music business who will have to be anonymous I'm afraid. Call him Nathan Nutter. I rang him and said: "Oh, hello, is that Nathan Nutter?"

"Speaking," he said.

"Oh, hello," I said, "Well you don't know me, but my name is Jean Atkins."

"Oh yes, hello George," said Nathan.

"Oh I see, it's difficult to talk is it. I suppose your wife's there?"

"Er yes," said Nathan, "yes, ha ha, er well?"

"It's Jean Atkins, darling, and we're having a little party, I'll just whisper it in your ear, don't worry, and Sean Connery and Roger Moore and Pete Murray and a few others are coming.

"Only it's rather embarrassing, because it's about three girls to one man, and all the girls are such darlings, you know? Well, you've been recommended, and we'd just love you to come over."

"Well, George, if you insist I suppose I'll have to come out tonight, in spite of this weather. You're sure it can't wait till tomorrow?"

"No, darling, it can't," I said.

"Well, where shall we meet, George?"

I gave him an address in a well-known block of flats. 'And bring a bottle, darling."

And that's where I left it, just as a bit of amusement for the few friends who were with me. It was a terrible night, with a thunderstorm and cloudbursts, and besides, Nathan lived miles out, deep in the stockbroker belt. So I never believed he'd do anything about it.

Three hours later, at 11.30, when the others had gone home, my phone rang.

"Pete, it's Nat here." He sounded agitated.

"What's the matter?" I asked.

"Where's this bloody party?"

"What party?" I said, forgetting what I'd done earlier.

"Well, a few hours ago this bird called me, some girl called Jean Atkins. Do you know her?"

"No, never heard of her."

"Well, I had this call from her," continued the miserable Nat, "and she said there was going to be this party at Chelsea Cloisters, and that you and Sean and Roger would be there, and the sex ratio would be three to one in our favour."

"Sounds like a great party," I said, enthusiastically.

"You think so," he said. "I just went there, with a bottle of brandy, and knocked on the door. There was the sound of rattling chains and a voice said: 'Yiss. Vot do you vont?' I said I'd come to the party, and the voice said: 'Vell, go away or I call the police'."

I confess I felt really sorry for him, particularly when he told me that the thunderstorm had been the last straw for the faulty roof on his convertible, and that the drive up to London had left him soaked to the skin. So I invited him round for a hot bath, and he had several large brandies from his bottle.

I never let on, but about two years later he and I were having lunch with Geoffrey Everitt from Radio Luxembourg, when Geoffrey, for no particular reason, did an imitation of a girl's voice. Nathan rounded on him and said: "It was you, you bastard."

"What on earth are you talking about?" asked Geoffrey.

"It was you who did that girl's voice, and got me out in the middle of the night to a non-existent party."

He never accepted Geoffrey's protestations of innocence. To this day he's sure he knows the culprit. But if he recognises himself, he really will know now.

That May, I had what for me was the real honour of being asked to go to London Airport to meet Tony Bennett, who was due to tour with Count Basie, to present him with a silver disc for the quarter-million sale of 'I left my heart in San Francisco'. The reason it was such a pleasure was that it summarised everything I believe about

217

music.

The record had been issued in 1963, had never been in the hit parade, and yet it had sold a quarter of a million, because it is a truly good song, in music and words. It's curious, that although those are the songs that last, and make the big money in the end, the record companies never seem to learn. They go for what they think are the obvious hits, which sell a few thousand, get into the Top Twenty, and are then forgotten.

A recent example was Charles Aznavour's 'She'. It was Number One. In years to come it will be forgotten, but Aznavour will be remembered for 'The Old-fashioned Way', which was never a hit, and which in the end will sell far more records than 'She'.

That summer I finally persuaded Miss X, the girl who didn't want to be seen with me, to come on holiday in Beirut. After about four days we both realised that the relationship was at an end, but we stayed, as they say, good friends. I remember going with some other people up into the mountains one day and having a meal in the company of some old man who looked as if he didn't have two pennies to rub together.

After the meal he announced that he would pay. Horrified, I turned to one of our friends. "That old man can't be allowed to pay," I whispered. "It'll break him."

"Don't worry about that old man," I was told. "He's on holiday from Nigeria, he comes originally from the Lebanon, and he's a multi-millionaire." How wrong can you be?

I know I was very nearly in the wrong with the authorities. It was just after the Six Day War, and my dear, helpful friend Tony Lewis, he of the Arabic gibberish, sent me a telegram which read: "Muzzel Tov. Hope all is well with you. Congratulations on the Aswan Dam." This was not calculated to endear me with Lebanese officialdom, and I had to explain that this was a joke from a mad English friend, without going into the fact that he was also Jewish.

Having escaped internment, I then proceeded almost to suffer interment. We met a local madman who had a marvellous speedboat on which he took us to Baalbek. After a fantastic lunch at a sea-side restaurant, and some water-skiing, we were on the way back when the motors suddenly spluttered to a halt. It was then that I was unhappy to discover that this Lebanese landlubber knew nothing whatsoever about boats. Nor, of course, did I. Nor did anyone else aboard.

Darkness, as it does in that part of the world, dropped as quickly as a safety curtain, and we drifted helplessly some five miles off shore. Next he tore open one of the lockers and discovered an SOS rocket. He ripped the end off, and lit it. Nothing happened. The instructions were in English, and he'd torn off the wrong end.

Indeed, even if he'd done it properly it wouldn't have made any difference, because every night seems to be fiesta night in Beirut, and they would have thought it was just more fireworks. As for his wife, at home, we learned later that she wasn't worried because she though he'd probably gone to Cyprus for the day.

For five hours we drifted, and I was starting to practice my 'Abide with Me' and other suitable sinking songs, when we were practically run down by a fishing smack, whose skipper had the decency to stop and help the group of expiring idiots.

But most memories of that holiday were, I am happy to report, rather more joyous, and a few months later, after I had written to thank various people there, I had an invitation from Middle East Airways to compère and produce their first-ever beauty contest, at the Casino in Beirut.

The title to be contested was 'Miss Beautiful Airlines', but clearly a number of the one thousand people who turned up, and who had never seen a beauty contest before, regarded the exercise as a sort of showcase for harem-fodder. Miss Air France decided the whole thing was just too humiliating and said she was going home, sorry 'ome. As organiser I had to do something, so I practically went on my knees begging her to compete.

"All right. I do 'eet," she said, and promptly won the contest and a trip to Miami. So *she* was 'appy.

I, too, was happy when towards the end of 1967 I was initiated into the Grand Order of Water Rats, the mainly show business charity organisation. But there was one problem. I had no-one to take to their annual ball.

Now whenever I had done a 'Top of the Pops' I had noticed a girl who used to come into the studio to watch. She looked the sort of nice homely girl that I had always looked for. Besides, she always carried a shopping basket identical in shape and form to one my Aunt Dorothy had.

The double attraction of her looks and the basket proved too much for me, so finally I went up to her and said: "Excuse me, do you accept invitations?"

"It all depends on what the invitation is," she replied coolly.

"Well, would you like to come to a ball with me?" I asked. "It's in two weeks' time."

"Yes," said Valerie Singleton, "I would."

In the intervening fortnight I was down at Henlow Grange Health Farm, where I naturally managed to lose her telephone number. The day before the ball I finally managed to get hold of it, and phoned her.

"I thought you'd forgotten all about it," she said.

"No I haven't," I said. "Are you still coming?"

Well, she was, and we got on marvellously well together, but there was one immediate snag. While in Beirut I had invited an Arab girl to come to spend Christmas with me, and there was no way of cancelling the arrangement. I explained the situation to Val, who was very understanding. So the Arab girl came. She was very good to me, and spoiled me in a way Miss X never did. I love these little attentions, and the feeling that I am not just wanted for my body (for lack of a better word.)

The snag with the Arab girl was that she had a brother. The brother wrote to me enquiring how serious I was about his sister. The sister wanted to know the same thing. I had to make it clear that I had no long-term plans in her direction.

Both the brother and the sister were unhappy with this clarification.

I was still living at Montagu Mansions at this time, and Val, who was a very successful commère on 'Blue Peter', had her own flat in Earls Court. We never lived together, which was just as well, because in many ways we were total opposites. She liked museums . . . I liked football matches. She liked browsing . . . I didn't. I liked lying in the sun . . . she didn't. But we still had many, many happy times together. She is a very soft and warm person, with a great sense of humour.

Our friendship became public knowledge when the Daily Express did a story about us, and the fact that she chose to wear an antique ring I had given her on her engagement finger. I simply told them that it wasn't official, and left it at that.

The papers also made something of a furore of an unfortunate episode on 'Juke Box Jury' in 1968. Jimmy Savile, Simon Dee and I were on this particular show, and we were fooling around as usual when suddenly they played us a record called 'The Addicted Man'. I'm afraid I really blew my top. I am so totally against all drugs it isn't true, and I made my feelings forcibly known. I demanded to know why air-time was being given to such a disgraceful record. Luckily the BBC agreed, and fortunately the programme was recorded. The record, and my comments, were completely cut from the show. I think that was one of the very few times when I've blown my public cool.

In March of that year, I had the Royal cool blown on me. Robin Scott told me that, together with Brian Matthew, Jimmy Young and Ed Stewart, I had been summoned to meet Princess Margaret, who was to do a tour of Broadcasting House. We were to take tea in the royal presence.

Thus I found myself in the office of the Director-General, a hallowed area, and the seat of all wisdom, where I had never previously set foot, and indeed am unlikely to ever again. I remember that a few people came in, led by a girl, and I thought to myself: "My God, there's no doubt about it, the D.G's got himself a very nice-looking secretary. And doesn't she dress well." Then I realised it was Herself.

So we proceeded to tea, which was very pleasant, and I remember her saying to Brian Matthew how sorry she was that his 'Saturday Club' was no longer on, because she used to listen to it every week. I made a couple of harmless cracks, at which she was kind enough to oblige me with a modicum of royal Mirth.

Then Ed Stewart, who was doing the 'Junior Choice' programme, asked her: "Would you like me to play a record for the kids, Ma'am?" We had all had the "Ma'am" drilled into us. At this, the Presence went a trifle rigid, and I felt sorry for Ed, who had clearly committed lese-majesty at the very least.

"If you make remarks like that," I told him, "you'll finish up in the Tower."

Silence. A tinkle of tea-spoons. The royal Eyes swivelled in my direction. And she spoke to me. What she said I cannot remember, because even as it was being uttered I was aware that I was undergoing

221

the royal put-down in no uncertain way, and I blushed to the roots of my hair. It was one of those remarks where everyone present sort of goes "Phew!"

Happily, the BBC obviously didn't think I had cost them their Royal Charter, because Michael Mills, head of the Comedy Department, asked me to his office and offered me a part in a new series called 'Mum's Boys'. After thinking about it for three weeks, I decided on another gamble.

And that suited my part, which was of a gambler and a rake, a prodigal son returned to the bosom of my family, which consisted of my brother Bernard Bresslaw and our mother Irene Handl, whom I had first met at the Kew Theatre back in 1943. She was marvellous. She got so deep into the character she was playing that she started cossetting Bernard and me in real life. Rehearsals ran right through from ten in the morning till three in the afternoon, and she made it her business to keep us supplied with tea, coffee, and sandwiches.

Irene was then in her late sixties, but a marvellous personality, and a devoted fan of Elvis Presley, who, she declares, "turns her on". She has all his records, though she prefers his rock and roll!

The BBC had told us that if the series did well in the ratings it would come back, but although it came number two in the TAM ratings for the London area, and did well elsewhere, the critics were so hard on us that the BBC, who thought it was a bit risqué anyway, took it off after the first run of seven shows. For me, another gamble had failed.

But at Radio Luxembourg, things changed for the better. They decided that the long affair they had had with the record companies, allowing them to do whole programmes of their own records, should stop, and that they would revert to mixed programmes.

This suited me fine, because as readers may have gathered, I can't bear out-and-out pop. And for some time, anyway, I had been doing a Saturday evening show in which I selected my own favourite tracks from LPs. This show actually got the top Saturday night listening figures, but the powers at Luxembourg declared that this was "just a twist of fate", a curious attitude in view of the fact that people were ready to stand or fall by their listening figures.

It worried my wonderful, loyal Aunt Dorothy too. She was so concerned that I should get good figures, that if a rival DJ came on

222

BBC radio, Luxembourg, or television, she would turn off the set. But when I was one, she would rush around the house turning on all the five radios in her possession. She believed that this was how figures were measured, and she was determined to play her part!

That year, 1968, was the first time I had been asked to commentate on the Eurovision Song Contest, for radio. It took place at the Albert Hall, and Cliff Richard came second with 'Congratulations'. He takes these matters very seriously, does Cliff, and he was desolated that he hadn't won.

The following year, in March, the contest was held in Madrid, and I went out there to cover it with John Billingham, the producer of 'Pete's People'. We decided that on the way back we could do a 'Pete's People' from Paris, so on the way out we stopped over in Paris to set up the interviews.

For help, we went straight to Ginette Spanier, of Pierre Balmain, whom I knew well; a remarkable woman who seems to know everyone, and who in the past had been instrumental in getting people like Noel Coward and Lena Horne for us.

Ginette provided us with a list of numbers, and we started to ring round. The first person I managed to contact was Yves Montand. "I would be only too 'appy to appear with you," he said, "but unfortunately you 'ave just got me going out of the door. I am on my way to Brighton, to do some filming with Barbra Streisand." It was not an auspicious start.

Jean Sablon, Jean-Pierre Cassel, Danielle Darrieux, Michele Morgan (with whom I have been in love for years) . . . nobody could make it. So we had to place our hopes in the hands of Ginette as we flew on to Madrid.

The hospitality there was just unbelievable. It was the one Eurovision Song Contest I have seen which had real style, including liveried flunkeys to deliver champagne to the commentators. I remember John Billingham had lost one of his stop watches, which in the BBC is one of the cardinal sins, and when we went off to the Gala dinner he discovered that he had left his other stop watch at the theatre, ten miles away. That would probably constitute a hanging offence! We were just finishing the first course when the technician attached to us arrived with the watch, for which he had driven all that way back. I can't think of many people who would have done that.

And I had a boost when we went in for this dinner, because I was greeted by a tall and very handsome Spanish major-domo who said: "I have a very special meal for you, Senor."

"That's very kind of you," I said, "but why specially for me?"

"Because we have met before, Mr Murray," he said. "I was the head waiter in the French restaurant at the Midland Hotel in Manchester. And I know you are a vegetarian."

So not only did I get my vegetarian meal without having to ask for it, but everyone thought that these attentions marked me as a star of some kind.

Back in England, there was certainly no doubt about the night Liberace and Danny La Rue came on the show together. A lot of people came into the studio to watch the performance, including my next door neighbour Mrs Welland, sister of Brian Epstein's mother Queenie. Queenie came too, together with Clive Epstein and my own mother.

Whatever they all expected, I don't think they were disappointed, because the show went something like this . . .

"A very good evening, and welcome to Pete's People. First of all we give a warm welcome to Lee Liberace. Hello Lee, nice to see you."

"Why, it's just a pleasurebecause the show went something like this . . .

"A very good evening, and welcome to Pete's People. First of all we give a warm welcome to Lee Liberace. Hello Lee, nice to see you."

"Why, it's just a pleasure being here, and I just love London, and it's just the greatest city in the world."

"Also with us is Danny la Rue. A very good evening to you, Danny."

"Hello Peter. Lovely to see you."

And that was pretty well the end of my contribution. It immediately became a mutual admiration society of two.

"Well, I've just got to say this before I say another word," said Liberace, who was clearly going to say many another word. "Danny is just the greatest artist I've ever seen in my life, and I am going to tell you something, I have never seen anything greater. We have nothing like him back home in the States, you know."

Danny was not to be outdone. "Well, as far as I'm concerned, nobody has it over Lee, and I'd go anywhere to see him. I think he's one of the greatest showmen I've ever seen in my life."

"Well, as soon as mother comes," said Liberace, "I'm just going to rush her along to the theatre to see you, because she'll just love it."

"Oh well, if you're going to bring your mother, I'm going to bring my mother too," said Danny. "We can make a little party."

I felt it was time to remind them of my presence. "While you're about it," I said, "I suppose I might as well come along with *my* mother.

The papers got on to it quickly and phoned to ask me when the great event was to take place. There was no pulling back, and in the end it turned out to be a marvellous evening at Danny La Rue's, pictured, of course, in all the press.

That May, John Billingham, who was a good wheeler-dealer, persuaded the BBC to let us do the programme from the Cannes Film Festival. After some argument they agreed, and we arrived at Nice airport on the Wednesday, due to do the programme on Saturday. The BBC had arranged a hire-car for us, but I took one look at it and was filled with horror. It was like the original tin can.

"John," I said. "In all fairness, we can't drive that bloody thing."

"Well, that's what the BBC has fixed for us," he said, like a true-blue Corporation man.

"That's all very well, but we would have every chance of being roasted alive in that damn object."

"So what do we do?"

"Tell you what," I said. "I'll go to the Hertz people, tell them we want a convertible, and I'll pay the extra."

Thus we arrived with some degree of style at a Cannes where we immediately discovered, to our utter misery, that there wasn't a star in sight. The Festival was in rapid decline, and no-one had told us. We were, however, immediately told of a film show we *must* see that evening. We took with us a couple of English women whom we had met at the hotel, and who said they would like to come.

This first piece of filmic enlightenment turned out to be an American version of *Romeo and Juliet,* porno-style. Just about everything happened in it, and there were so many orgies going on at once that it looked a bit like one of the 'Laugh-In' shows, but so terrible that one of the women with us was promptly and violently sick.

I remember some weird character who kept on coming in front of the camera in doublet and hose and saying: "I reckon they should re-title this film *Romeo and Screwliet.*"

We were kept sane by giving running commentaries as the action proceeded, and I remember remarking, as some hunchback (where did HE come from?) mounted the unfortunate Juliet: "I don't know about the Hunchback OF Notre Dame, but they should call this the Hunchback ON Notre Dame."

We were not happy about this introduction to the famous festival, nor were we happy about the total absence of anyone whose name meant anything. But help was at hand. A big, and now demolished, film company was making *Julius Caesar* in Spain at the time, and they brought in a whole host of stars. We managed to wangle our way into the reception for them, together with a tape recorder, and I got interviews with people like Peter Ustinov, Charlton Heston, Richard Johnson and Richard Chamberlain, so at least we would have a show.

The next day we heard that there was another bevy of names at a fabulously expensive hotel up in the hills at St Paul de Vence. Thither we sped in our convertible, and discovered Simone Signoret, Yves Montand (not about to leave for Brighton, this time), and Vanessa Redgrave. I thought it rather curious that people of such celebrated left-wing views should be staying at probably the most expensive hotel in the South of France, but at least we ended up with about twelve good interviews for the show.

So on the Saturday we drove to the ORTF studio at Antibes, where John spent the day editing the tapes into a usable form. About a third of the programme was to be records, and the rest interviews and taped music.

About ten minutes before we were due to go on the air, the French technician came in and asked John: "'Ave you got ze spool?"

"What spool?" asked John.

"Ze right spool," said the man.

It turned out that French spools are different from English spools, and we were faced with disaster.

Luckily, there was a second technician there, and he was set to work winding our spools on to his by hand. The net result was that I had no cues, nor clues, as to what was being played, the names of the records, or anything. But we blundered through, and when I got back to London a friend said: "You sounded a little confused on Saturday."

"Confused?" I said. "You've got it wrong. I didn't have the slightest idea what was happening."

But at least we had got the BBC interviews with a group of stars that would have cost them a fortune in other circumstances, which may be why, when the bill for the famous convertible came in at £96, they paid up and never said a word.

From that mess, I became involved in the summer in anti-mess, in the form of a Litter Campaign. They had a lot of T-shirts filled with pretty girl students and inscribed with: "For Pete's Sake, Tidy Up" or something like that. I fear it didn't do much good for our litter-loving nation. It was rather like the Wombles, who had a great idea, but with the unsatisfactory off-shoot that all the kids went on to Wimbledon Common and left litter there so that they could see the Wombles come to clear it up.

Whether in honour of this devotion to national sanitation, I don't know, but that autumn I was invited to 10 Downing Street, along with a number of other show business people, to meet the American astronauts. Harold Wilson greeted me with: "It's wonderful to welcome you to one of my parties. I've been to lots of yours (meaning Pete's Party), but it's the first time you've been to one of mine."

I must say that, with politics aside, I found him a marvellous host. And I had an early demonstration of that famous memory at work. He talked about a programme I had done a year before about some people at the Stoke Mandeville Hospital, in which he is specially interested.

I mentioned some names to him, and he said: "No, these were the people." Of course, he was right.

Off-duty, like this, I found there was no cant about the man. One actor got rather drunk and said loudly: "Well, I'm not a bloody socialist." Not that anyone had asked him. At this, the CID heavies started to move in tactfully, but it wasn't necessary, because Wilson dealt with him with grace and good humour.

I was to go to several parties at Downing Street and Lancaster House, and I particularly remember one which was in honour of a

Rumanian Trade Delegation, a good, communist, comradely party. But with one surprise, best summed up by Harry Secombe who turned to me and said: "Hey, look at this, boyo, My God, here I am, a conservative, having dinner with a socialist MP and all these communists, and by God, they've got hand-made shoes, and hand-made suits . . . they all look as if they're millionaires."

He was right, and they all had these ultra-smart haircuts, as well. There was no doubt they were far smarter than the rest of us wicked capitalists.

Soon after my first visit to Downing Street I was approached by a sort of delegation of BBC radio men: Derek Chinnery, Teddy Warrick, Michael Bell, Stewart Grundy, and Robin Richmond, who had been one of my heroes as a kid, and whom I had seen play at the Paramount Tottenham Court Road. (This building has now, of course . . .)

"We've got an idea for a new daily programme for you," they said. "It will be called 'Open House'."

Chapter Eighteen

I am not a great sportsman.

Sporting, I hope yes, but one of the neo-Olympians, definitely no. But I include this separate chapter on the subject because I have always enjoyed playing games, watching games, and talking about games, especially in those instances where, unlike rugby, people have been kind enough to tell me the rules.

First of all, I must clear from readers' minds the possibility that, like many showbiz folk, I might be a reasonable golfer. As with rugby, though for different reasons, I played but the one game.

It was in Luxembourg, and I was persuaded on to the course by some friends determined to make a swinger (in the sporting sense) of me. A small crowd of locals, hearing of our intentions, and no doubt convinced that an English foursome would be well worth watching, gathered round the first tee.

With confidence I placed my ball, swung at it, and missed. The locals looked sympathetic. I re-addressed myself to the obstinate globe, took a second swing, and missed again. There was muttering among the natives.

Undaunted, I returned to the attack, swung more mightily than before, missed the ball, missed my balance, and lost my dignity as I landed on my backside. I looked up to see what the audience reaction might be. They had gone.

I did not return to the game of golf.

But when I got back from Luxembourg I did return to football. With my son Michael, Patrick Westwood, and the Brothers Barnett, who used to run the Curzon House and Embassy clubs, I used to kick a ball around in Regents Park. Joan Collins' father Jo was also one of our regular company.

One day a bunch of lads arrived, a local team, and when they saw us they said: "We're a bit short. Do you fancy joining in?" We did, and at the end of the game a bloke called Alf came up to me and said: "You turned in a fair performance there. You want to sign on?" I think I got more thrill out of that than signing the contract for '6.5 Special', which was about the same time.

The team was called The Strollers, and they certainly had no idea who I was, but I thoroughly enjoyed it, playing at such illustrious venues as Hackney Marshes and Parliament Hill, both without benefit of showers.

I know that we were bottom of the league, but what league it was I never had any idea.

From the Strollers I graduated to a team consisting mostly of show business people who played on Sunday mornings at Wormwood Scrubs. (Some might have said that our standard merited a spell *inside* the Scrubs.)

Jimmy Henney, who at that time was with Chappells, said to me one day: "You know, I reckon we ought to start a charity football team, like the cricketers do in the summer. We'd enjoy it, and at the same time we'd be doing something useful."

I liked the idea. "What's more," I said, "I know what to do about getting some gear." I knew a fellow called Fred Ripper at Jaytex, for whom I'd done some work, and I went to him with the idea. He said he'd be delighted to fit us out, and with my hankering after being a cowboy still not assuaged, we settled on a sort of gunslingers' outfit, black shorts, black shirts, black socks, and white saddle-stitching throughout. Very chic. We decided that there was only one possible name to give ourselves . . . 'The Showbiz Eleven'.

Our first match was at the stadium at Hayes, in Middlesex, and we announced on '6.5 Special' that it would be occurring. Little could we guess that 12,000 people would turn up. Our team included Ronnie Carroll, Glen Mason, who was on the Jack Jackson Show, and Franklin Boyd, a music-publishing friend of mine. Our opponents were the Twickenham Corinthians, and they really had a go at us. I recall being kicked up into the air by one of their players. Franklin Boyd, a very quiet fellow off the field, turned out to be a maniac once he donned football gear. Disturbed by the opposing aggro, he proceeded to engage in a fight with their left-half. I attempted to separate them.

"Come on, Frank," I said hopefully," you can't do this in front of 12,000 people."

"I don't give a sod about the 12,000 people," he said tersely.

I tried another tack. "Look, what about the image of the team?" I said, desperately conscious that it was our first game and that as yet the team HAD no image.

"Sod the image of the team," said Frank. "I'm going to kill him."

I made the final appeal to reason. As I held them at arm's length, I turned towards Frank and whispered in his ear: "Look Frank, you've got a higher I.Q. than he has."

"Oh, yeah, you're right," said Frank, and abandoned the attempted murder.

The Showbiz XI, despite these early hazards, began to go from strength to strength. I think we raised enough money that first year for three coaches for handicapped children. But then, gradually things started to be taken seriously. Some of the members began to think they could really play. Ex-professionals started to be drafted on to the books.

ITV began to televise the matches every other Sunday, and instead of playing, I sometimes used to do the commentaries, of which I was rather proud, not that I think Brian Moore has any need to look over his shoulder. We started getting enormous crowds – 26,000 at West Ham, and 18,000 at Charlton, the biggest crowd they'd had there in years. And when we went back for another match at Hayes, I did the commentary there.

The next day I happened to see Lew Grade in Isow's restaurant, and he told me he thought my efforts had been hysterical. But the following weekend, when I was coming back from Portsmouth, where Arsenal had been playing in a Cup match, a bloke on the train said to me: "Are you an Arsenal supporter?"

"Yes, I am, I have been for years," I said.

"Well, I heard your commentary on the Showbiz XI on TV last week."

"Oh, really?" I said, expecting some little nugget of praise.

231

"Yeah," he said. "You know sweet bugger-all about football, don't yer?"

I was not happy with this remark. Put it another way, I was flaming angry.

"What do you do for a living?" I asked him.

"I'm a plumber."

"Yes, and I bet you're a bleeding awful plumber," I hissed.

"There's no need to be like that, mate," he said. But I thought there was.

The team included some good chums, like Sean Connery, a very good footballer, Des O'Connor, Dave King, and Mike and Bernie Winters. And it was the Brothers Winters who finally led to THE BIG TRANSFER. Things had got serious beyond belief. We even had dressing room arguments! And people began to be offered half-games, so that other, better players could be drafted in.

Mike and Bernie were treated in this way at the second Hayes match, and it was the last straw. They said: "Right, we're going to form another team, and call it the TV All-Stars. We've not going to have professionals playing for us unless it's to make up a number. It's essentially going to be for show business people."

I went with them, together with a lot of the real showbiz members of the Showbiz XI, like Lonnie Donegan. We were joined by people like Tommy Steele, a then almost unknown Anthony Newley, and Jess Conrad, who played in goal.

The TV All Stars were an instant success. Very soon, to the utter consternation of the Showbiz XI, we started alternating with them on the Sunday TV spot. And I *still* had to fight to preserve the team image.

One Sunday we played against The Jockeys. They were a pretty tough bunch, and champion jockey Geoff Lewis went into a crunching tackle on Bernie Winters. Bernie was unhappy about this tackle. Bernie arose in a rage, smashed the diminutive cavalier in the face, and knocked him out cold all in close-up on the TV screen.

I rushed up to the enraged Bernie. "Do you realise what you've done?" I muttered at him.

Bernie, off the field a sweet and lovely man, could not care less what he had done. As far as he was concerned, it was justice.

"Bernie," I urged him, "you're on TV. If they think you've really done this, your fans are going to be very upset." This at least got his attention. "You've got to do your funny walk, right now," I went on, "and we've got to *pretend* that you hit Geoff, and *pretend* he's knocked out. And we'll carry him off as if it was a joke."

Bernie saw the force of the argument and did his funny walk, with a horrible grimace all over that famous mug, but of course it wasn't a joke, and the remainder of the game was one of the dirtiest I ever played in. The jockeys, being small, came in at us low and painfully, if you know what I mean.

A rather gentler game was the one we played against a girls' team at the Huntley and Palmers ground in Reading – our lads were keener on scoring with the girls than scoring with the goals. But again the team managed to present me with image problems.

They gave us a marvellous tea in the factory afterwards, and Tony Newley got up to make a speech of thanks. For some reason best known to themselves, Harry Fowler and Kenny Lynch decided that this was an appropriate moment to try to debag Tony. I was horrified. After all, it was mixed company as well as mixed biscuits.

At the end of it all, Lord Palmer came up to me, shook me by the hand, and said: "Thank you very much for all the help you've given our charity. We appreciate it very much indeed. It's a pleasure to shake the hand of the only gentleman in the team." I never thought the day would come when anyone said that to *me*!

Apart from the jockeys, I think our best games were against the Speedway Riders. My one ability, if I was given a decent pass in front of me, was to run at great speed down the wing and cross the ball. And against the Speedway Riders I had what for me was the ultimate accolade – they put two men on to mark me, as the danger man.

I remember Bernard Bresslaw played in that match. He and Ronnie Corbett, another of our regulars, used to do a regular little act, in which Ronnie would pretend to get into a scuffle with one of the opposing team. Bernard would come over, sort the man out in a gentle sort of way, and then he, standing six foot eight or so in his socks, and Ronnie, at five foot nothing, would walk off the field hand in hand. It never failed.

Rivalry with the old Showbiz XI was getting pretty tough. At times it was even petty. I remember that at my son's suggestion, we went down to play at Stroud, near where he was at school at Wycliffe College. I still have a cutting from the local paper which reads: "The Secretary of the Showbiz XI points out that the Showbiz team is still very much in existence, and the TV All Stars team has no connection with the Showbiz team – except that some of their players have played for them in the past. Mr Andrew Ray is a registered player in the Showbiz XI and is not likely to play in the Stroud Match."

There was only one way to settle the rivalry, and it was decided that we should play them for a cup. It was televised, and we were certainly marked as the underdogs; they were supposed to be the slick footballers, with Ronnie Carroll (an ex Irish Youth International), Glen Mason (formerly of Falkirk), Des O'Connor (who had played for Northampton Town), and Wally Barnes and Billy Wright who should need no introduction.

We, on the other hand, boasted only one professional, in the elegant shape of Malcolm Allison, who had to put up with the likes of me, the Winters Brothers, and Jess Conrad, who spent most of his time in goal combing his hair in case the TV cameras should alight upon his locks.

Well, the long and short of it was that Malcolm Allison scored what should have been the goal of the century for us, we managed to keep their forwards at bay, and won.

A big party had been organised for after the match, but they were so furious, not to say humiliated, that only Billy Wright from their side had the grace to turn up to tea. The rest got into their coach and fled the battlefield.

A few months later, by chance, there was a re-match, at Brentford, where a knock-out competition had been organised with several teams competing. There was a great turn-out of players, including Stanley Baker, Richard Attenborough, and John Gregson for the actors' team.

We beat the sports writers, and got into the final, where our opponents turned out to be the Showbiz XI. Ironically, I was playing on the left wing, and the opposing right back, who was marking me, was my old chum Jimmy Henney, with whom I had started the Showbiz team in the first place.

There was a lot of needle in that match. Let's face it, it was dirty. In fact I have to admit that Jimmy Hill, who was refereeing, called me up and said: "If you go on playing like that, you're so dirty that I'm going

234

to send you off." It was my one and only public warning.

Then disaster. Whom should I foul but Jimmy Henney, and in the penalty area. The penalty was given, the goal was scored, and that was the single goal by which they won. Nobody in the All Stars would talk to me for a fortnight!

The All Stars even did their own version of a continental tour...well, one match actually. The Army invited us to play in Dusseldorf. We nearly didn't get there in one piece.

A group of us, including Harry Fowler, Andrew Ray, and Peter Prichard, who had come along for the ride, were having dinner on the boat, when Andrew got coffee spilled on his trousers. With what I considered to be a fair degree of logic, he immediately decided that the best course of action was to remove the said trousers.

Admittedly, it *was* in the middle of the restaurant, and three burly Dutch sailors picked him up, carted him off, and locked him up for unruly behaviour. Disaster now threatened, because the captain announced that he was going to turn round at the Belgian port with Andrew still clapped in irons, and that he was going to hand him over to the police at Dover.

Leslie Wise, the brother-in-law of Mike and Bernie Winters, Arsenal supporter extraordinary, prince of the rag trade, and manager of the All Stars, finally managed to dissuade him from this course of action, explaining that Andrew had had a nervous breakdown, that he was a key member of British show business, not to mention our team, and that if we didn't play at full strength the next day the British Army of the Rhine would probably collapse of a broken heart.

In fact, I think, the Army *were* a little disappointed, because the only member of the team they could recognise was Dave King. But Peter Prichard cheered them up, for a short while. Peter's nickname among us was 'Major', because he loves the army, collects military bits and pieces, and generally has a very upright bearing. So he was in his element when we were entertained in the Officers' Mess.

The officers, I'm sure, reckoned he was clearly one of them, and after lunch he was walking across the square, with an officer on each side of him, and myself trailing along behind rather like some abject batman.

We were half-way across the square, when one of the officers said to him: "Of course, you must have been in the War, Major?"

Before he could reply I chirped in from behind: "War? Major? He's nothing but an officer's servant!"

That night, after the match, I was supposed to get back to London for a TV rehearsal, but managed to miss the plane at Dusseldorf airport. It was to prompt, behind my back, one of the best lines I ever heard. I got a message through a friend to the TV people to explain what had happened, and said that I was coming the following morning.

So when rehearsals started, the director told the people on the set: "Oh, Peter Murray will be late for the rehearsal this morning. He's stuck in Dusseldorf."

"Yes," said his assistant. "Ann Dusseldorf."

On the day that we were televised, the All Stars were paid a fee towards their charity fund by the TV companies, and one way and another we raised a lot of money. And it ALL went to charity, mostly for the coaches for handicapped kids.

Such is not always the case. There is charity, and there is charity. I first learned my GREAT LESSON about that when I compèred a show at the London Palladium for some blind charity, back in the fifties. After I had done my bit, the organiser said: "Thanks very much, Pete. That was very kind of you. We'll send you a few hundred fags."

"No thanks," I said. "I don't want anything like that."

"Well, how about some nice silk ties?"

"No, really," I said. "If there's anything going spare, give it to the charity." With that, I walked off to my dressing room, which I was sharing with a couple of fairly well-known singers. To my utter astonishment, they were counting out about £500 between them.

"What the hell are you doing?" I asked.

"What's the matter?" they said. "Haven't you been paid yet?"

"What, paid for a charity?" I said. "I've never heard anything like it."

A couple of days later I happened to bump into an agent I knew on the street. "'Ere Pete," he said, "I 'eard you done that show fer nuthin the other night. You're a right berk, ain't you?"

On the other side of the coin, there was the occasion when I did a charity fashion show for a woman in Surrey. I asked for nothing, but in the end regretted it. Tricia came down with me, there was no-one to meet us, we even had to ask for a cup of tea when we got into the place, and when it was all over they said, rather condescendingly: "We have booked a table for the two of you at an hotel. You can charge it up to us."

They didn't even offer to take us there, and yet the woman had sold about £5,000 worth of clothes. Them I *should* have charged, whereas to open the garden fête for the rather poor little school at Wandsworth, near where I live, I wouldn't even ask for petrol money. They couldn't afford it.

It's a question of sorting the genuine ones from the rest. On the one hand, I see some charity organisers living in grand style, with lots of houses and cars, and I hear stories like one charity which gets only three pence out of every pound from its flag day, after all the expenses are paid.

On the other hand, with organisations like the Stars Organisation for Spastics, or the Variety Club of Great Britain, nobody gets a farthing out of it, and I think if anyone was caught with so much as a little finger in the till they would have their heads chopped off.

It's the same with the people who give their time for charity. I personally cannot stand showbiz personalities who make a song and dance about all that they are doing. In some cases it seems almost to be built into their act. But again, there are people like Sylvia Sims, Vera Lynn, Roger Moore, Dickie Henderson, Leslie Crowther, Brian Rix, and even my 'enemy' David Jacobs, who give a massive amount of their time free to help others less fortunate, and yet the public never hears a word about it. That is not meant to be an exclusive list. It is just a few of the names which occur to me as people who go about their business quietly.

But now it is the readers who must be charitable as I turn my thoughts to cricket, in which, you may recall, my techniques were based on sheer mimicry.

I remember with special affection a game soon after the war in which most of the team was composed of out-of-work actors like myself. The captain, suitably enough, was Peter Crouch, who was then working in the offices of Spotlight, the actors' directory. Our number included John Gregson, the slobbering Patrick Westwood, Peter Finch and Bonar Colleano, who probably thought it was a kind of baseball.

237

We were playing the local team at a very beautiful place called Matching Green, in Essex.

It was a colourful occasion, on account of the fact that only two of our team possessed whites. The rest sported a Hawaiian assortment of flowered shirts and multi-coloured trousers. The other team batted first, and John Ainsworth, now a film-director, announcing that he was a very fast bowler, was permitted to open our attack. At the end of his first over they had scored about 95, including an enormous number of wides, no-balls, overthrows, and other miscellaneous items not entirely due to our opponents' batting ability. In the end they declared at 375 for five, and because Patrick Westwood and I were the only two members of our team to wear whites, it was rashly assumed that we might know how to bat.

We opened the innings. Patrick scored one run. I scored three, then was given out to what I still claim was a dubious catch at the wicket. But in fact it proved to have been a great stand, because the rest of the team contrived to amass only one further run between them. We were all out for five.

Now we repaired to the pub, and a different sort of competition was proposed . . . a beer-drinking tourney. As their champion, they put up, to our surprise, a fresh-faced youth of about seventeen. Against this David we arrayed our Goliath in the shape of Peter Finch.

Some twenty pints later, the fresh-faced youth remained happily in that condition. In the matter of Peter Finch, I regret to say, the end came less happily, since he completely passed out, and we had to send for an ambulance to take him to the local hospital for resuscitation.

Mind you, it wasn't all laughs. Oh no. I once did a hat-trick against Mill Hill while playing for Cardew Robinson's team, which happened almost by accident as I matched my imitation of Compton with what I thought was a passable Alec Bedser.

I went off Alec Bedser, though. I played in some testimonial game at the Oval, captained by none other than Peter May. I was put to field quite close to the wicket, and suddenly one of the opposing batsmen hit the ball with great speed and authority in my general vicinity. Somehow I managed to take a low diving catch of great importance, and Alec Bedser said: "Oh yes, well that was just a reflex action." Such gratitude! I could do without that.

I am told that what I bowl are known as 'cutters'. Colin Cowdrey even told me once that he thought I had missed my vocation (and I *think* he meant it kindly!) But I do have one little problem, that of keeping to a length. Opposing batsmen have an unkind awareness of this fact.

And I very nearly played for England. Oh yes. I was on holiday in Corfu, where the locals play cricket in the town square. At the hotel where I was staying I met Robert Carr, the Tory Home Secretary and Lord Orr-Ewing, who had taken a team out there.

They told me that they were playing the Greeks on the following day and that they had an injury problem. Assuming mistakenly that I was a good cricketer, they asked: "Would you care to play for England tomorrow?"

Would I care to? That would have been IT, for me. Unhappily, I had to leave that night, since I was due to do a show the following morning. My great chance had gone.

And there is tennis. My great achievement there came in a charity Pro-Am match at Weybridge. I was partnered by Alan Mills, and the actor William Franklyn played with Mark Cox.

Mills and Cox pretty well played between themselves, sending Bill and me the occasional ball to make things look good. It was all a very friendly affair until the moment that we reached match point. Some inner instinct told Mark Cox, who was serving, and who has one of the biggest services in the game, not to give in without a fight. He wasn't fooling.

He sent down an absolute humdinger, which I was sure was going to remove my left ear-lobe. Hopelessly, I smashed wildly at the ball, unbelievably I connected, and to everyone's amazement, Mark's included, the ball sped hard and low over the net and down the tramlines, leaving him straddled. I took my bow.

There was rather less glory in the Tony Bennett match. Tony had been on 'Open House', and announced that he was taking up tennis. I offered to have a game with him, and rather like the Danny La Rue/Liberace Mum's Party, the thing escalated from there. Jack Jones was originally going to join the foursome, but he fled the country in terror at the prospect, and in the end Sacha Distel and Malcolm Roberts were named as our partners.

We went up to Tony's flat at Grosvenor House for pictures, since he had declared: "No way is any photographer going to see me play tennis." After the photos were taken, I asked him about the game. "I have further news for you," he said. "No way am I going to play tennis."

During the next couple of weeks a great many listeners wrote in to ask who had won. Since Sasha and Tony were no longer in the country, I said that Malcolm and I had. Well, so we had. By default.

But much as I enjoy playing, my great love, as readers may have gathered, is watching the Arsenal. I remember at the start of 1971, as Arsenal were on the way to the Double, I wouldn't take any work because I *had* to see every match, home and away.

For the match against Tottenham which was to decide the League title, I was given a place in the Spurs directors' box. Ray Kennedy scored for the Gunners, and I stood up and screamed my head off with delight, until I suddenly realised where I was, and that this was scarcely the most tactful line of behaviour.

After the match, one of their directors came up to me and said: "You know, I've been a director of this club for many years."

"Oh yes?" I said.

"No matter where you go," he said heavily, "it is the accepted rule that if you are in the directors' box, no matter how much emotion you may feel — and we all of us feel emotion — you should not express it in any way."

"I'm very sorry," I said contritely.

He was not to be put off. "Your performance today, I have to say, was unlike anything I have seen in all my life."

"Well, I must apologise," I said, "but you must realise one thing."

"What's that?"

"We haven't won a bleeding thing in years."

The following Saturday was the Cup Final, and I went to cheer with Leslie Wise. Now Leslie had a coat, a lucky coat, and he never saw Arsenal lose while wearing this garment, except once against Leeds; but that was a disputed goal, so we forgave the coat.

But the coat was a warm one, and the Cup Final was a hot, sunny day. It was all I could do to persuade Leslie to wear the coat at all. Throughout the match he kept insisting that he was about to pass out.

Ten minutes from the end, he left. He could stand neither the tension or the heat. And after it was all over, and we had won, I found him sitting in his car in the park, listening to it on the radio.

Anticipating victory, we had organised a party at the Portman Hotel, that night to which all supporters were welcome. We charged an entrance fee that we thought would merely cover the cost. It didn't, not by a long way. The party cost Leslie and myself a lot of money.

But it was worth it. It always is.

Chapter Nineteen

I am not a star.

The word has become vastly over-used in the past few years, and should be reserved for the special few — and the word superstar for the special even fewer. Of course, by being instead one of that strange new race of people, the media personalities, I would probably attract more customers to the opening of a new supermarket than Laurence Olivier.

But that is merely the product of being well-known, which is a completely different matter. Olivier is a star. I, much as I might like to be, am not.

And curiously, I viewed the idea of doing a 'strip' programme, which is what they call a daily show like Open House, with some trepidation. I had always had a way of being anonymous. People would say: "Oh yeah, there's old, um, er, old um . . . got his name on the tip of my tongue." I didn't particularly like the idea of people being able to point and say: "There's Pete Murray."

The disadvantages of recognition had been brought home to me a few years ago, when I happened to walk into the Caprice restaurant at the same moment that an awesome threesome composed of Olivier, Sir John Gielgud, and Laurence Harvey were approaching from the opposite direction.

Outside the door a dustman was emptying bins. "Pray God he doesn't recognise me," I thought. God wasn't listening.

"'Ullo Pete," he shouted, past the earholes of the theatrical trio. "Saw you on telly last night."

"Oh, oh yes, how very kind," I muttered, directing my remarks at the pavement.

"Yeah," he shouted. "Load of old rubbish, wasn't it?"

So much for my chances of playing Hamlet.

The original plan for 'Open House' was that there would be a girl on it with me, but I baulked at that. As I told them: "If we don't happen to get on it will be a bit difficult to present a friendly programme."

"Then what about a different guest every day?" they asked.

"Okay," I said. "That's fine. We'll do that." I also insisted on having a hand in the building of the programmes. I didn't want to be landed either with the dreaded sharp end, or with the hackneyed choice of music that had filled the previous 'Housewives' Choice'.

On September 29th 1969, to a signature tune by Brian Fahey called appropriately, Open House, the show began, with the first guest, Cliff Richard. In those early days, the guests would simply say what they were doing at the time, and read a few requests. There was no real interview or participation.

The start was not too auspicious for some. Our third guest was Graham Hill, who went off to America later in the day and broke both his legs in a race-crash. And we had our little worries. Kenneth Williams was an early guest, and very funny as usual, but he recounted how he had walked to the studio. It was during a dustman's strike, and on his way he had been spotted by a dustman who shouted: "'Ullo Kenneth, 'ow's it goin'?"

Kenneth's reply was; "You get on with your bleeding strike, and get my dustbins done." He told me this over the air. The dustmen were not happy.

After the first six weeks the listening figures for that time in the morning still hadn't changed, and were still bad. The hierarchy thought they would have to take off the guests, and I had to beg them to give it a bit longer. "I'm sure it's going to be a success," I told them, "but please give it time."

There were still a lot of bugs to be ironed out, and there was still a great deal that we ourselves had to learn about doing a show like that. For instance, Gerald Nabarro and Manny Shinwell were two guests in the early days. Each of them raised a storm of protest from listeners who thought we were giving publicity to 'the other side'. Our audience, too, had to learn what to expect.

243

And I had to learn to cope with the unexpected, like the morning Alfie Bass came on. "Morning, Pete," he said. "I would like to say something."

"What's that, Alfie?" I asked.

He put his face close to the microphone and shouted: "Enoch Powell is a black Welshman."

I had no idea then, nor have I now, what this meant, but it was clearly not going to be a subject for discussion so I simply said: "Oh well, very interesting, you've just come back from Russia haven't you?" For some reason, his statement brought no complaints. Perhaps the audience were as bemused as myself as to its meaning.

But at least Tony Blackburn brought the chance of a little light relief. He was doing the early morning show then, and I was listening to him one morning. After he had played Petula Clark's 'Don't Sleep in the Subway, Darling', he gave in to one of his little bits of facetiousness.

"Oh yes, that was one of my better songs," he said. "Matter of fact, I wrote that with Petula Clark in the bath."

I got to the studio a little early that morning, and went to the continuity studio, where there is an outside line. I phoned the BBC number and asked to be put through to Tony's studio. Having got through I said in a thick French accent: "Oh, I would ver' much like to speak wiz Mr Blackburn, please."

"Well, he's on the air at the moment," said the assistant.

"But zis ees ver' important, 'e 'as just made a slanderous statement about my wife. My name ees Claude Wolfe. I am ze 'usband of Petula Clark."

"Oh, I see, well just a minute, I'll put you through," said a harassed voice.

"Oh, h-hello," said Tony.

"My name ees Claude Wolfe," I said.

"H-hello, Mr Wolfe," said a clearly worried Tony.

"Don't come all zis stuff wiz me, all zis pleasant sings," I said. "You 'ave made a statement about my wife, making zis disgusting sing, of being in ze bass togezzer. I sink zis ees slanderous, and I want a public apologise."

"Oh well, er, I can't do anything like that. It was just a joke," Tony stammered.

"Ees not a joke," I said angrily. "Ees not funny. I 'ave spoken to 'Arold Davidson, your agent, 'e ees a great friend of mine, I want a public apologise."

"No, no, no, ... oh, hold on a minute, there's another record coming up," said Tony.

After the quickest introduction to a record he's ever done, he was back. "Yes, Mr Wolfe."

"Now, I want a public apologise," I said firmly. "You 'ave not written zis song wiz my wife, eet was written by Tony 'Atch and Jackie Trent, and zis ees a falsification."

"Yes, but it was a joke," said Tony. "Look, just a minute, my producer's here."

Now, I reckoned, I was in trouble, because his producer was my old friend Derek Chinnery. I assumed he would guess immediately that it was me. "Now, what's all the trouble?" asked Derek.

I repeated the whole rigmarole, "Come on, Claude, it's just a little joke."

"I don't sink eet's funny."

"Oh come ON, Claude, it IS funny, it's funny to us anyway, you know."

"It's funny to you? What are you trying to say?" I demanded.

"Perhaps because you're French you don't understand it," said Derek.

"Ah, so, zis ees racialism as well, you take eet so far, racialism."

"Oh no. Come on Claude. This is ridiculous."

"I want a public apologise," I said, returning to my theme.

"Well, I'm afraid I can't give it to you," said Derek.

"Ver' well, zen, I shall 'ave to take zis matter furzer," I declared, and slammed the phone down.

Now I knew that when the programme was handed over, they always listen to the first announcement you make, to make sure everything is all right. My guest that day was Francis Matthews. So at nine o'clock, when Tony handed over to me, I thanked him for his programme and said: "Welcome to Open House. Our guest on the programme this morning is Francis Matthews, alias Paul Temple, who this morning is investigating the case of Petula Clark and Tony

Blackburn in a bath.''

It took about ten seconds flat for the phone to ring. I will not commit Tony's remarks to paper.

At the end of that year, Alan Freeman and I left 'Top of the Pops'. I can truthfully say that I was less than broken-hearted. For one thing, I am a great believer in some sort of a Providence that seems to open one door for me at the moment another door closes. The only thing that I really regret ending is a play, because one becomes so involved, though admittedly I'll be sad when 'Open House' ends, because that has become part of my life.

I had never tried to be part of 'Top of the Pops' in the same way, nor did I *feel* a part of it. In fact, I appeared on it many times in a grey, pin-striped suit and tie, rather than try to be with-it.

That summer, I had joined the Roehampton club, where I had spent months trying to perfect a pathetic game of tennis, and where, infinitely preferable, there was a lovely swimming pool by which to laze. It was while paying some of these devotions to my sun-worship that I first saw a lovely, bronzed, blonde lady, whose name I didn't know, but whom I liked instantly for the fact that she was always smiling.

Val Singleton, who didn't like sunbathing, was rather suspicious of this club. I remember her saying: "You're going to meet a girl here, and you're going to fall in love, and that will be the end of our relationship.''

"Nonsense,'' I said. But as usual, she turned out to be right.

But we were still together for the Boxing Day of 1969, when, together with Kenny Lynch and Harry Fowler we were invited to Chequers for a party for twelve of the patients from Stoke Mandeville Hospital.

Before the patients left, after the tea party, I recorded a few of them for Open House, and when I had finished I turned to Harold Wilson and suggested: "What about you saying a few well-chosen words for the Open House listeners?'' He agreed, and as I switched on the tape recorder I saw the most incredible transformation, something I had never seen with actors, singers, or anyone else. He became an entirely different person.

It was almost as if he had become a part of the machine. But the thoughts were genuine enough. He talked about people in hospital and sick at Christmas, and tears were coming down his face as he was talking, in spite of the fact that it was only to a tape recorder. I'm sure a lot of people would have been surprised by that, and the cynical might say that he turns it on, but I believe he is being honest on occasions like this.

At any rate, after showing us round Chequers he asked: "Do you fancy staying for dinner?" I said that would be lovely, and it was, a family affair, completely natural even to the extent that when I pulled a cracker with Mary Wilson I regret to say that it sent her flying on her – yes, well even that was taken so well that I thought what a good guest she would make for Open House, and suggested as much to her. She told me she would think about it.

Barbara Mullen came on the show, an incredible lady who had just been in 'Doctor Finlay's Casebook'. I hadn't realised that she was once a jazz singer in America and was very keen on drumming. This she demonstrated by picking up some pencils from the studio desk and doing a neat riff to the music. "Dere's only one ting wrong with it," she said, "It's too square. I like de hard rock music."

Reg Varney proved a little more embarrassing. He was doing 'On The Buses' at the time, and at the end of the interview he told the viewers: "Don't forget to tune in tonight, eight o'clock, ITV." The BBC were not happy with this exhortation.

1970 started marvellously for me with the announcement in the New Year's Honours List that I had been awarded the OBE, a great honour for me. The immediate reaction of the newspapers was: "Why?" Now since the citation did say "For Services to Broadcasting" I thought the reaction was less than generous, and I seemed to be interviewed by all the trendy-lefties in radio, asking me my opinion on awards of this kind, and wondering whether I didn't think they were an anachronism. (Which was actually what *they* thought.)

In fact, my view is that no matter where you live there are awards for all kinds of people, even though the right people don't necessarily get them. I would be loath to have to say that I was entitled to the OBE, but Russia, China, Cuba, all have awards, so why shouldn't Britain have the OBE for lowly people like myself?

Having fended off the knockers, I was summoned at the end of January to a meeting and told: "Open House is going to come off Radio One in March, and will just continue on Radio Two. Of course, this does mean a squarer programme. I don't know how you feel about this."

He obviously expected me to have a breakdown at the rearranged geometry of the programme, and was startled when I said: "Actually, it couldn't worry me less." The fact was that even when we were also on Radio One, the number of request for pop records was so tiny that it was hard to find any to play. Generally speaking, I don't think the public want them.

"I see," he said. "Well it will, of course, be the blunt end rather than the sharp end."

I refrained from asking what other design details he had on this square, blunt programme, and merely nodded. Then he went on to say: "In addition, of course, we will be making changes from time to time."

"How do you mean?" I asked.

"Well, for instance, you might come off it for a couple of months, and we'll put someone else in your place."

I continued to nod, but now I was quite worried. I didn't like the sound of a square, blunt, show, if it was also going to be Murrayless. But as I said earlier, I'm a great believer in my providential doorman, and sure enough, that same evening, another door opened in the form of a phone call from my old friend Renee Stephan.

"Peter," she said, "how would you feel about doing a summer season in Bournemouth?"

"Starting when?" I asked.

"Starting in May. It's *Not Now Darling*. It's at the Strand Theatre at the moment, so why don't you come and see it, and make up your mind?"

What she didn't know was that at that moment it would have to have been a pretty frightful play for me to turn it down, but in fact I liked it, and thought it an extremely good comedy of its kind. Besides, I knew that it was going to be done well, with good sets and so on, and at an excellent venue, the Pier Theatre in Bournemouth. So right afterwards I said: "Yes, I'll do it."

248

The following morning, I realised that Providence had this time arranged a double-door for me, because I got a call from the Press Office at Downing Street, to say that Mrs Wilson had agreed to do the show. We set the date for February 5th.

Armed with this information, I made my way once again along the senior corridor at Broadcasting House. I gave them the Mary Wilson news to start with. This appeared to cause a mixture of delight and terror. While they were still deciding whether to cheer or run, I chucked in my other news. "I'll be leaving 'Open House' in the middle of May," I said.

There was what they call a stunned silence. Then someone asked: "Why?"

"Well," I said, "I have been given to understand that you would be making changes anyway, and I thought that it would be a very good opportunity for you to do that and for me to do something else for a few months. Actually, it's from May 30th till . . ."

"Till when?" someone asked worriedly.

"October 2nd," I said.

Another pause for digestion, then Douglas Muggeridge, Controller of Radio One and Two said: "You finish on October 2nd. How would you like to start Open House again on October 4th?"

"Done," I said.

Roger Moore came on the show. I had first met Roger during the War, when he was a Captain in the 'Stars in Battledress' outfit. We met at the Arts Theatre, whose lounge he used to frequent.

He reminded me of a famous showbiz story of those days, when he had under his command a number of fairly unmilitary thespians like Brian Forbes and Joe Baker. The general deportment of the outfit was not of a nature calculated to win wars, and finally Roger was hauled up in front of the Adjutant.

"Now look here, Captain Moore," said this worthy. "This has got to stop. Your men must cease referring to you by your first name. They must show respect for your rank. In addition, will you kindly tell them to stop wearing suede shoes and khaki satin ties."

Roger called the "men" together in a room of the hotel in Hamburg where they were all staying, and relayed the Adjutant's instructions. The following morning he was entering the hotel in the company of the Adjutant and a visiting

General, when Joe Baker, who was a sergeant, came hurtling down the staircase, rushed up to him, cried: "Hello Roger darling!" and kissed him full on the lips.

The Army was not happy with this mode of address.

People often tell me I look like Chuck Connors, the Western actor. In fact, on a good day I look like Roger Moore on a bad day. A couple of years ago I went to some film premiere when a woman came up and started gushing all over me.

"Oh my dear, how wonderful," she drooled. "I've met my dream man. This is the most exciting moment of my life. I wonder if you could persuade one of the photographers to take a photo of us together."

Bemused by the ferocity of the onslaught, I looked desperately at the gathered lensmen. "I'll do it, Pete," said one of them.

"This is the moment I've been waiting for," said the woman, gathering herself in to me ready for the big moment. "I never miss the Saint."

"I'm terribly sorry," I said, "but I think you've made a ghastly mistake."

"What *do* you mean?" she said.

"Well, I'm not Roger Moore."

She disentangled herself as though suffering from snakebite.

"So who are you?" she demanded aggressively, as though it was I who had made the approach.

"I'm Pete Murray," I admitted.

"Oh, dear, how *very* disappointing," she said, and faded away into the crowd.

There was rather more protocol involved with Mary Wilson's visit to Open House. I had to go first to their cosy and comfortable private flat in Downing Street, where I have to say that at no time did I see any trace of a bottle of HP sauce. I remember her telling me how much she liked sunbathing, but how she couldn't go into the garden there, because as soon as she did, everyone started peering. I didn't feel that she was very happy there, because she wasn't really able to be herself.

We discussed her favourite artists, around whom we were going to build the programme, which wasn't difficult since they included Ken

Dodd, Cilla Black, Tom Jones, Alan Price, Peter, Paul and Mary, and Danny La Rue. While I was there I decided to record their cat, Nemo, which purred louder than any other cat I've ever heard. We played this message from Nemo to the cats of Britain on the show, and Mrs Wilson read a verse she had written for the patients of Stoke Mandeville. I only remember that it started: "The flowers are so gay, the grass is so green . . ."

All in all it was a very successful broadcast, and got massive coverage the following day in all the papers, with headlines like: "Meet Mary, DJ from Downing St," and: "Pop goes the PM's Missus."

In a less ecstatic vein I received a few days later a letter from a woman listener which read something like this: "Dear Mr Murray. I listened with interest to your programme with THAT woman. It is quite obvious to me that you have been awarded the OBE, following which you have paid your debt to the man who bestowed it upon you. THAT man Harold Wilson. I'm sure you must feel very satisfied at having paid your debt."

Now I don't get a lot of rude letters, and I don't usually bother to reply when they do come, especially as they are usually anonymous. But on this occasion the name and address *was* given, and I *was* rather incensed, so I wrote, as follows:

"Dear Madam, Thank you very much indeed for your letter. I regret that Mrs Wilson's appearance caused you so much pain. If it is any consolation to you, whenever we have anybody of any political persuasion on the programme, we get problems with people from the other side.

"With reference to my OBE, this was bestowed upon my by Her Majesty the Queen. As yet, I have no plans for her to appear on the programme."

The day after Mrs Wilson was on, the guest was Barry Humphries. He planned to do a cod version of Mary Wilson's poem, but was persuaded from doing so as it was felt to be in bad taste. It ran as follows: "England is a cup of tea with warm and friendly neighbours. England is a pack of corgis trained to sniff cannabis."

Everyone seemed to think that my appearance at some of the Wilson's parties indicated that I was necessarily a staunch Labour supporter. That was not so. It was on a purely personal basis.

And at one of the Downing Street parties in 1970 I had something of a set-to with Clive Jenkins. He told me that show business was very corrupt. "About as corrupt as the Trades Union Movement," I said.

"There's nothing wrong with the Trades Union Movement," lilted Clive.

There was no answer to that!

On March 3rd, despite the lady listener's objections, I proceeded to Buckingham Palace to collect my gong. Michael Caine had been the guest on the programme, and after it finished I dashed to pick up my mother and Auntie Dorothy, clad in a dark suit and grey tie (me, not Auntie Dorothy, I just couldn't face tails). We had to queue when we got there, rather like queueing for buns, I thought at the time, and were ushered to seats by extremely senior Service gentlemen. One of them was an admiral I happened to know because he was a friend of Frank Barnes, and he took charge of us, resplendent in his uniform, and made me feel at home. I thought that was rather good for someone who never got higher than AC2 (i/c glider-batteries).

I remember the Equerry saying out of the corner of his mouth: "You got here quite quickly, didn't you. Been listening to you on the wireless all the way from Windsor." And the Queen Mother, who was doing the honours that day, said: "You did get here quickly. I thought Michael Caine was marvellous this morning."

"That's very kind," I said. "I'm sure he'll be delighted to know that."

Then she asked: "Was this programme 'Open House' your idea?"

"I regret to say no, Ma'am," I replied. "It was basically the idea of Derek Chinnery. I'd like to take the credit for it, but unfortunately I can't."

"Well," she said, "I thoroughly enjoy it, and listen every morning." And with that she pinned the OBE on my lapel, 27 years after presenting me with the bronze medal at RADA. (I don't think she remembered!)

And that is the first and last time I have worn my OBE. Since then, I've never been at an occasion where "medals will be worn". On the other hand, unlike so much that has been mislaid by my incredible absent-mindedness. I *do* know where it is, should occasion arise. It's in the sock drawer.

On April 1st, that year, I decided to let my weakness for practical jokes stray into the show. Leslie Crowther was the guest that day, and I let him in on it, since he is a naturally funny man anyway.

When the programme started I said: "Forgive me if I sound a little confused this morning, but today we have cameras in here, and for the first time ever 'Open House' is on TV. In glorious colour."

Leslie joined in. "Oh, how wonderful to be on television at the same time," he said.

We played the record of Richard Tauber singing 'You are my heart's delight', and I said how grateful we were to the film company for allowing us to show the clip of him singing in the film. "Isn't it great to see him actually singing the song?" I said. Leslie chimed in with hearty agreement . . . and the phones started to ring.

It appeared that there was consternation throughout the land, with people everywhere trying desperately to find the non-existent TV station. Even my mother phoned up, among the multitudes who jammed the switchboard at Broadcasting House.

In May, I duly went down to Bournemouth for *Not Now Darling*. It was a great summer and a really happy season, especially working with Joe Baker, who is naturally a very funny man, though I'm happy to say that he had abandoned his army mode of greeting friends!

My son Michael, meanwhile, had got a job working at the Repertory Theatre in Whitby. A heartfelt letter he wrote me brought back memories of my own early tours. It seemed that he was paying £4 out of his weekly £11 for digs whose walls were so running with water that they should have called the house 'Niagara'. Michael was not happy with this accommodation, and as soon as it was over, he came down for a month to stay with me in Bournemouth, where he worked as a pinball-machine attendant to make some money.

The only slight blight on the summer came when Peter Pritchard rang me to say that a journalist wanted to come down and do an interview with me.

My immediate reaction was: "Why does he want to come and talk to me? There's nothing particularly interesting about me at the moment. I mean, a summer season in Bournemouth isn't the end of the world." Some little sixth sense warned me about it, but my agent kept phoning back, and eventually I agreed, after Peter had said that the journalist wanted to talk about pop music.

He came down, and we had a very pleasant lunch together at the Royal Bath Hotel, and then he started to ask me about pop music, as promised. I noticed that he didn't take any notes, so it was hardly surprising, when the article appeared, that he got Mike Gibb instead of Maurice Gibb, and a reference to Englebert Humperdinck was all wrong. But all that I could have forgiven.

However, when the interview was over, he started talking to me about his personal life. There was a lot about his problems with women, and how difficult it was when models and so on were earning more than he was, and what could he offer them? This, he said, was why he never got married. I just sort of nodded, and sympathised, and said yes I understood the situation.

Then, when the article came out, it was headlined: "Pete Murray says: I'm scared of marriage." About half of it was devoted to problems with women, HIS problems with women, which had been put into my mouth.

I didn't bother to complain, or sue, or anything like that, although it made life very embarrassing for a week or two. As far as I'm concerned, the papers seldom do anything about it, unless it is an outright libel. And I should add that although this, and some other remarks I have made about the press, might make readers think that I am agin' them, I'm not.

On the whole, throughout my career, I've been treated very fairly. Of course there has been a good deal of criticism, but then, if you are in the public eye, whether it's in sport, politics, or entertainment, I think you have to pay that as part of the price. It's all part of the game.

Many journalists, on the other hand, have been very kind, and have become good friends. There's only one thing I wish they wouldn't do, apart from misquoting out of context, and that is to rely so heavily on the cuttings.

When I was in New York in *Power Without Glory*, one lone critic, as I mentioned earlier, described me as giving the performance of the season. When I came back to England I was interviewed, and when I told this to the journalist, I was asked who else was on Broadway at the time. Well, among others, Marlon Brando was at a theatre down the streeet, and I said so.

The way the whole thing was phrased in the article, it appeared that I had beaten Marlon Brando in the choice of the performance of the year. And the mistake has been repeated in dozens of articles by people who merely read the cutting and didn't check with me. I should like to state here and now that I have never beaten Marlon Brando at anything, nor am I ever likely to.

Not Now Darling was a typical Ray Cooney farce, in which I played a businessman running a chic furrier shop and having affairs left, right and centre with as many girls as he possibly could. I enjoyed this role, which proceeded with only two more interruptions.

One was when I became a godfather (no, I *wasn't* trying to do a Brando) to the son of Johnny Gordon, a music publishing friend of mine, and one of nature's gentlemen, who has never once tried to put any pressure on me to play one of his songs.

The other was, inevitably, a phone call from Peter Pritchard, who said that ATV wanted me to do a series called 'The History of Pop', later retitled 'The Melodies Linger On'. I liked the idea very much, but it involved me in having to get up at 7.30 in the morning to be in London in time to record the voice-links for the series.

Now several of my predecessors on the pier had suffered illnesses or worse, through overwork. Sid James had had a very nasty turn, and Freddie Frinton had actually died there.

Determined to escape a like fate, I hired a private ambulance. It would pick me up at 10.30 at night after the show, and once in the back I would remove my clothes and sleep during the drive to London. When we got there I would go straight to bed (having replaced my clothes during the transfer, I hasten to add), and thus managed to combine the two activities in something approaching comfort.

The series, which featured Jack Parnell's Band, dealt with the whole story of pop, from 'Greensleeves' onwards. Unfortunately, when it went out in 1971, the ITV companies were terrified of it because it had been given the Council of Education's seal of approval. So they put it out at 11.30 on Sunday nights, hardly the guarantee of a good audience, although I reckoned it was one of the better things that ITV ever put on.

Certainly the reaction was enormous from those who did see it. I even got letters from older viewers who said that they went to bed at

255

7.30 and then set the alarm so that they could wake up to watch it. At the other end of the scale, I even got a mass of letters from teenagers. Once again, TV had underestimated the intelligence of its audience.

At the end of 1970 I was booked to be the compère for a variety show at the Palladium. Russ Conway and Herman's Hermits were in it, and Dick Emery, with whom I did a sketch, but in general I was dreading it, because I'm really not a compère. I prefer a situation, or people heckling me. So I racked my brains working out some funny lines to suit the various introductions.

Half an hour before the curtain on the opening night, Billy Marsh came up to me. Billy is Bernard Delfont's right-hand man at London Management, a laconic character rather like a priest in mufti, and usually with a cigarette in his mouth from which the ash cascades over his lapel. Occasionally he reaches up to remove this extrusion from which he then takes a long, ruminative drag.

He now went through this rigmarole, and then muttered through a haze of smoke: "How are you Pete?"

"Oh, I'm quite well, thank you Billy," I said, praying for an oxygen mask. Billy gave another long pull on his fag.

"Enjoy your summer season in Bournemouth?"

"Yes thanks, Billy, great, wonderful, I had a lovely time. All that sun, and a really funny show. I really enjoyed it."

A pause, another long drag on the offending weed, then: "You're not going to try to be funny tonight, are you?"

That first night was total disaster for me. I kept muffing my lines for fear that some element of humour might have crept into them. The audience might laugh, heaven forbid. I was not happy with Billy Marsh that night.

While I had been away, 'Open House' had been done by Keith Fordyce and George Elrick. Now, in 1971, I was asked to take over, during Bob Monkhouse's holiday, in the 'Golden Shot', a show that is known in show business by a not dissimilar name. I was filled with my usual quota of trepidation, but at Peter Pritchard's urging I had a go, failing completely to get the hang of it. The ghosts of 'Hit the Limit' came rushing back to me.

It was total chaos, with people rushing round with boards painted with huge letters telling me where to go next. I felt dizzy and quite faint at the end of it, and my admiration for Bob rose dramatically with the thought that he coped with it every week.

1971 was also the end of my 21-year association with Radio Luxembourg. It had been decided that in future all programmes would be done live from the Grand Duchy, and it was another gift from my providential doorman, because as it happened I was invited that year to sign a three-year contract with the BBC which precluded working for commercial radio.

Geoffrey Everitt threw a party for me at the Wellington Club, and the guests included Frank Barnes, who sixteen years earlier had said I was passé, and now had become one of my greatest friends, and Beecher Stevens of Decca, who had been responsible for so much of what I had done. At the end of the lunch, Geoffrey – the man who had given me my first advice on the advantages of ad-libbing – took out and presented me with an ornamental silver microphone with the inscription: "For loyalty and Integrity to Radio Luxembourg. From Your Friends." There's no way I can be funny about that moment. I was simply very touched.

Open House was starting to get a greater variety of guests with a greater variety of stories. There was Patrick Moore, the astronomer-cricketer, describing how aggrieved he was, when playing for a team in Sussex, to have one of his rare batting successes ended by being caught out from a rebound off a goat.

I remember Jilly Cooper, who had been a judge in the Miss UK contest, with her marvellously apt description of Michael Aspel "looking as if he was suffering from crumpet-fatigue."

There was Lord Soper, for whom, knowing he was a Fats Waller fan, we had moved a piano specially into the studio. It was quite something to have the Head of the Methodist Church thumping out and singing 'My Very Good Friend the Milkman'.

On April Fool's Day 1971, the guest on the show was Kenneth McKellar, he of the dry Scottish humour and the ability to swim in freezing California pools. I told him what I had in mind, but kept it secret from Robin Richmond, who was producing the show.

It went something like this.

"Kenneth," I said, after the preliminaries, "I had no idea, until I read a little biog of you, that you were born in Barry in South Wales."

"Oh," said Kenneth, "I don't know where you got that from. It's not widely known that I was born there."

"Then that's one up for us," I said.

"Yes, I suppose you could say that."

"But of course," I said, "you were born of Scottish parents."

"Noo, noo, noo," declared this most Scottish of Scotsmen. "I wasn't. My real name is not Kenneth McKellar but Blodwen Jones."

"Oh, they were Welsh, were they?" I said. "That's very interesting. Do you put down your singing voice to the fact that you were born Welsh?"

"Oh, certainly, certainly. There are no good singers in Scotland at all. I'm fortunate enough, and proud, to have been born a Welshman."

At this point Robin Richmond made it clear that he thought I was being a bit cruel bringing this out, particularly since he was having to cope with the Scottish Daily Mail and the now-demolished Scottish Daily Express who were anxiously on the line. Clearly one of the pillars of Scottish identity was about to fall. But worse was to come.

Half an hour later I played a record by another Scottish artist, after which Kenneth said: "Yes. Very good. But of course, he can't sing, because he's Scottish. Of course, you know about Sir Harry Lauder?"

"No, I don't," I said, not daring to imagine what was coming.

"He wasn't Scottish at all," declared Kenneth, heretically.

"Really?" I said.

"Noo, noo. He was actually a Czechoslovakian. He left during the Putsch. His real name was Heinrich Laudervich."

By now it appeared that the entire Scottish nation was on the streets. We had irate phone calls from as far as Aberdeen. And nobody guessed, even when I ended the programme with: "I wish you all a happy April 1st."

Robin Richmond said somewhat testily: "I think you came on a bit strong with all that Scottish stuff."

"Robin," I said, "you're kidding. Haven't you realised what day it is?"

The penny dropped with a massive clang, and *all* the organ stops came out!

In May of that year, Val Singleton and I went on holiday to Antibes.

I mention that only because of a near disastrous expedition with Dickie Henderson and his wife in a hired motor boat. The engines broke down, and we were left drifting helplessly past the rocky islands off Cannes, and after my Beirut experience I should have known that boats and I do not happily combine.

In fact, I had had an early inkling of this many years before when I took a boat on the Thames at Maidenhead. When going through a lock, I tied the boat happily to a stout post, inconveniently forgetting that the water was going down. After a short walk along the bank, I returned to find the vessel dangling in mid-air, to the astonishment of the lock-keeper.

That holiday was really the beginning of the break-up with Val. It wasn't anything to do with my unsatisfactory sailing, but a bit of the sparkle had gone out of the relationship, and we agreed to go our own ways.

In my case, that meant life at Montagu Mansions with Michael who had descended upon me. The flat was in a terrible state, because whereas I at least have some conscience about clearing up, Michael doesn't. He's the original gypsy. Into this chaos, Uncle Bill would merge most evenings in order to watch the television.

One evening, after working very hard all day on a Dickie Henderson Show, I arrived back about eight o'clock exhausted, to find Uncle Bill putting on his overcoat.

"Where are you going?" I asked.

"Well, Michael's going off to Liverpool tomorrow," he said.

"Yes, I know he is. So what?"

"Well," said Bill, "he's in there with his girl-friend. I think we ought to leave them alone and let them have a couple of hours together."

"And where do you suggest I go?" I demanded. "It may be of small importance, but this does happen to be my flat."

I walked through into the living room, where Michael and the girl were heavily entwined. The place looked like a lunatic asylum, but I will give Michael his due, he did break off for approximately three and a half seconds to say: "Oh, hello Dad," before returning to the lips of his loved one.

"Hold on a minute," I said. "I'm delighted that you two are very happy with each other. But I'd like to be happy too. Do you think that there's a chance that at some time your girl-friend might be good enough to get off her arse and make me a cup of tea?"

"Yes, all right," said my long-suffering son. The girl did as bidden, and when she came back with the tea, I saw a little twinkle in Michael's eyes which I had started to recognise.

"By the way, Dad," he said. "Sharon doesn't believe this. We do have coloured blood in the family, don't we?"

I got the picture instantly. We had already formed the opinion that the girl was rather racialist. "Yes, of course," I said. The girl looked up. "Of course we do," I went on, "your grandmother was from Africa."

"Yes," said Michael, "that's what I told Sharon, but she wouldn't believe me.

"You know your Auntie Agnes, don't you?" I said. Now by chance, he had been talking about Auntie Agnes to the girl earlier, and saying that for some reason he had never met her.

"Well, no, I've never met her," said Michael.

"Well, you know you get throwbacks," I said. "That fact is, Auntie Agnes is coloured. That's why we haven't let you see her."

"Oh, is that a fact?" said Michael interestedly.

The girl Sharon could take no more. She removed herself from Michael's embrace, stood up in a determined way, and said: "I'm sorry, but I can't stay here with coloured people."

It was the most frightening piece of prejudice I ever heard, but it wasn't really a joke that misfired, because it taught Michael how much *she* was worth . . . and it got me a free flat for the evening!

That Autumn, John Billingham took over as producer of 'Open House'. The show now ran for an hour and a half, and he had a lot of ideas for it, including the notion of taking it on the road. We had no idea how it would go, and our first experiment was at a small studio in Bristol, which held about 150 people. We announced that we were coming, and expected just a few people to turn up, not the 600 who did.

Our guest that day was Arthur Negus, and I'll always remember his reply, in that marvellous West Country voice, when I asked him to describe the furniture at the BBC studios. He looked round carefully, mulled it over for a few seconds, then said: "Well, I'd say it was early nineteen-thirties . . . and rubbish."

For our second attempt we went to the Paris Theatre in Lower Regent Street, which holds about 450 people. Again we failed to issue tickets. This time 1,000 turned up, some from as far as Bristol. (They were probably the ones who couldn't get in the first time!)

The guests were Max Bygraves and Val Doonican, and there was one slight embarrassment when Max asked Val: "Have you been over to Ireland lately?"

"No. No I haven't," said Val.

"I have. My grandmother's over there," said Max.

"Oh, really?"

"Yeah," said Max, "she's a rear-gunner on a milk-float." It was a great line, but for some reason, perhaps because he was talking to the Irish Val, it died a rather awkward death.

In October of 1971, Cyril Drake, the Executive Producer of 'Open House', said he thought that it would be a good idea to do a Christmas Day special version of the programme. My first thought was how to avoid having to go into the studios, so before I could think what I was doing I said airily: "I've got it. I'm going to get you the unobtainable. I'm going to get you the sort of stars you'd never get on the programme."

"What sort of people?" asked a dubious Drake.

"Oh," I said, thumbing carelessly through a mental file of all the most famous show business personalities I could think of, "Noel Coward, Maurice Chevalier, Rex Harrison, Robert Morley, Richard Burton, Liz Taylor, Morecambe and Wise . . . you know, that sort of thing."

"Would you really?" he asked.

"Certainly," I said. I had absolutely no idea what I had let myself in for. I had to work on that show continuously through till Christmas. It's certainly the last time I'll make such a rash promise.

For the interview with Noel Coward, John Billingham and I went to the Savoy, where we were shown into his suite by Graham Payne, whom I'd known for many years. He ushered us into the presence of The Master, who was looking very poorly and lying in bed. Thankfully, he agreed to do the interview, and we took out our little recorder and switched it on.

Nothing happened.

Now it's always difficult getting someone to talk into a tape recorder. I always feel as though I'm soliciting, like some old tart. And when it doesn't work, especially in the face of Noel Coward, the whole thing is just too embarrassing. So I breathed a great sigh of relief when he just gave a little smile and quipped: "Typically BBC."

I found him charming, gentle, unassuming, unexpectedly shy, and very reticent about talking about himself and his wit. But I did get the chance to ask him, NOT for the programme, whether a story that was currently going the rounds was true.

The story went that he had been to the first night of the stage production of *Gone With the Wind*. He had loathed it. Not only was one of the leading parts played by an extremely bad actress, who must remain nameless, but the horse that was brought on stage for one of the big scenes did something that no self-respecting equine performer should do in public.

Noel Coward was reported as saying afterwards: "If they had taken that actress, and stuffed her up the horse's arse, they might have averted two major catastrophes."

Did he? "Yes, dear boy, I confess I did. I'm glad you appreciated the remark."

Another interviewee was the fearsome Robert Morley at the Lyric Theatre. Over the years he always sort of waved at me in corridors. "Hello, dear boy," he would call, not knowing at all where he had seen me before. This time it was no different.

"Come in, dear boy, want to do an interview, do you? Can't think what you want to interview me for, but come in nonetheless, what do you want me to talk about, Christmas? All right, dear boy." The monologue delivered, he sat firmly in his chair and started to read the Evening Standard. I felt like a 17 year-old again.

"Well, do you think we might do the interview?" I asked nervously, feeling rather as if I were meeting my old headmaster.

"Yes, of course, dear boy, carry on," said Morley, eyes glued to the paper. There was only one thing to do. I crouched on the floor, microphone in hand, and thrust it up under the newspaper, which he continued reading. At least he managed to tell me that his favourite comedy programme was 'Stars on Sunday'.

"And what do you want most for Christmas?" I asked, a trifle weakly.

"That there will be a Christmas 'Stars on Sunday'. I like to be amused."

During the whole interview, and even when I said my farewell, he never once looked up from the paper, and I retired crestfallen, and more terrified than ever of Robert Morley.

On a later occasion I was talking to David Tomlinson, and recounting my terror to him. "You must never be frightened of Robert," he said. "He's terribly nice. Gentle as anything. Wouldn't hurt a fly." He then told me how he, Robert, Vanessa Redgrave, and Wilfred Hyde White, a real political rag-bag, often used to go out together.

At this I expressed some surprise.

"Could only happen in England, dear boy," said David, who has himself a fair bit of Morley's avuncular manner.

"But what about Vanessa and all her chat?" I asked.

"Mad as a hatter, old boy. But what a lovely girl. We used to go to her meetings. I confess I tended to go to sleep. So did Robert. So did Wilfred. We love her."

At the end of 1971, Dorothy Squires came to me and said: "I'm doing another show at the Palladium, and I'd like you to compère it."

"If you don't mind, I'd rather not, Dorothy," I said. "It's not really my scene." I had visions of getting schizophrenia about whether to be funny at the Palladium or not.

"You're going to do the bloody thing, you see?" said Dorothy, for whom the answer "No" does not exist. So I did it.

After introducing the four acts in the first half of the show, I sat in my dressing room during the interval waiting for the second half. Then it began to dawn on me that it was becoming rather a long interval. I went along to Dorothy's dressing room to find out what was happening, and there I was confronted by, Dorothy Squires in *negligee*.

"What's the matter, Dorothy?" I asked, attempting, gentleman that I am, to keep looking her straight in the eyes.

"The bloody dress hasn't arrived," she fumed. "It'll be another five minutes at least."

"Don't worry," I said, "I'll go out and explain what's happened. Are you sure it will only be five minutes?"

She nodded, and I went on stage. I told a few stories, and glanced into the wings. Nothing was happening. I told a few more stories. Still nothing. By now I was starting to get desperate. What's more, I was rapidly running out of clean stories. Then the dream happened.

A woman from the audience shouted out: "I know you."

"Thank you very much," I said.

"Yes," she shouted, "you've been up to my flat, and I made you a nut cutlet."

It was a gift from Heaven. The audience went into hysterics, and she gave me at least ten more minutes of material to last until Dorothy finally came on. I don't know who that woman was, nor, I regret to say, do I recall her nut cutlet, but if she reads this ... Thank you Madam.

At the end of the show I stayed to give Dorothy her bouquet of flowers. The audience loved her, and she burst into tears, and put her head on my shoulder.

Now there are quite a number of gay people among Dorothy's devoted following, and at the party afterwards one beautiful young man came up to me. "You know, I never liked you," he lisped. "Never liked you. Thought you were a hard man, a hard, shrewd man. But the way you picked up those flowers for Dorothy, well, it was a sight for sore eyes. I thought to myself, here is this hard man ... you're all heart Pete, you're all heart. And then when you put your arm round her to comfort her ... Oh my God, I'd like to put central heating into your Open House any time you like."

I did not avail myself of this offer.

The 1972 Eurovision Song Contest was in Edinburgh, because Monaco, who had won it the year before, didn't feel that it had the facilities to stage it. We took the chance of doing a couple of Open House Road Shows from there, one of them with Moira Anderson, a delightful lady and the epitome of fun. We took her to lunch at the Royal Caledonian Hotel, and she and I waltzed together into the dining room. Then she suddenly realised where she was, and decided she ought to worry about her image. "They don't like that sort of thing up here," she said.

The other show included the New Seekers and Chic Murray as guests. I thought Chic seemed a bit down, and only discovered later that they had announced his divorce that morning. Certainly the audience seemed very glum, and I thought we had died the death.

After the show one of the attendants came up to me and said: "Mr Murray. I've been a studio attendant here for twenty-five years."

"Really?" I said.

"Aye, twenty-five years, and by Christ, I've never seen anything like it today. They went raving mad." They had me fooled.

Every night, while we were up there, a party of us got together to eat at the Caledonian. There was a pianist there, playing away very nicely to absolutely no reaction from the dour diners. At John's suggestion, we got a number of sugar bowls one evening and went round to all the tables making a collection for him. Fourteen pounds ten shillings. It wasn't bad.

Another evening we saw an engaged couple at a table who were obviously having an argument. John called over the maître d'hôtel, a very deadpan Scotsman. "Look, we want to play a gag on those people," John explained. "Could you possibly get us an empty bottle of champagne, fill it with ginger ale, seal it, and take it across to them with our compliments to wish them a very happy time here in Edinburgh."

The Maître looked sternly at us, and said: "No ... ' a very long pause, and then " ... trouble at all Sir." He did it beautifully. He then did as John had asked, the coupled poured out their ginger ale, toasted each other happily, and by the end of the bottle were completely and utterly drunk, Let no-one say it isn't in the mind.

With the contest finished, I had to dash back to London where I had been asked to do the interviews in the foyer for the Royal Film Performance. It was a touch of the trepidations again, because I thought it a peculiarly thankless task, and remembered Mike Parkinson the year before being lumbered with a particularly monosyllabic Ryan O'Neal.

The whole affair started less than auspiciously for me when I discovered, with a quarter of an hour to go, that my absent-mindeness had left me without my black shoes, only brown ones to go with my dinner jacket. A panic-stricken phone call to Michael produced the correct footwear with thirty seconds to go. Not that he was unused to these dramas. During our days as brother bachelors, I frequently used the 'Open House' airwaves to send him desperate pleas like: "Don't forget to buy some bread. We're out," or: "Where have you put all my socks?" There was in fact one occasion when he took *all* my socks away with him, and I had to beg him publicly to return me a pair.

The Royal Film Performance was hair-raising. In those days there was just the one commentator. I wore earphones, and as people arrived a directorial voice in my ear would say "That's Fred Nurge."

"Ah yes," I would promptly tell viewers, "there's Fred Nurge, and with him the lovely, the lovely … " "Jean Snooks" went the voice in my ear. "Ah yes, the lovely Jean Snooks."

I then had to turn immediately to interview whoever was standing next to me, going boss-eyed with the effort, since I'm not a cinemagoer and didn't recognise half of them anyway.

This fiasco was then interrupted by the arrival of The Queen, at which point I had to move into a fresh position and whisper into the microphone the details of the unidentifiable but frightfully important beings to whom she was talking, together with a description of her attire, which had arrived from the Palace (the description, not her attire) about ten minutes before.

I was struggling through this hopeless situation when suddenly there was a shot of Princess Margaret. "There's Margaret," I whispered confidently to the viewers, delighted that at least there was someone I could recognise. I was deafened by a voice screaming down my earpiece. "She's a Princess, you fool."

The following day I was panned in the Press. It has become a sort of annual fiesta to pan the Eurovision Song Contest or the Royal Film Performance.

Or preferably both.

Since I do both, I am in for an annual bad time.

Not that I think *all* the criticisms are valid. They often come from people who have no idea of the real problems. Regarding the Film, I think that the public still like a good old bit of glamour, and it's certainly not the occasion for an in-depth interview, which is what some of the critics seem to want.

As for the Song Contest, it still gets an audience of hundreds of millions, and it still produces a mass of good songs, whatever the more ignorant of critics may say. Of course, the best songs are not always the winners, but in the end they show their true merit. 'Arriverderci Roma', 'Love is Blue' and 'Walk Away' are just three songs that first became known in the contest, but came nowhere in the voting.

When I said this year that the good songs don't always win, one critic asked: "What is the criterion?" A man who asks a question like that is a fool. It's easy to talk about a hit *after* it's a hit, but not before.

And whereas 'Go, before you break my heart', which did not win in 1974, will become a standard, 'Waterloo' which *did* win will never be heard of again.

Since 'Open House' is neither rehearsed nor researched, but simply done off the cuff, we are never quite sure what people are going to say, or how the audience will react.

For instance, Virginia McKenna came on a road show we did from Liverpool, and recited the poem that was used as a code in the film Carve Her Name With Pride. *We had about 4,000 enquiries about this poem, and the end result was that Virginia recorded it.*

In a less literary vein, Arthur Askey came on a road show at Eastbourne. Now Arthur, a great showbiz veteran, can get away with things that other people wouldn't dare try. It's just as well, because Wimbledon was on at the time, and Arthur said: "I wish they could do for me what they do for the players."

"What's that?" I asked.

"Well, it's the way they keep calling 'New balls please'!"

Raquel Welch inadvertently followed a similar track. I was delighted (naturally) to have her on the programme, and was flattered to learn that she had always wanted to be asked, since she used to listen to it while filming over here.

But when I asked her to read the first card she rather fluffed it, and said: "Oh gee, I made a bollocks of that, didn't I? ... Oh gee, I shouldn't have said bollocks, should I?"

"Um, er," I said. There were no complaints.

Nor, surprisingly, were there any when Brian Clough came on, in his typically forthright way. After talking about his buying plans, and how he would like to buy Charlie George and make him get his hair cut, I asked him why he had never gone into politics. He said he would have done had it not been for his views on immigration. He's agin' it.

For the Spring Bank Holiday of 1972 we went to Woburn Abbey, with David Nixon and Katie Boyle as the guests. David, John Billingham and I stayed the night there, and had dinner with the Bedfords, who were the epitome of easy-going. I remember that their son kept telling me he was a Marxist, having just bought, I think, a Lamborghini.

I also succeeded in one of my more notable faux pas, when I looked around at the impressive pictures on the walls and said: "Those paintings are marvellous. And especially those Canellonis. They're excellent." To this day they think I was making a joke. I didn't disillusion them.

Up in the suite I had been given, I discovered that all my clothes had been unpacked and laid out for me, an experience I was unused to, and which enable me to find not a single thing. The following morning I was extremely embarrassed to discover that I couldn't find my clean underpants anywhere.

I phoned the valet, who didn't answer, and in desperation rang the butler, who gave me the impression that he was not accustomed to dealing with vermin such as myself.

"Your underpants, SIR?" he intoned heavily. "I brought your breakfast up this morning, SIR, and I think," he said with utter distaste "that SIR will find them on the chair in the bedroom." It was a heavy hint that I should have used the dressing room.

The situation called for a counter-attack. "Yes," I said, "but those are Sir's used underpants, and Sir would like to know where Sir's clean underpants are located."

'I will send a lady up,' said the voice from Downstairs.

Miraculously she produced them from a drawer in a place I would never have thought of.

The Duchess, who was a great sales lady for Woburn, appeared on the programme, and once I had introduced her she launched into a six minute speech about the glories of the place, which left me no chance of interruption. Suddenly she came to a full stop, having done her piece, and blessed inspiration descended upon me. "The Morning

268

Story this morning," I said, "was read by the Duchess of Bedford."

She too took it very well, which is more than I did the haggis. They had a haggis-eating contest, but knowing my eating habits they had made a special vegetarian haggis for me (if that's not a contradiction in terms.) I came second in the contest, for the simple reason that the haggis, even in its vegetarian version, was so utterly revolting that I couldn't wait to finish it.

The road shows took us to some pretty unlikely places, The Royal Opera House, Covent Garden, actually rang up and invited us to do it from there, which was how I came to be doing a rock-and-roll dance at Covent Garden with ballerina Antoinette Sibley.

Rather more down to earth was the City Hall in Hull. The first person in the queue, at three o'clock on the previous afternoon, was Elsie Perry, all the way from Cleethorpes in Lincolnshire, and aged 79. "We can't let her stay there all night," I said. "We must guarantee her a place and arrange an hotel for her."

The following day I brought her on to the stage, and she said: "I've queued for the Coronation, I've queued for the Royal Wedding, and now I've queued for 'Open House'." I couldn't have asked for a better write-up.

"How will you get back to Cleethorpes?' I asked her.

"Don't worry about me," she said. "I'll get the train."

"Well, I'm going to see my son at Skegness," I said, "so I can give you a lift most of the way."

She thought that was marvellous, and talked non-stop all the way. When I arrived at the ferry at Hull, where I was going to drop her, British Rail, bless their hearts, had laid on a fantastic bouquet of flowers and a bottle of champagne for her.

That may seem a bit of a sob story, but I include it because I often sit down and wonder why I don't do something worthwhile or useful, and it's moments like that which make me think that perhaps it's not all as trite and useless as it may seem to be.

Rossano Brazzi came on the programme and told the audience that he had once been a professional goalie in Italian football. I think it shook a few people. It hardly went with 'Some Enchanted Evening.'

Then there was Mrs Mills who told the story of how, after a visit to Melton

Mowbray, she was booked to stay at some very posh hotel. "Lovely to see you, Mrs Mills," said the manager as she walked into the foyer. At that moment her bag burst, and a couple of dozen Melton Mowbray pork pies were scattered among the ankles of the astonished guests.

And Ilie Nastase actually failed to throw a single tantrum, and confined himself to announcing his engagement.

In September of that year I went on holiday to Majorca where it rained continuously, and I returned with one day left to discover that for once the English weather was beautiful. So I went down to the poolside at Roehampton.

By chance, the blonde lady whom I have mentioned earlier, and whose name I had discovered was Tricia, was there.

"Oh, I'm going to the club dance on Saturday. Are you going?" I asked her.

She said she was. In the smooth-talking way that I have I then said: "Oh, well maybe I'll see you there then."

"Well, are you inviting me?" she asked.

With a piece of manly decision I said: "OK, then, I'll definitely see you there."

We had a great evening, and I danced a great deal with her, and after the dance took her home and said goodbye. And that seemed to be that. Then, out of the blue, a bombshell arrived in my morning post. It was a letter from a solicitor, the gist of which was: "Regrettably a divorce case in which you were involved ten years ago, and which was then dropped, has now come up again. You are involved as a witness." I gathered I was to be mentioned in despatches.

I went to Tricia, who by now had been called to the Bar, to ask her advice, because anything to do with litigation frightens the life out of me. She said: "I'm afraid you're going to have to defend yourself." And there, for the moment, the matter rested.

That autumn, we did a road show from the Thornaby Pavilion. There were about 3,000 people there, and at the end of the show a lady who had been queueing up, said: "Can I have your autograph? It's the first time I've been out in six months." She was very smart, with a green costume, and above all she had these lovely eyes.

"Why so long?" I asked, as I signed the autograph for her.

"Look at my hands," she said. I looked. She had plastic knuckles, the result of severe arthritis.

"God, that's terrible," I said. But she had none of the bitterness you sometimes find with people who have ghastly afflictions.

"Well, life's like that sometimes," she said. "My husband's dead, but now I'm hoping to get an old banger so I can get out and about again."

When I left Thornaby, I thought what a shame it was that I hadn't taken her name, because I would have loved to try to help her. So the following morning, on 'Open House', I said: "Would the lady with the green costume and the arthritic hands and the lovely eyes please write to me, as I might be able to help in some way."

In the event she phoned me, and I asked her for her address, since I thought I might be able to help her, though I didn't say what I had in mind. I then wrote to all the people who had ever been on 'Open House', told them the story, and asked if they would care to send a pound ... not for a large amount of money, because it's always assumed that people in show business earn, and can afford vast sums of money, and it just isn't true.

Well, they did her proud. We raised about £450, which I sent to her, and she bought herself her old banger.

Just before Christmas that year, I went to the Royal Albert Hall to compère a Syd Lawrence concert. It was about two-thirds of the way through when I was called to the phone. On the other end was Rodney Collins, then publicity man for Radio One and Two.

"Peter, I think you might have told me," he said reproachfully.

"Told you? What about?" I asked.

"About getting married on Saturday."

"What ARE you talking about?" I demanded.

"Come on, Peter," he said, "I've had all the Press on to me."

"I'm sorry, I really don't know what you're talking about," I said.

He wasn't to be put off. "You don't have to lie to me. Peter. I'm here to protect you. I know you're getting married on Saturday."

"Look, Rodney," I said, feeling that the situation was getting out of hand. "I tell you I'm not getting married on this or any other Saturday. Perhaps you could kindly tell me whom I am supposed to be marrying."

"Hang on a minute," he said. "I'll call you back."

271

Towards the end of the concert he did call back. "Yes, Peter, you're marrying your former secretary."

It was starting to be a mixture between high farce and a nightmare. "WHAT former secretary?" I asked. "I've never *had* a secretary."

"Ena Owen," he said, with a note of triumph in his voice, as if he had caught me smoking behind the bushes.

"Ena Owen. My conscience guided my memory over a quick tour of the past twenty years. Have I ever known an Ena Owen? Have I ever known an Ena? I've never even known an Ena. "I don't *know* any Ena Owen," I protested.

"Well that's unfortunate Peter, because you're marrying her. The banns are up."

"WHAT?" I shrieked, the sweat now pouring down my face. "For God's sake Rodney, get on to the Press, tell them it isn't true, I'm not marrying anybody, and especially not anybody called Ena Owen."

"Are you sure about this, Peter?" he asked cautiously, but with an element of doubt creeping into his voice.

"Rodney, I swear to you on my life, my mother's life, my son's life, anybody's life, Ena Owen's life, I'm not getting married. I don't know anybody to get married to."

"All right, Peter, don't panic," he said, somewhat unsympathetically I thought, in the face of these hypothetical nuptials.

The concert was over, and I emerged, shaking like a leaf, to find a group of reporters and photographers from the National Press outside. "Pete, what's this about you getting married?"

"I'm not getting married, I don't understand it," I said, thinking that I had better put this refrain on tape, but quickly. They pressed me, disbelieving my story, and I fled home, where more pressmen were waiting. As we were going through the same rigmarole, there was a call from a newspaper in Manchester.

"We hear you're getting married, Peter."

By now I was getting hysterical. "I swear to you, I'm not getting married."

"Come on, don't give me any crap, Pete," said the nerveless newshound. "We've got confirmation from the girl's mother."

"Look, describe to me what's happened," I pleaded.

"It's like this," he said. "Your future mother-in-law —"

272

"Cut that OUT!" I yelled.

"The girl's mother went to the local paper to put in an advert about a choir concert. She said to the editor that she hoped he would mention her daughter, because she was getting married on Saturday. He asked her who she was marrying, and the mother said Pete Murray.

"He asked if by any chance it was you, and she said yes it was. And of course, the editor then got on to all the national papers."

"Look, do me a favour," I said. "Get on to the woman and find out if she's ever met me."

"We asked that," he said, "and she says you've been going to meet her on several occasions, but each time there's been a hitch. The last time, apparently, your car broke down on the M1."

"The M1 to get to Oswestry?" I said, "I never even knew that was the route, and besides, the last time I was in Oswestry was with Robert Morley in a play during the war."

They didn't believe me, and the following morning it was in the early editions of the papers. In desperation I went to Rodney and got him to phone the mother.

"Have you ever met Pete Murray?" he asked her.

"No," she said.

"Well, Mr Murray says he's never met your daughter."

There was a long pause, and then she said: "Oh my God, she's done it again."

And that was the last I heard of it. Who she was, why she did it, whether she was sick, I never found out.

Chapter Twenty

I am not . . .

going to start this last chapter with a negative, because in it I did the most positive thing I have ever done, which was to marry Tricia. But that comes a little later.

1973 started marvellously for me, when I went to the Talk of the Town for the New Year's Eve Royal Variety Awards. I was given the award for the Radio Personality of the Year.

It was an emotional moment for me. I thought back to the producers who had worked with me on the programme, Peter Bell, Colin Chandler, John Billingham. I had often heard people on these occasions trot out the same speech about how they owe it all to their producers, and so on. But when it came to it, I told the audience, there was no alternative to saying the same, because it happened to be true. You are as strong as your producer, who is there to inspire you, to berate you, and to take the can back for you. I confess that a little tear came into my eye.

That year, of course, was when we first entered the Common Market, and someone, in one of those secret rooms where the BBC's thought processes occur, decided that it would be a wonderful idea if the BBC showed the flag. Murray, it was decided, would be the flag.

The plan was that I should travel through all the Common Market countries in one day, ending in Britain, and the original idea was that I should fly to Amsterdam at the crack of dawn, do a quick broadcast from there, then for some reason beyond my comprehension (but probably to do with air schedules) fly back to London, before racing off to the Continent once more.

These things, however, don't always work out as intended, especially if the Clerk of the Weather hasn't been informed. To my intense relief, on January 2nd a thick fog descended upon Europe; I was confident that I could spend the day in bed instead of doing this hectic Cook's tour. But no.

The BBC power-that-was said: "Marvellous. You and Steve Allen, the producer, will go by ferry to Belgium, and make your own way to Brussels."

Thus it came about that at some god-forsaken hour we set sail from Dover, to arrive in Belgium at two in the morning. The hotelier woke us at six, and we phoned through to London to do the first broadcast-insert of the day. Unfortunately, no-one had told the BBC operators what was happening, and there was a long hassle over whether they would accept a reverse-charge call. Well, we certainly weren't going to trundle round Europe with a sackful of coins for long telephone calls, and in the end they accepted it.

After a quick and pointless chat with Tom Edwards, who was doing the early morning programme, I said that we would be speaking to David Hamilton from somewhere in Holland. This was actually rather a rash promise, since we had not the faintest idea where we were. There was only one solution for rational beings . . . we hailed a taxi.

"Where do you want to go?" the man asked.

"Holland," we said.

The man put his machine back into neutral and turned off the engine in order to check what he had just heard.

"Where?!"

"Holland."

"Ah, you *did* say that. But where in Holland?"

"Just take us to the nearest village," I commanded, with the feeling that he couldn't have been more surprised if I had asked him to take us to his leader.

The nearest village in Holland was shut. All of it. No-one had told us that the Dutch New Year holiday had a tendency to spread. "Where now?" asked the taxi driver. "The next village," I said, trying to make it clear by my tone of voice that his question was a stupid one, but inwardly feeling great sympathy for him.

At the next village there was actually one café open, a sleazy place with a radio playing and about four people sitting around in a desultory way. We asked if they spoke English, and when it transpired that they did, we asked them to switch to the BBC on the long wave.

After some muttering among themselves, they quickly did as requested, and when I asked if there was a phone, in order that we might call London, the proprietor rushed with a great show of nervousness to show me where it was. It later turned out that, since both Steve and I wore macs and carried brief cases, they were sure that this early morning visitation was from the IRA.

"Where are you?" asked David Hamilton.

"That is an extremely good question," I said. I looked out of the window and saw a sign carrying some word, which might well have been a name, and gave it to him. For all I know, I might have been giving him the way to the public toilets, but he was satisfied, and after further futile chat I said that I would be speaking to Mike Parkinson, who was sitting in for me on 'Open House', at approximately 10.45 from Brussels.

Outside the café, our taxi-driver waited with an air of Belgian resignation. "Where to now?" he asked wearily, when it became clear that we were not about to pay him off. "Brussels airport," I said, conveying the impression that that was the most natural thing in the world.

We got to the airport at 10.25, just in time to hear Mike Parkinson saying: "Pete Murray should be arriving at Brussels airport about now, and should be giving the taxi-driver something in the region of £20,000." He was actually spot-on, except that it was francs, not pounds.

During the quarter of an hour of 'Waggoners Walk' we rushed around trying to find the studio from where this historic broadcast was to be made. We finally found it, a truly Heath Robinson affair that looked like something from the early days of 2LO. The idea was that from this oddly-wired venue I should interview Mr Average Brussels Man. He was nowhere to be seen. The only soul in sight was Ward Bogart, the representative of Radio Brussels. "Where is Mr Average Brussels Man?" I asked him.

"There is nobody here," said Ward, whom I had met at Eurovision Song Contests.

276

"In that case, I shall have to talk to you," I said, making a quick Hobson's Choice.

"You can't talk to me as me," he said.

"Very well. Who do you want to be?" I asked. "But hurry up and choose, because Waggoners Walk is about to finish."

"Tell you what," he said. "I'll be the owner of a sauna and massage parlour."

So for ten minutes he talked to me, very convincingly, about his non-existent massage parlour, and the joys of a Brussels rub-down; at two minutes to eleven we said goodbye; and at five past eleven we were on the plane to Luxembourg.

The Grand Duchy, for some reason, was fogless. It was a beautiful day, and we were met by Germaine who got us through Customs quickly and into a fast car for the studios, where I got Michael, who was visiting his mother, to join in the broadcast. We talked to the Tony Brandon show, and then hurtled off to Frankfurt.

By now I was getting punch-drunk. I did a quick interview at a beautiful studio at the airport about the cost of living and the price of cauliflowers in Germany, and then took the plane to Milan, where we only had a few minutes. To our consternation, the studio there was on the other side of the airport, so after a frantic sprint we got there to find an unbelievable set-up right next to a booking office.

Waiting there was some unknown pop group and Mr Average Italy, so after some cursory remarks to the former, and a quick chat about the cost of living and the price of cauliflowers in Italy to the latter, we sprinted back to catch the plane for Paris. We got there with five minutes to spare before my chat with David Jacobs (combined with an interview with Mr Average Paris about the price of living etc).

"Hello, Peter, what a terrible waste of time this all is," said the imperturbable David at his most imperturbable. I refrained from agreeing with him, which was just as well. The BBC were not happy with this comment.

Steve Allen and I were about to expire. At nine-thirty we arrived back at Heathrow, and at ten-thirty I was on the Late Night Extra programme with Keith Fordyce.

"What was it like, Pete?" he asked.

To that, as they say, there was no answer. Besides, I was just about to fall asleep.

In March of 1973 we did an 'Open House' road show from Llandudno. There was a lot of Welsh Nationalism about at that time, and we were afraid they might cut the power lines . . . not that I have given any particular offence to Nationalists, that I can recall.

Half-way through the show some girls came on to the stage, declared that they were going to make an announcement, and unleashed a torrent of Welsh of which Kenneth McKellar himself would have been proud. It turned out to be a protest, of course, but the greater protest came from the audience in the hall, who were screaming for them to get off and let me get on with the programme.

But that was nothing to the protests the day Sheila Graham, the gossip columnist and one-time mistress of Scott Fitzgerald, came on the programme. Michael Crawford was due that day, but he couldn't make it, and when the producer told me that she just had a book out, and suggested her as an alternative, I happily agreed. Little did I know what I was letting myself in for.

I asked her what advice she would give to someone of similar circumstances to her own, who wanted to make it to the top. She said that her first advice to women who wanted to succeed was to find themselves a very wealthy man.

"My first husband was a multi-millionaire, and he owned a department store," she said. "I worked for him in the software department, which was rather appropriate, because he was impotent."

What do you say to that? What I did say was: "I'd like to dedicate the next record to you." The record was 'Call me Irresponsible.' And the phones started to buzz.

While this unexpectedly suitable music was playing, I said: "I do realise that your book includes a fair amount of detail about your sexual life, but do you think we could talk about something else?"

"Certainly, food," she said.

So when the record ended I said: "I believe you are something of a gourmet?"

"Oh yes, indeed I am," she said. "Can I tell you about my favourite meal?"

"Please do," I said, confident that sex had now been eliminated from the subjects for discussion.

"Well, it was at the Waldorf, here in London," she said. "I was eating with this man whom I fancied like mad. I knew we had a very limited time, because he had an appointment at three o'clock. But I was loving this meal. The dessert

came, and it was twenty to three. Coffee arrived at ten to three.

"But I'm happy to tell you that it was not only the best meal I've ever had, but it was also the best lay, because it was short and very sweet."

Without any planning at all, the programme then went into the theme music from 'Love Story'. People rang in from all over the country, some even suggesting that I apologise the following morning for her appearance on the show. And one man I know was telephoned in the middle of a board meeting to tell him to listen to the show whatever he did. He broke up the meeting and got it on tape, now one of his most treasured possessions.

The BBC, however, were not happy with this interview.

That spring the divorce case finally came to court. For me, the whole affair was a horrifying experience.

The extraordinary thing, for me, was that for all those years I had kept the various letters and papers involved.

The Press, as usual, managed to find out that someone well-known was involved, so that all the photographers were awaiting my arrival at the court.

My only previous experience with the law had been in 1947, during the power cuts, when Patrick Westwood and I used to go to watch cases being fought, not from any great legal interest, but because it was warm. There was one divorce case where the woman was complaining that her husband wanted sex all the time.

"How would you like it," she asked the judge, "if you were pushed up against the stove and had your skirts lifted up five times a day." We never heard how the judge would have liked it, because we dissolved into hysterical laughter and were removed from the court for misbehaviour.

Apart from this, my knowledge of court procedure was limited to watching 'Crown Court' on television, but luckily Tricia was able to give me a load of tips on how to behave.

At the end of the afternoon, the judge, who was very courteous, said that he was sorry, but that I would have to come back again to give more evidence. He asked what my commitments were the next day. I told him that I had 'Open House' in the morning, and in the afternoon was due to go off for the Eurovision Song contest. But the case couldn't be delayed, and I had to miss 'Open House' the following morning.

The whole thing was very unpleasant. I was a minor cog in a very major divorce case that ran for about five weeks, but to read the Press you would think that I had been named as the co-respondent of the century. Nor did the Press realise that had I been found guilty of helping to break up the marriage, it could have cost me a fortune.

Instead they only reported on my supposed night out with the woman involved, and Jean Rook and Lynda Lee Potter, those twin guardians of public morality, wrote scathingly about me trying to save my innocence, and who was I trying to kid?

It had all happened ten years previously, and I had only become involved through a simple act of trying to help someone, and at the end of it the judge, while saying that I had been rather stupid to become involved at all, awarded me half my costs. What that actually meant was that I got a paltry £50 or so. My defence of my own name cost me a great deal more.

Throughout the whole unpleasant business, Tricia had been an unbelievable comfort, and I had discovered what a warm, kind, and emotional person she was.

Frank Barnes had once said to me: "What you want, Pete, is a wife, a mother, a friend and a lover. The day you find that girl, don't muck about, marry her."

Tricia seemed to fulfil all Frank's nominated requirements, and many more. They do say that opposites attract, and maybe they do, for some people. For me, that theory doesn't work, certainly not as a basis for marriage or even long relationships.

But here I had found a girl whom I not only loved, but liked. I enjoyed being with her, whether it was on a visit to the Savoy, or at some Bingo Hall in Wigan. We took pleasure from the same things ... tennis, swimming, sunbathing, watching the telly (even Match of the Day!)

As far as I was concerned, I had found perfection, and I certainly wasn't going to let it slip away.

When the case was over, I took Tricia out to dinner at a quiet little candle-lit restaurant by the Thames at Sonning. A coward to the last, I had to do it in French, perhaps to avoid the embarrassment of a refusal.

"Est-ce que tu veux me marier?"

"Quoi?" she asked.

"Est-ce que tu veux me marier?"

Now she was sure what I was saying. Thank the Lord, she answered: "Oui."

We married within a month, on May 25th. I had seen so many showbiz weddings turned into a circus that we kept it very quiet. It was at Morden Registry Office, which is not internationally known for celebrity weddings. We only invited my mother, Tricia's parents, Auntie Dorothy and Uncle Laurie, Michael, Uncle Bill, my producer Harry Walters, and Peter Prichard and his assistant Joan Anderson. And Freddie, my clairvoyant friend.

But of course, just as we were cutting the cake at the house of my parents-in-law, the phone rang. THEY were on to it. And this time, naturally, I had to admit it was true, and that her name was *not* Ena Owen.

Mind you, my parents-in-law had taken a bit of adjusting to my madnesses anyway. Shortly before we were married I had to phone up Tricia's mother, Mrs Crabb, and it was actually as I was dialling that the devil moved me.

"Oh, er, I'd like to speak to a Mrs, er, one minute please, er Mrs Betty Crabb, please."

"Yes, speaking, who's that please?"

"Oh, er, Wimbledon Police Station here."

"Oh yes? What's it about?"

"Well, the question is, erm," I said in my best station sergeant voice, "would it be more convenient if we actually came round with the car to pick you up, or would you like to make your own way round to the station now?"

"In conjunction with what?" demanded my prospective mother-in-law.

"Well, madam, you do, er, shop at Sainsbury's don't you?"

"Yes, I . . . I do."

"Oh yes, well it's a question of shoplifting, and we would like to interrogate you," I said, in a voice that hinted darkly at glaring lights in the face and very probably the thumbscrews.

There was a scream at the other end of the phone, and I heard her yell for her husband, of whom I was fairly terrified. I dropped the phone like a hot brick, and let Tricia explain. The Crabbs were not happy with this early episode in our relationship.

But once we were safely married, I felt secure enough to have another go. Now Tricia was interested at one time in doing commercials, and the one commercial the four of us used to laugh our heads off at, despite thinking it pretty terrible, was the one for Kentucky Fried Chicken.

So one day I phoned up the long-suffering Mrs Crabb, this time with the voice of Peter Beninson, Tricia's agent.

"Em, Peter Beninson here, I've been trying to contact Tricia."

"Oh yes?"

"Yes, I'm trying to contact her desperately urgently, because we want to put her up for a commercial."

"Oh, that's wonderful, wonderful," said Mrs Crabb enthusiastically. "I don't know where she is at the moment, but as soon as I contact her I'll ... "

"Yes, well will you please tell her it's very important. By the way, er, your daughter, she is a sort of fun girl?"

"Oh yes," said the proud mother.

"I mean, she would do anything?"

"Oh yes, I mean she's good fun, but why? What is the commercial?"

"Well," I said, "It's, er, I don't know if you've ever seen them on television, the Kentucky Fried Chicken ones with a man going ker cher, ker cher, ker cher?"

At this the enthusiasm audibly waned. A spot of humming and hahing ensued. I could hear her mind thinking: "My daughter's a barrister. How could she humiliate herself by pretending to be a chicken?" But she promised to get her to phone.

Some time later Tricia happened to call her, and her mother said: "Peter Beninson has been on about you doing an advertisement for Kentucky Fried Chicken."

"Oh, that's wonderful," said Tricia.

"But you don't really want to do that, do you dear?" said the devoted mother-hen soothingly. "I mean, they want you to make ker cher, ker cher chicken noises!"

Some time later I phoned again.

"Well, Mrs Crabb, have you managed to contact your daughter

yet?"

"Yes, Mr Beninson, I have."

"Well? How does she feel about Kentucky Fried Chicken?"

"Oh well, I don't know … " she began.

"If I might make a suggestion, you can stuff it," I said, charmingly.

"I beg your pardon!"

"This is your son-in-law here. Bye." The wounds from that took a little while to heal, as well.

But at least, that December, I was deservedly "had" myself. We went to the charity evening for the Stars Organisation for Spastics, and arrived a bit late. I was dancing with Tricia when Tony Blackburn came up to us with a very worried expression on his face.

"Where were you, this evening?" he asked.

"What are you talking about?" I replied.

"Pop Score," he said. "You should have been recording Pop Score. We tried to get you everywhere. In the end we had to get Alan Dell in as a replacement."

Disaster! It was unthinkable and utterly unprofessional to miss a recording. "Oh my God," I said, panic-stricken. "I didn't know anything about it."

"Yes, well, I did think you might be doing it tonight," said Tricia, rubbing salt into the wound.

"Oh God, what on earth can I do? What will I tell them?" I said feeling utterly drained, and the evening ruined for me. Then a little smile flickered across Tony's face, and he said: "I've waited four years to get my own back on you."

And he did. He had me absolutely cold.

That same evening we were sitting with David Jacobs and his girl-friend Caroline. "How's married life, Peter?" asked David.

"Tremendous," I said. "When are you and Caroline going to get married?"

"You know," said David at his poshest, "it's an extraordinary thing you should ask me that. We were in the kitchen the other day, and I was peeling the potatoes, and I said to Caroline 'I think we ought to get married.' And she agreed with me."

"You proposed, then, did you David?" I asked.

"Well, yes, I suppose I did," he said. "I hadn't really thought about it."

"Would you say you were engaged?" I asked, pressing the point.

"Yes, I suppose I am," he said, dubiously.

"In that case, would you mind if I announce your engagement on 'Open House' tomorrow?"

"No, that would be quite pleasant," he said. So I did. Perhaps at last people would realise that we are not arch enemies!

On December 11th of 1973 my producer, Harry Walters, told me that Marjorie Wallace, Miss World, would be a guest on the programme. "I hope you don't mind," he said, "but they are filming a day in the life of Miss World, and there will be a film crew in the studio."

"No, not at all, that suits me fine," I said, making a note to wear something a bit more respectable than my usual casual wear.

At the end of the programme Harry came in and said: "That was a marvellous interview Peter," and at that moment I did a double-take, because behind him was Eamonn Andrews with that red book under his arm. I turned to Marjorie Wallace and said: "Darling, they've done you."

But she looked straight back at me and said: "Sweetheart, they've done YOU."

'This Is Your Life' was an eerie experience. Looking back on it, I realised that Tricia had been behaving a bit peculiarly during the previous three weeks, but I had no idea what was happening. All those people have been ganging up on you, and you have no idea.

When the show was over, a terrible fit of depression came over me. It had been a 'once-off' situation. There was a feeling that, now they had done me, that WAS my life. But I was lifted, not for the first time, by Diana Dors who, as we were leaving the studio said: "That was great. Now let's do his *real* life!"

As a way of getting another view of the characters of the guests on 'Open House', we used for a time the services of graphologist Fraser White. I'll never forget his description of Michael Crawford, which ended with a line to the effect that he had a certain coy virility. Michael gave one of his high-pitched laughs and said: "Does that mean I like doing it with the lights out?"

He also talked about the film The Games *in which he played the part of an*

Olympic runner. Being a perfectionist he did many hours of hard graft under the coaching of Gordon Pirie, and actually got down to something around a four minute six second mile, which is incredible. I said as much.

"Ah, well," he said, "I did my training on Wandsworth Common, and if you saw some of the things that go on at six in the morning on Wandsworth Common, you'd run a four minute mile too."

1973 had been a good year, but with one enormous sadness. In October my great friend David Hughes died, a dreadful shock, especially as he was so careful about what he ate, didn't smoke, and seldom drank. His wife, Anne, asked me if I would do the tribute at the Memorial Service in St Paul's, Covent Garden.

I dashed down there after 'Open House' had finished, to be met by the vicar who said: "You're on after Verdi's Requiem."

"When's that?" I asked.

"It's on now," he said.

As it finished, I made my way through the huge orchestra and choir and up to the pulpit where, inwardly shaking, I paid tribute to my friend. I read out a beautiful poem by an Indian philosopher, which had been given to me by a member of the National Theatre. I hope I did David proud that day. When I had finished the audience rose, and I thought for a horrified moment that they were about to give a standing ovation. Then I realised it was just the next hymn.

A couple of months later I recorded a tribute to David for the BBC. It was again a very emotional experience, and I'm afraid we had to record the last part no less than six times, because I was crying. But the reaction from the public was overwhelming, and the best I have known in all my years of broadcasting, so I was happy for Anne's sake.

The other worry in my life at that time was Michael. We had lived together, off and on, for quite a time by then, and I had tried to make up a bit for what he had lost through Germaine and I parting. But after I got married again I think he believed our friendship had gone, and on top of that he was desperately unhappy about his career. He was very keen to act, but was still an assistant stage manager, working at a London theatre where Rex Harrison was starring.

Now I had never met Rex Harrison, and to him Michael was just a very junior young man working in the company. But when he heard that Michael was so miserable, he took him out to dinner, talked him through it, and said that if he got to the end of his tether he could go to stay at Rex's villa in the South of France.

When I heard about this I was unbelievably touched. It's not often you find an international superstar (*really* a superstar) going to that sort of trouble. To my chagrin, I never wrote him a note of thanks. I simply couldn't think how to express myself. Perhaps he will take this as the gratitude properly delivered.

My other memory of 1973 was the 'Open House' programme for Princess Anne's wedding. Actually, my only previous contact with the lady had been in a letter I wrote to her, suggesting that she might like to be a guest on 'Open House'. (Well, it still wasn't inviting the Queen!)

I had a reply from her lady-in-waiting saying: "Princess Anne has heard your programme, and thinks that she is eminently unsuitable to appear on it" . . . my second royal rebuff.

For the wedding, we had to go from point to point in three-minute dashes, with a police motor-cycle escort, while records were playing. And to cover the trip from the Horse Guards Parade to Buckingham Palace, which nobody could have done in three minutes that day, we played the tape of an interview I had done with Mark Phillips' parents and old headmaster.

When we finally did get to the Palace, I introduced a record called 'Trotting to the Fair' and at that moment the Life Guards came by, the rhythm of their hoofbeats by some weird chance matching exactly the hoofbeats on the record. It was actually the first time that Open House really was televised, but I'm sure a lot of listeners, once bitten twice shy, didn't bother to turn their sets on, even though it wasn't April 1st.

I remember once convulsing myself with laughter while listening to the radio in the car. Some unfortunate interviewer asked James Stewart how he had enjoyed making McKenna's Gold. *He told them: "Fine, except that I wasn't in it." And when he later came on to 'Open House' his first remark was: "You're not going to ask me about* McKenna's Gold *are you?"*

Then, in 1974, Burt Lancaster was a guest, and a little bit uptight since he had been surrounded by newspaper photographers all morning. I knew this, and was a little bit edgy myself, which may explain how I came to say: "May I remind you that our guest on this part of the programme is Burt Bacharach." He gave a little hint of a smile and said: "I've never written a good tune in my life."

To Ken Dodd I owe my thanks for a marvellous story about Dame Edith Evans. It seemed that she had been rehearsing a play with a young, 'nouveau vague', director. "Dame Edith, do you think you could do that line this way," he said. "No dear, I think I'll do it my way if that's all right." And so it went on. At the end of a week, in desperation, he declared: "Dame Edith, I have to say this. I feel totally superfluous to this production."

"Never mind, dear," she said. "I'm sure we can find something for you to do."

Then there was Sammy Cahn, who has an anecdote to match every record. We played one of Dean Martin's, and he said: "I know Dean. Matter of fact, we were flying over Greece together the other day, when one of the plane's engines caught fire. Dean looked out of the window, put his glass to his lips, took it away again and said: 'Say, what a crazy place to hold a barbecue!'"

And we owe a great debt of thanks to Telly Savalas. "Great to see you," he said. "Now I'm not saying another word until I get a cup of coffee." At that time we were having problems, because the BBC, in one of its great economy waves, had decreed that there would be only one serving of coffee, at ten-thirty. Now, thanks to 'Kojak', we have a large supply of coffee-filled flasks.

Peter Sellers was another guest in 1974. He had previously been at what was possibly my favourite of all the 'Open Houses', a road show from the Prince of Wales Theatre, with Harry Secombe and Sacha Distel. He hadn't been a guest then, but was sitting in the audience indulging his favourite hobby of video-taping the proceedings. But as soon as I spotted him I got him on stage, and he and Harry did a marvellous unscripted and utterly hilarious turn.

When he did come as a proper guest, it was to follow Clive Dunn. Unfortunately, just as I was about to announce 'Waggoners Walk', Clive came back into the studio and announced that he couldn't leave since the door was jammed. I went to inspect the situation, and through the glass there was a goonishly frantic Peter Sellers trying to get in. I am happy to say that the BBC has an army of men equipped to solve such matters.

In mid-1974, Tricia and I did an appearance on a TV show for Border Television, called 'Mr and Mrs'. She did so well on it, that they now employ her regularly doing a legal advice spot on one of Derek

Batey's programmes. By chance, it was at about the same time that I was asked to do a pilot for a new series to be called 'Husband of the Year'.

The wives of the prospective competitors had to write to the TV Times giving their opinion of their husbands, and Tricia decided to write about me. She scored me as follows ... Love, 8 out of 10. Consideration, 8 out of 10. Tact, 4 out of 10. Resource, 3 out of 10. And practicability, Minus 30.

I couldn't really blame her. The very first day we were in our new flat I managed to drop the only key to our new car down the lift shaft. Soon afterwards, I managed to lock her out on the balcony while she was sunbathing. I, meanwhile, had gone out to post a letter, taking the balcony keys with me, and leaving the flat keys locked in the flat. It was four and a half hours before she was rescued.

And even if I haven't yet actually forgotten my trousers, I think she's caught my disease a bit. One morning I was frantically trying to find my glasses for reading the requests on the programme. I was already late in leaving, and we searched for about fifteen minutes until she suddenly looked at me and said: "God, you've got them on."

I don't suppose I'll ever be anything but absent-minded, nor do I suppose that practical joking will ever disappear, even though it sometimes has unfortunate side-effects. One day quite recently Teddy Warwick got a telephone call from a very senior BBC man whom I shall call Mr. Righteous-Indignation.

"Yes, who is it?" he asked.

"Hello, Warwick? Righteous-Indignation."

"Why don't you piss off, Pete," said Teddy.

The BBC hierarchy does not take kindly to such remarks.

But at least I was delighted, one morning recently, to walk into the studio and discover that they had given me a new clock. For years I've been criticised for giving the time wrongly, and now at last they had given me a huge timepiece in place of the old, little (indeed to me nearly invisible) clock. At last I could really see the time. Delighted, I gave my first time-check. And, by the time proclaimed by the clock, I was spot on. Alas. The clock was wrong.

What the future holds for me, I have no idea. Perhaps Buster Reed's prediction *will* come true, and I'll end up doing a Personal Appearance in the cloakroom at Victoria Station. And I suppose that programmes like 'Hit the Limit' will be reincarnated under other titles, to haunt me, to confuse me, and to earn the inevitable brickbats from the critics.

But at least the stability of my personal life more than compensates for the worry. Not for me the carrier-bag in the King's Road on a Saturday morning, but a lovely, honey-haired wife with big, blue, smiling eyes to welcome me home, and a warm, comforting shoulder on which to rest my head; someone the public have taken to so much that, should I be asked to do a personal appearance, it is not complete if she isn't with me. In fact, since her own success on TV and radio she's been asked to officiate at garden fetes in her own right. Sometimes she is even told: "Perhaps you might like to bring your husband along."

I have in Tricia a loyal, trusting partner; someone who spoils me to the utmost, and someone whom I love with all my heart. That, at least, makes me a rich man.

I have no plans. I maintain that unshakeable sense of insecurity that has always been with me, and can only pray that my Providential Doorman is still keeping an eye on my progress, or lack of it. I really mean that. The truth of the matter is that I am STILL waiting to be discovered.